THE LIFE OF SOLOMON

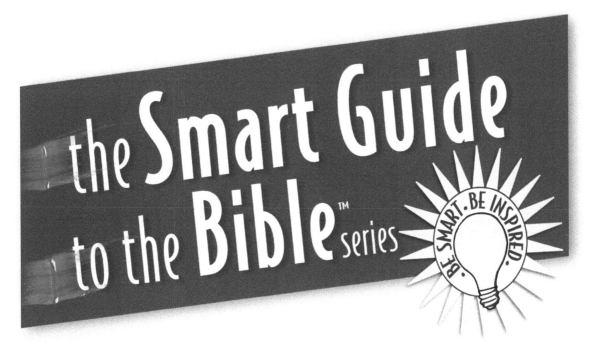

the Smart Guide to the Bible™ series

BE SMART · BE INSPIRED.

Angie Peters
Larry Richards, General Editor

THOMAS NELSON
Since 1798

NASHVILLE   DALLAS   MEXICO CITY   RIO DE JANEIRO   BEIJING

The Life of Solomon
The Smart Guide to the Bible™ series
© 2009 by GRQ, Inc.

Published in Nashville, Tennessee, by Thomas Nelson. Thomas Nelson is a trademark of Thomas Nelson, Inc.

Thomas Nelson, Inc. titles may be purchased in bulk for educational, business, fundraising, or sales promotional use. For information, please e-mail SpecialMarkets@ThomasNelson.com.

Scripture quotations are taken from the New King James Version® (NKJV), copyright © 1982 by Thomas Nelson, Inc. Used by permission. All rights reserved.

To the best of its ability, GRQ, Inc., has strived to find the source of all material. If there has been an oversight, please contact us, and we will make any correction deemed necessary in future printings. We also declare that to the best of our knowledge all material (quoted or not) contained herein is accurate, and we shall not be held liable for the same.

General Editor: Larry Richards
Managing Editor: Michael Christopher
Scripture Editor: Deborah Wiseman
Assistant Editor: Amy Clark
Design: Diane Whisner

ISBN 10: 1-4185-1012-2
ISBN 13: 978-1-4185-1012-1

Printed in the United States of America
09 10 11 12 RRD 9 8 7 6 5 4 3 2 1

Introduction

The Bible features hundreds of personality profiles. To note some of the variety, these include up-close-and-personal biographies of businessmen and beggars, warriors and weaklings, the selfless and the stingy, the wise and the foolish, and the arrogant and the unassuming.

Regardless of how they each one played out, taken together the unique stories that God chose to highlight in the pages of His Word offer His followers a broad range of valuable truths about living. Studying the assorted cast of colorful characters who populate the pages of the Bible can help readers figure out many things. For example:

- How God interacts with His people
- What God expects from His followers
- Some of the best and worst ways to handle challenges
- The habits of godly people
- Advice about avoiding costly mistakes

Why Study Solomon?

Of all the people mentioned and described in the Bible, why is it important to study Solomon? To begin with, God used Solomon in a number of special ways. We can't always know why God does everything He does, but it's obvious that He singled Solomon out for several clear distinctions:

- ***To be a wise guy.*** No, Solomon wasn't a smart aleck—at least, nothing in the Bible suggests he was! But in answer to Solomon's famous request for wisdom, God granted him more of it than anyone who lived before him or anyone who came after him. Solomon applied his great gift of insight and discernment to every facet of his life, from business, government, politics, and the economy to science, zoology, architecture, and law, using his wisdom to benefit nearly everyone whose path crossed his. Plus, his writings in the biblical books of Proverbs, Ecclesiastes, and the Song of Solomon preserved his wisdom for the benefit of all succeeding generations.

- ***To build His house.*** Solomon built the temple atop Mount Moriah to house God's holy presence and to place worship of God back at the center of the Israelites' hearts.

- *To pave the way for His Son's arrival.* If you read the study about the *Life of David* in this same Smart Guide to the Bible series—or maybe even if you didn't—you know that David was called "a man after God's own heart" and is a central figure both in the Bible and in God's plan for the nation of Israel. Even more important, David was a central figure in God's plan to provide for the salvation of all mankind. God promised that a descendant of David would be the Messiah God planned to send to earth to make it possible for everyone to be saved from the eternal consequences of their sins. That great-, great-, great-grandson, generations down the line, of course, was Jesus Christ! And since David was one of Christ's forefathers, Solomon was an ancestor of the Lord Jesus, too. Most would agree that anyone in Jesus' family tree is worth a closer look.

However, in addition to all that, Solomon was quite simply—to put it in today's language—a celebrity. If the *paparazzi* had been around in the tenth century before Jesus Christ was born, they would have staked out every entrance to this man's sprawling estate. His unsurpassed wealth (a layer of gold coated practically everything within his reach); his uncanny knack for turning enemies into friends; his ambitious and magnificent accomplishments (the temple and his palace, for starters); his impressive wisdom; and his extravagant lifestyle would have placed him on the front page of the ancient world's tabloids for sure. Even long after his death he has not lost his prominent place on history's "List of the Most Rich and Famous People in the World." And a person would be—well—"foolish" not to want to learn more about the man whose name became synonymous with such universal themes as wisdom, wealth, power, and splendor.

Things to Learn from Solomon's Story

Oswald Chambers, in his classic devotional book *My Utmost for His Highest*, said: "The test of a man's religious life is not what he does in the exceptional moments of his life, but what he does in the ordinary times…" (entry for October 12). But where Solomon is concerned, it doesn't seem like there were any ordinary times. He spent his childhood as a prince; his young adulthood preparing for and securing the throne of Israel; his middle years expanding and fortifying the nation, collecting an obscenely large harem, building the temple, and embarking on many of the other fantastic endeavors that marked his life's work; and his latter years dealing with—and reflecting upon—the consequences of the poor choices he had made a few years earlier. Yet even though little about his existence would remotely resemble that of today's average Joe (or Jane), there is much to learn from him. Otherwise, God wouldn't have included Solomon's story (or the books he wrote) in Scripture!

When studying Israel's third king, be on the lookout for lessons having to do with:

- *Wisdom*—its source, how to gain it, and how to put it into practice.
- *Obedience*—the importance of obeying God's laws, the blessings that follow obedience, and the consequences of disobedience.
- *Faithfulness*—what it means to be faithful to God and to be a faithful steward of the resources He gives, whether these include time, wealth, influence, wisdom, or creativity.
- *Worship*—what worship meant to the ancient Jews, how it was carried out in the temple, how it affects all aspects of a believer's life, and the characteristics of authentic worship.
- *God's Dealings with People*—how God communicates with His people, how He blesses and disciplines His people, and how He carries out His plans for His people—when they obey and cooperate as well as when they disobey and rebel.

Of course, there are many more truths to be discovered in Solomon's story. Here are some strategies for making sure you don't miss any of them:

1. *Pray.* This is a good habit to practice when undertaking any endeavor, but it's especially helpful when studying the Bible. Prayer opens up the lines of communication with God. His Holy Spirit can serve as your personal tutor, helping you better understand what you're reading.

2. *Read the account of Solomon's life directly from the Bible.* There isn't space in this book to record every word of the biblical biography of King Solomon, so it's important that you keep your Bible open to the passages being discussed. God says His Word is powerful and dynamic; only when we open it up and read it for ourselves can we experience firsthand its impact.

3. *Ask lots of questions.* Try to figure out why certain details and events in Solomon's life might have been included in Scripture. Search for ways the king's motivations and reactions to his circumstances are similar to yours, and notice how they differ. Make it a goal to find ways to apply your discoveries to your everyday life. Solomon himself offers this advice in a passage of one of his books. In Proverbs 2:2–4, he said to "incline your ear to wisdom," "apply your heart to understanding," "cry out for discernment," "lift up your voice for understanding," "seek [wisdom] as silver, and search for her as for hidden treasures" (NKJV).

Those who do all that, he promised, can count on exciting results: "Then you will understand the fear of the LORD, and find the knowledge of God" (2 Proverbs 2:5 NKJV).

About the Author

Angie Peters has written several books, including *A Survey of the Life of David* from this very same Smart Guide to the Bible series (Thomas Nelson, 2008); *Celebrate Home: Encouragement and Tips for Stay-at-Home Parents* (Concordia Publishing House, 1998, 2005); *Designed to Influence: A Woman and Her Testimony* (Bogard Press, 2004); and *Designed to Build: A Woman and Her Home* (Bogard Press, 2005). She has also written articles for publications such as *Today's Christian Woman, Christian Home & School,* and *ParentLife*. Angie has pursued her passion for teaching and encouraging others by leading women's Bible studies for more than fifteen years. Angie lives in Benton, Arkansas, with her husband, Kurt, and their children—Nick, Lindsey, and Erin. She dedicates this book to her family and friends, with thanks for the love, encouragement, interest, and prayers that kept her afloat and moving forward during her yearlong visit with this magnificent king.

About the General Editor

Dr. Larry Richards is a native of Michigan who now lives in Raleigh, North Carolina. He was converted to Christianity while in the Navy in the 1950s. Larry has taught and written Sunday school curriculum for every age group, from nursery through adult. He has published more than two hundred books that have been translated into twenty-six languages. His wife, Sue, is also an author. They both enjoy teaching Bible studies as well as fishing and playing golf.

Understanding the Bible Is Easy with These Tools

To understand God's Word you need easy-to-use study tools right where you need them—at your fingertips. The Smart Guide to the Bible™ series puts valuable resources adjacent to the text to save you both time and effort.

Every page features handy sidebars filled with icons and helpful information: cross references for additional insights, definitions of key words and concepts, brief commentaries from experts on the topic, points to ponder, evidence of God at work, the big picture of how passages fit into the context of the entire Bible, practical tips for applying biblical truths to every area of your life, and plenty of maps, charts, and illustrations. A wrap-up of each passage, combined with study questions, concludes each chapter.

These helpful tools show you what to watch for. Look them over to become familiar with them, and then turn to Chapter 1 with complete confidence: You are about to increase your knowledge of God's Word!

Study Helps

The thought-bubble icon alerts you to commentary you might find particularly thought-provoking, challenging, or encouraging. You'll want to take a moment to reflect on it and consider the implications for your life.

Don't miss this point! The exclamation-point icon draws your attention to a key point in the text and emphasizes important biblical truths and facts.

death on the cross
Colossians 1:21–22

Many see Boaz as a type of Jesus Christ. To win back what we human beings lost through sin and spiritual death, Jesus had to become human (i.e., he had to become a true kinsman), and he had to be willing to pay the penalty for our sins. With his <u>death on the cross</u>, Jesus paid the penalty and won freedom and eternal life for us.

The additional Bible verses add scriptural support for the passage you just read and help you better understand the <u>underlined text</u>. (Think of it as an instant reference resource!)

How does what you just read apply to your life? The heart icon indicates that you're about to find out! These practical tips speak to your mind, heart, body, and soul, and offer clear guidelines for living a righteous and joy-filled life, establishing priorities, maintaining healthy relationships, persevering through challenges, and more.

This icon reveals how God is truly all-knowing and all-powerful. The hourglass icon points to a specific example of the prediction of an event or the fulfillment of a prediction. See how some of what God has said would come to pass already has!

What are some of the great things God has done? The traffic-sign icon shows you how God has used miracles, special acts, promises, and covenants throughout history to draw people to him.

Does the story or event you just read about appear elsewhere in the Gospels? The cross icon points you to those instances where the same story appears in other Gospel locations—further proof of the accuracy and truth of Jesus' life, death, and resurrection.

Since God created marriage, there's no better person to turn to for advice. The double-ring icon points out biblical insights and tips for strengthening your marriage.

The Bible is filled with wisdom about raising a godly family and enjoying your spiritual family in Christ. The family icon gives you ideas for building up your home and helping your family grow close and strong.

something significant had occurred, he wrote down the substance of what he saw. This is the practice John followed when he recorded Revelation on the **Isle of Patmos.**

What does that word really mean, especially as it relates to this passage? Important, misunderstood, or infrequently used words are set in **bold type** in your text so you can immediately glance at the margin for definitions. This valuable feature lets you better understand the meaning of the entire passage without having to stop to check other references.

the big picture

Joshua
Led by Joshua, the Israelites crossed the Jordan River and invaded Canaan (see Illustration #8). In a series of military campaigns the Israelites defeated several coalition armies raised by the inhabitants of Canaan. With organized resistance put down, Joshua divided the land among the twelve Israelite

How does what you read fit in with the greater biblical story? The highlighted big picture summarizes the passage under discussion.

what others say

David Breese
Nothing is clearer in the Word of God than the fact that God wants us to understand himself and his working in the lives of men.[5]

It can be helpful to know what others say on the topic, and the highlighted quotation introduces another voice in the discussion. This resource enables you to read other opinions and perspectives.

Maps, charts, and illustrations pictorially represent ancient artifacts and show where and how stories and events took place. They enable you to better understand important empires, learn your way around villages and temples, see where major battles occurred, and follow the journeys of God's people. You'll find these graphics let you do more than study God's Word—they let you *experience* it.

Chapters at a Glance

Part Three: Building a Temple

Part Four: Peace, Prosperity, and Public Relations

Part Five: Solomon's Downfall

Part Six: A Legacy of Wisdom

Part One
Chosen Before He Was Born

2 Samuel 11, 12; 1 Chronicles 20: Conceived in Sorrow

Let's Get Started

To be a son of the nation's most beloved king: Surely there was no greater honor in all of Israel than to call King David *Abba,* or "Daddy." Solomon was one of the few people who could claim that distinction; in fact, he was the only of David's many sons singled out by God to become his father's successor to the throne.

Much of Solomon's story springs from the positions, virtues, and behavior of his father and his mother, Bathsheba. That's why it's essential to begin a study of Solomon's life with a close look at that famous couple, especially during the period leading up to Solomon's birth.

A Famous Father

PSALM 78:70–72 *He also chose David His servant, and took him from the sheepfolds; from following the ewes that had young He brought him, to shepherd Jacob His people, and Israel His inheritance. So he shepherded them according to the integrity of his heart, and guided them by the skillfulness of his hands.* (NKJV)

More space in the Bible is devoted to David than to anyone else—that is, than to anyone else other than Jesus Christ Himself. The books of 1 and 2 Samuel, part of 1 Kings, and part of 1 Chronicles sketch out a roughly chronological and very detailed biography of David. Plus, his poetry and songs—many of them offering rich personal insights into the extraordinary events that he shaped, influenced, or was affected by—comprise more than half of the book of Psalms.

There isn't room to go into the full life story of David here. That's for another book in this series! But here's the "short version" of the biography of Solomon's father:

go to

anointed
1 Samuel 16:12–13

people had demanded
1 Samuel 8:19–22

Goliath
1 Samuel 17

victory over the Philistines
1 Samuel 17:52–54

celebrated warrior
1 Samuel 18:7

David fled
1 Samuel 19:18;
20:1, 42; 21:10; 22:1

Saul's death
1 Samuel 31:3–6

man after God's own heart
1 Samuel 13:14;
Acts 13:22

no one is without sin
Romans 3:23

God delighted in him
2 Samuel 22:20

Bethlehem
a city about five miles south of Jerusalem; birthplace of Jesus Christ

anointed
set apart by God through a ritual of applying oil

Saul
Israel's first king

Philistine
fierce warriors and perpetual enemy of Israel

Goliath
Philistine soldier David killed as a young man

Jerusalem
the city he established as the capital of Israel

Bathsheba
Solomon's mother

When David was just a boy, watching over his father's sheep in the countryside outside of **Bethlehem**, he was <u>anointed</u> to one day become Israel's second king. God had chosen him as the one who would politically, economically, and religiously unite the nation that had been floundering under the rule of **Saul**, the man the <u>people had demanded</u> as their first king in their self-centered, short-sighted focus on becoming a nation like those that surrounded them.

David's public career had been launched on a rocky riverbank where, with one smooth stone, a lion's share of righteous indignation, and limitless faith in God, the teenager killed the **Philistine** giant **Goliath**. That feat—and the subsequent Israelite <u>victory over the Philistines</u> that followed—thrust David into the spotlight as Saul's most <u>celebrated warrior</u>. Jealousy over the young man's popularity and success, however, soon triggered a rage in Saul so unrelenting and irrational that it drove him to seek the younger man's life. <u>David fled</u>, living as a fugitive until <u>Saul's death</u>.

When David's time finally came he first became king of Judah, then king of all of Israel. He set up his new government in **Jerusalem**, which quickly became the political, economic, and religious center of the nation. By the time David met **Bathsheba**, he was a seasoned leader. He had spent his most recent years subduing Israel's enemies, strengthening the nation's political alliances, expanding its economy, and—most important of all—fixing the nation's spiritual focus once more onto God.

For all of David's successes, his most significant accomplishment by far was being designated as a <u>man after God's own heart</u>. He didn't earn that title because he was an overachiever or a perfectionist. Neither did he get it because he was a mighty warrior or a gifted administrator. And he certainly didn't obtain it because he was without sin, because absolutely <u>no one is without sin</u>—and David demonstrated that monumental truth in a monumental way!

Instead, David secured God's eternal favor and blessing because of what was in his heart, which was all about God. Because David delighted in God, <u>God delighted in him</u>.

Robbie Castleman

In today's world, as in David's, we must discover and define what it means to be people "after God's own heart," determined to bring him delight by our love and obedience.[1]

Uriah
2 Samuel 11:3–26;
12:9–10, 15;
1 Kings 15:5

Uriah
one of David's mighty men

mighty men
David's heroic and loyal supporters

Joab
general of David's army

Rabbah
capital city of Ammon; modern-day Amman, Jordan

A Snapshot of Bathsheba

Solomon's mother, Bathsheba, is not nearly as well-known as David. In fact, her file of biblical press clippings is quite flimsy compared to David's overstuffed folder! Nonetheless, she enjoyed an enviable position in Israel during the tenth century BC. Her first husband, **Uriah**, was one of David's **mighty men**, who had first rallied around the king while he was still hiding from Saul in the wilderness. Once David became king of Israel, these men—the best of the best—formed David's inner circle of military officers and advisers. So Bathsheba's marriage to Uriah—which gave her a prestigious address in Jerusalem near the palace of the king himself—practically guaranteed the beautiful young woman provision and protection during this turbulent yet exciting time in the history of Israel.

Not His Usual Routine

Less than two years before Solomon was born, Uriah, as usual, was out on the battlefield and Bathsheba found herself, like the other warriors' wives, passing the hours at home in the capital city with the children and the men who were too old to fight. The city that had become the hub of politics, commerce, and religion in Israel must have seemed eerily quiet, with its streets and common areas emptied of all of its able-bodied men—that is, all of them but one. For some reason, this time the king had chosen to stay behind.

> 2 SAMUEL 11:1 *It happened in the spring of the year, at the time when kings go out to battle, that David sent **Joab** and his servants with him, and all Israel; and they destroyed the people of Ammon and besieged **Rabbah**. But David remained at Jerusalem. (NKJV)*

go to

Ammonites
Genesis 19:36–38

idol worship and
human sacrifices
1 Kings 11:5, 7

Hanun
2 Samuel 10:1–14

Ammonites
descendants of the
family of Lot

Gilead
a mountainous
region east of the
Jordan River

Nahash
Ammonite leader

Age-Old Animosity with the Ammonites

David, his general, Joab, and their extensive army already had put Israel on the map as a nation among all nations. They had worked hard to secure its borders and vanquish its enemies. So why were Joab and the other Israelite soldiers so eager to hit the battlefields this time? Because they had a bit of unfinished business. They wanted to wrap up what they had started with the **Ammonites** the previous year. Israel had long been at odds with the Ammonites, whose religion included idol worship and human sacrifices.

> **what others say**
>
> **Easton's Bible Dictionary**
>
> [The Ammonites] were of Semitic origin, and closely related to the Hebrews in blood and language. They showed no kindness to the Israelites when passing through their territory, and therefore they were prohibited from "entering the congregation of the Lord to the tenth generation" (Deuteronomy 23:3).[2]
>
> **Holman Bible Dictionary**
>
> The proximity of the Ammonites to **Gilead** . . . destined them to be constant enemies of the Israelites, who made claims to Gilead and actually controlled it during the reigns of certain strong kings such as David, Omri, Ahab, and Jeroboam II.[3]

When the Ammonites had attacked the city of Jabesh in Gilead during Saul's reign, the Ammonite leader, **Nahash**, made a gruesome offer. He said that, in exchange for the Israelites' surrender, he would gouge out every man's right eye. And that was supposed to be a tempting proposition! The threat infuriated King Saul, who responded with his own bloody warning in the form of two butchered oxen. The gory message terrified the Ammonites, and Saul quickly gained a victory.

Years later, when David became king, he had managed to forge a friendship with Nahash in spite of the pair's conflict-riddled past. When the Ammonite monarch died, David sent a message of sympathy to Nahash's son, Hanun. But the gesture wasn't well received. Hanun's men told the king the Israelite ambassadors were nothing more than malicious spies. Then they greatly insulted David's messengers, touching off a full-blown war whose outcome was unresolved throughout the winter that brought the fighting to a standstill with its cool temperatures and frequent rain.

go to battle
1 Samuel 8:20

"Spring"-ing into Action

The first signs of spring made the Israelite warriors eager to get back out on the battlefield to finish their business with the Ammonites.

Springtime was wartime because it featured conditions ideal for battle:

key point

- Dry ground replaced the soggy turf that came with the winter rains and cool temperatures, making the roads better suited for traveling and setting up camp.
- Vegetation sprouted, providing men, warhorses, and pack animals with a steady supply of food.

What's a Warrior Like David Doing in a Place Like Home?

It was out of character for David to stay at home when his men were at war, especially since it was standard practice for all kings to go to battle. David was a fighting man, a soldier of soldiers. His reputation as a fearless warrior had been built on a military record that included not only slaying the Philistine giant but leading Israel's armies to numerous victories.

Too Tired to Travel? Too Pampered to Camp?

No one can say for sure why the king chose to bid his soldiers good-bye instead of marching out to battle with them. There's only speculation. Having passed his fiftieth birthday, he might have lost some of the strength, energy, and stamina required for hiking, camping, and combat. He might have simply become spoiled by the sedentary lifestyle of luxury and leisure he enjoyed in the palace. Or, as at least one commentator notes, he might have settled into the easy chair of arrogance.

temptation
1 Corinthians 10:13

what others say

Robert Deffinbaugh

David seems to have come to the place where he believes his abilities are so great he can lead Israel into victory, even though he is not with his men in battle.[4]

As noted in the book on David's life in this same series, "Whatever the reason, Bible commentators across the board agree that staying home was the first in a spree of poor choices David made during this period of his life. Even though the Law didn't specifically prohibit kings from refraining from military duty, sitting out on this campaign ultimately placed David in graver danger than any posed by spears, arrows or slingshots."[5]

Being at the right place at the right time doesn't completely immunize a person against temptation, because everyone is vulnerable to facing <u>temptation</u> at any time. But being at the right place at the right time certainly helps. When the Lord scolded Cain after he failed to give the Lord an acceptable offering, God warned him that refusing to do what is right opens the doorway to sin: "If you do not do well, sin lies at the door" (Genesis 4:7 NKJV).

what others say

Kathy Collard Miller and D. Larry Miller

[David] was vulnerable to the temptation of adultery by being where he shouldn't have been and by looking where he shouldn't have looked.[6]

The Girl Next Door

2 SAMUEL 11:2–3 *Then it happened one evening that David arose from his bed and walked on the roof of the king's house. And from the roof he saw a woman bathing, and the woman was very beautiful to behold. So David sent and inquired about the woman. And someone said, "Is this not Bathsheba, the daughter of Eliam, the wife of Uriah the Hittite?"* (NKJV)

Rising from a late-afternoon siesta, David decided to take a twilight stroll on his rooftop patio. What he saw from his bird's-eye viewpoint took him by surprise. A woman was bathing next door. Captivated by her beauty, the king immediately sought information.

Who was she? And perhaps even more pressing to David: Was she available for him to take as a new wife?

Ahitophel
one of David's
counselors

what others say

Jamieson, Fausset, Brown

The Hebrews, like other Orientals, rose at daybreak, and always took a nap during the heat of the day. Afterwards they lounged in the cool of the evening on their flat-roofed terraces. It is probable that David had ascended to enjoy the open-air refreshment earlier than usual.[7]

Charles R. Swindoll

The Bible never pads the record. When it says a woman is beautiful, she's fabulous. When it says she's very beautiful, she's a knock-out, physically attractive beyond description. Rarely will the Scriptures include the word "very," and when it does, rest assured, it is not an exaggeration.[8]

The Name Should Have Rung a Bell

The information the servant provided about Bathsheba stamped "Hands Off" on David's ravishing neighbor. Not only was she married, but her husband and father were both top-ranking soldiers in David's army. Further, Bathsheba's grandfather was **Ahitophel**, one of David's closest advisers. These red flags should have given David ample warning to stay away. Clearly, Bathsheba was not his for the taking.

> 2 SAMUEL 11:4 *Then David sent messengers, and took her; and she came to him, and he lay with her, for she was cleansed from her impurity; and she returned to her house.* (NKJV)

As one of Israel's top movers and shakers, Uriah spent much of his time away from home. All day, every day, as Bathsheba carried out her daily duties, she must have kept her ears open so she might be able to hear the distant cry of an approaching messenger bearing news from the battlefront—or even better, that she might hear the thunder of hooves signaling her husband's return home with the troops. It surely set her on edge, then, when a knock came at her door with a summons to the king's chambers. Did she think there was news from Rabbah about Uriah? Or did she recall with a shudder the moment she had felt the king's eyes upon her as she was

everyone sins
Romans 3:23; 8:10;
1 John 1:10

forbidden fruit
Genesis 2:17; 3:1–7

Eve
the first woman

bathing, and instantly suspect the messenger's mission? There's no way of knowing what was going through Bathsheba's mind; either way, she had little choice but to obey the king.

Everyone Sins

On one hand, it's difficult to understand how a person like David—a man after God's own heart whose usual mode of operation involved prayerful deliberation and a deep desire to be obedient—could be willing to risk so much for a fleeting evening of pleasure with the bathing beauty next door. On the other hand, as mentioned earlier, God's Word says _everyone_ sins.

How to Sin in Three Easy Steps

When it comes down to it, everyone sins in generally the same way:

1. *We see the temptation.* For **Eve**, it was the forbidden fruit. For a thief, it's an unattended cash register. For a sexual predator, it's the silhouette of a lone woman fumbling with her keys in a dark parking lot. For a cheating student, it's test answers left unattended on the teacher's desk. For David, it was a beautiful woman.

2. *We respond to the temptation.* At this first glimpse at temptation, we have two choices: We can look the other way, or we can keep staring. David kept staring.

3. *We yield to the temptation.* This is the first bite, the single-minded search for the phone number of the off-limits person, the grab for the cash, the step toward the lone shopper, or the glance at the answers.

The line between "safe" and "sinning" is stark. Temptation turns into transgression at the word *yield*.

go to

armor of God
Ephesians 6:13–18

Jesus was tempted
Matthew 4:1;
Mark 1:13;
Luke 4:2;
Hebrews 2:18; 4:15

death
Leviticus 20:10

Law of Moses
code of law God
gave His people
through Moses

what others say

Billy Graham

Temptation isn't the same thing as sin, and it isn't a sin to be tempted. Temptation is being enticed to do wrong; sin is actually doing it. It isn't a sin to be tempted, but it is a sin to give in to the temptation. The only way we can keep from yielding to sin is to put on the <u>armor of God</u> that gives us the strength to resist temptation.[9]

The Bible states that even <u>Jesus was tempted</u>.

what others say

Liz Curtis Higgs

Oh, that sin nature. It was born in the garden, beneath the spreading leaves of an attractive fruit tree where a woman saw something so pretty she convinced herself it had no power to wreak destruction in her life.[10]

Adultery: Risky Business

Adultery carries serious physical and spiritual consequences. Under the **Law of Moses**, the penalty for adultery brought the most severe physical consequence possible—<u>death</u> for both people involved. Participating in adultery destroys relationships and wreaks havoc on one's mental and emotional well-being. Further, it can greatly damage the person's relationship with God:

for your marriage

GALATIANS **5:19–21** *Now the works of the flesh are evident, which are: adultery, fornication, uncleanness, lewdness, idolatry, sorcery, hatred, contentions, jealousies, outbursts of wrath, selfish ambitions, dissensions, heresies, envy, murders, drunkenness, revelries, and the like; of which I tell you beforehand, just as I also told you in time past, that those who practice such things will not inherit the kingdom of God." (NKJV)*

As Solomon succinctly stated, "Drink water from your own cistern, and running water from your own well" (Proverbs 5:15 NKJV). In today's language, "It's best to drink water from your own faucet, mister!"

key point

The world's view of sex outside of marriage and God's view of it couldn't be farther apart. Many people regard sex outside of marriage as an activity of little consequence; God regards it as a lethal weapon: "Whoever commits adultery with a woman lacks understanding; he who does so destroys his own soul" (Proverbs 6:32 NKJV).

what others say

David Guzik

At this moment, David agreed with the world's understanding of the purpose of sex, seeing it primarily as the pursuit of a pleasurable experience. With his many wives, David may have *never* really understood *God's* purpose for sex: to be the "cement" that helps bond together a one-flesh relationship.[11]

The Blame Game

Bible scholars disagree about where to point the finger of blame for the affair between David and Bathsheba:

Bathsheba the Seductress—Some scholars believe Bathsheba was at least partially guilty for the illicit liaison. They point out that she would have known her bathing pool was visible from the king's terrace, and would have instantly realized she was being watched. They claim that her behavior paints the portrait of a seductress in action.

what others say

David Guzik

There is little doubt that this woman . . . acted immodestly. Though it was evening and apparently the time when most people were asleep, *certainly* she knew that her bath was visible from the roof of the palace. Any immodesty on Bathsheba's part did not excuse David's sin, but she was still responsible for her wrong.[12]

Robert Alter

Her later behavior in the matter of her son's succession to the throne (1 Kings 1–2) suggests a woman who has her eye on the main chance, and it is possible that opportunism, not merely passive submission, explains her behavior here as well.[13]

David the Rapist—Other commentators believe Bathsheba was an innocent victim and go as far as calling David a rapist. They suggest she would have had no reason to think that she was being watched by a man because most were off at war. They point out that Bathsheba complied with the king only because of his position; refusing the king's summons could have jeopardized her life. Further, a glance ahead at Nathan's parable condemning David's actions depicts Bathsheba as an innocent lamb.

what others say

Sue and Larry Richards

The text of Scripture makes it clear that we must view Bathsheba as a victim of David's lust, not the seductress which she is sometimes portrayed to be.[14]

Partners in Crime—Yet other scholars note that it does, in fact, "take two to tango." They suggest the most likely truth about Bathsheba's role in the affair is that she was neither manipulative nor completely innocent, but somewhere in between.

what others say

Charles R. Swindoll

I believe both David and Bathsheba were at fault on this occasion, but of the two, certainly David was the aggressor. He stopped. He stared. He lusted. He sought her. He lost control of his passion. He lay with her.[15]

A Different Kind of Adultery

Sometimes two people who aren't married to each other form a powerful emotional connection that goes beyond friendship. It often happens when one or both of those people have been either hurt or neglected by their spouse. Called "emotional adultery," it's shaky ground for anyone who desires to protect and preserve his or her marriage.

Sabrina Beasley, an editor for FamilyLife, an organization dedicated to helping couples strengthen their marriages, says it's critical to sever connections such as these because they can lead to trouble. She offers these strategies:

Abigail
1 Samuel 25:3,
14–42;
2 Samuel 2:2;
1 Chronicles 3:1

Nabal
1 Samuel 25:2–39

Abigail
wife of Nabal who
later married David

Nabal
wealthy, foolish
farmer who lived
near Carmel

- *Break all ties.* The first and most important thing you must do is sever the friendship. People express that they can still be friends with a person while maintaining a distance, but that is almost impossible.

- *Guard your heart and mind.* Hollywood and the media have a way of making us unhappy with real life. The hero of the romantic comedy may seem perfect and may make you wonder why your mate doesn't measure up. Then you become unsatisfied with your imperfect spouse.

- *Look beyond your spouse's faults.* No one is perfect. Your partner will fail and disappoint you at times. But that's why God has given us grace. How much grace have you given your husband or wife for his or her shortcomings? How much grace do you expect for your shortcomings? Start looking for the things that you love about your marriage partner. . . . If you look beyond the faults you will find a dear friend, and the disconnection that caused you to move beyond your marriage for physical love will begin to disappear.

- *Find a trustworthy accountability partner.* You need a good friend (of the same sex!) with whom you can be brutally honest. James 5:16a says, "Confess your sins to one another, and pray for one another so that you may be healed." Confess your feelings for the other person, and give your accountability partner permission to question your actions and hold you to God's Word.[16]

The Road Not Taken

Oh, the trouble Bathsheba could have prevented had she taken her cue from David's second wife, **Abigail**! When David, soon to be king, became furious at a foolish, arrogant farmer named **Nabal** who refused to extend common courtesy, he was ready to kill the farmer and all his men, too. In doing so, David would have broken God's law and jeopardized his reputation as a man of integrity. However, Abigail, who happened to be the farmer's wife, met the coming calamity head-on by confronting David and persuading him to cool off. It may be a "do-it-yourself" world these days, but the apostle James plainly stated how potent the power of godly influence can be: "He who turns a sinner from the error of his way will save a soul from death and cover a multitude of sins" (James 5:20 NKJV).

what others say

Charles Stanley

According to Scripture, we need to follow some guidelines when we intercede for others. We are to pray from hearts of love and compassion. We must ask the Lord to help us see what others see and feel what they feel. And we must be willing to be part of the answer.[17]

Details Matter

Truly, no words are wasted in the Bible. The small phrase "for she was cleansed from her impurity" (2 Samuel 11:4 NKJV) (meaning Bathsheba had been bathing for her monthly **purification ritual** following her menstrual period), divulges a piece of critical information: Bathsheba could not have possibly have been pregnant with Uriah's child when she slept with David. Don't miss the irony here! While David could rest assured that he was keeping the Law by sleeping with a ritually "pure" woman, he was in fact contaminating both himself and Bathsheba with sin by breaking the seventh commandment.

key point

Extreme Circumstances, Extreme Measures

the big picture

2 Samuel 11:5–25

Bathsheba discovered she was pregnant and sent David the shocking news. To resolve this desperate, life-threatening dilemma, David brought Uriah home from the battlefront on furlough and gave him two opportunities to sleep with his wife in order to create the impression that he was the baby's father. But Uriah, out of respect and compassion for his fellow soldiers at war, refused to do so. Finally, David arranged for Uriah to be placed in lethal danger in the fighting. Uriah was killed, just as David had hoped.

David's army
1 Chronicles 11:41;
2 Samuel 23:39

Francine Rivers

Bathsheba chose to rely on David to take care of "the problem." David chose to handle things himself. And Uriah became the scapegoat.[18]

Understanding Uriah

They didn't call Uriah one of David's "mighty" men for nothing! He was a commander of one of the thirty units comprising David's army. His name meant "my light is Yahweh," reflecting that although he was a foreigner—a Hittite—he had converted to the Jewish faith.

NKJV Study Bible

The Scriptures state that the mighty man is not victorious because of his strength (Psalm 33:16) but because of his understanding and knowledge of the Lord (Jeremiah 9:23, 24).[19]

Smith's Bible Dictionary

Like others of David's officers [Uriah] he was a foreigner—a Hittite. His name, however and his manner of speech indicate that he had adopted the Jewish religion. . . . It may be inferred from Nathan's parable that he was passionately devoted to his wife, and that their union was celebrated in Jerusalem as one of peculiar tenderness.[20]

Jamieson, Fausset, Brown

Uriah's refusal to indulge in the enjoyment of domestic pleasure, and his determination to sleep "at the door of the king's house," arose from a high and honorable sense of military duty and propriety.[21]

Richard D. Phillips

What was it that drove Uriah to refuse the respite David offered him? It was his solidarity with fellow soldiers who that very night would be facing hardship and danger. . . . Where did Uriah get such passionate devotion? From David, that's where. . . . Uriah, a Hittite by birth, has become the truest Jew in Jerusalem.[22]

The Cover-Up

go to

2 SAMUEL 11:26–27 When the wife of Uriah heard that Uriah her husband was dead, she mourned for her husband. And when her mourning was over, David sent and brought her to his house, and she became his wife and bore him a son. But the thing that David had done displeased the LORD. (NKJV)

Understandably, Bathsheba was devastated by the news that her husband had been killed in battle. Not only had Uriah been her protector and provider, but he had been a man of integrity as well. Now, she was alone in the world. The days she spent grieving her loss must have been all the more painful as she considered the vulnerable spot she was in: widowed, and expecting the arrival of a child conceived by a man who was not her husband.

David was the only one who could possibly help her, and much to her relief, that's what he did. Once her mourning period ended, the king swept the whole mess under the rug by bringing her into the palace as a new wife. Even though the child arrived sooner than onlookers would have expected, no one seemed to suspect foul play.

A Time to Mourn

Ancient Hebrews followed specific traditions for the way they grieved over a death in their family or community. A period of mourning might last anywhere from <u>seven days</u> to <u>seventy days</u>, and it usually included one or more of the following behaviors:

- <u>Crying</u>, which was sometimes in the form of lamentation, or loud wailing
- <u>Tearing one's clothes</u>
- <u>Wearing **sackcloth**</u>
- Smearing one's skin with <u>dust or ashes</u>
- **<u>Fasting</u>**
- <u>Silence</u>

seven days
1 Samuel 31:13

seventy days
Genesis 50:3

crying
Luke 7:38;
Ruth 1:9;
1 Samuel 6:19;
2 Samuel 3:31

tearing one's clothes
Genesis 37:24, 29;
Matthew 26:65

wearing sackcloth
Genesis 37:34;
Psalm 35:13

dust or ashes
2 Samuel 13:19;
Jeremiah 6:26;
Job 2:12

fasting
2 Samuel 1:12

silence
Judges 20:26;
2 Samuel 12:16;
13:31;
Job 1:20

sackcloth
rough, coarse cloth

fasting
going without food for religious purposes

what others say

Judy Bodmer

Jewish funerals were held either the same day or within twenty-four hours. The corpse was washed, anointed, and

bier
frame or stand on
which a corpse is
laid

prophet
spokesperson for
God

bound with special grave clothes and placed on a simple **bier**. Then it was buried or placed in a cave. There was a time of great lamentation and wailing for the dead.[23]

The Storm Beneath the Calm

David had everything under control—at least on the surface. But beneath the facade, sin was sickening David's spirit. He spent nearly a year suffering the physical, mental, and spiritual fallout of his actions. The following psalm he wrote sums up his frame of mind during this interval:

PSALM 32:3–4 *When I kept silent, my bones grew old through my groaning all the day long. For day and night Your hand was heavy upon me; my vitality was turned into the drought of summer. (NKJV)*

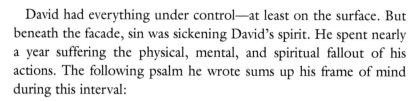

what others say

Matthew Henry

During all that time, it is certain, [David] penned no psalms, his harp was out of tune, and his soul like a tree in winter, that has life in the root only.[24]

A Prophet Makes a Point

2 SAMUEL 12:1–4 *Then the LORD sent Nathan to David. And he came to him, and said to him: "There were two men in one city, one rich and the other poor. The rich man had exceedingly many flocks and herds. But the poor man had nothing, except one little ewe lamb which he had bought and nourished; and it grew up together with him and with his children. It ate of his own food and drank from his own cup and lay in his bosom; and it was like a daughter to him. And a traveler came to the rich man, who refused to take from his own flock and from his own herd to prepare one for the wayfaring man who had come to him; but he took the poor man's lamb and prepared it for the man who had come to him." (NKJV)*

Being the persistent, loving parent that He is, God reached out to David through the **prophet** Nathan, probably the king's closest friend and most trusted adviser. It had been Nathan who had delivered the king the <u>promise</u> that David and his descendants would enjoy an everlasting reign. As discussed in the study of the life of David in this book series, "Confronting the man who wielded the most power and prestige in the nation would be a challenge. It could even be dangerous. That's why Nathan used the utmost tact in delivering his message that was designed to point out the king's offenses. To get the truth across with honesty, clarity and kindness, he wrapped the message in the language of a **parable**. He made the truth even more accessible to David by placing a lamb in the starring role of his tale. David, after all, was a shepherd at heart. If anyone understood sheep talk, he would."[25]

go to

promise
2 Samuel 7:12–16

parables
Matthew 13:1–23;
Mark 4:2–33;
Luke 8:10

restoration of stolen property
Exodus 22:1

parable
story that teaches a spiritual lesson

The Power of Parables

Jesus often spoke in <u>parables</u> in order to reveal sin and present spiritual advice. The Bible records thirty-five of His parables.

what others say

NKJV Study Bible

> Jesus' stories are like wrapped gifts. . . . When discovered, these lessons prove extremely valuable. The testimony of millions of changed lives over two thousand years attests to this fact.[26]

David Doled Out Judgment

2 SAMUEL 12:5–6 *So David's anger was greatly aroused against the man, and he said to Nathan, "As the LORD lives, the man who has done this shall surely die! And he shall restore fourfold for the lamb, because he did this thing and because he had no pity." (NKJV)*

Nathan presented his tale so clearly and powerfully that it provoked a passionate response from David. The king pronounced a severe judgment—the death penalty as well as <u>restoration of the stolen property</u>—for the imaginary man he thought to be real. David didn't realize that, by declaring the rich man's guilt, he had in fact established his own!

key point

apply it

This is a fitting illustration of Jesus' colorful counsel in Matthew 7:3–5 and Luke 6:41–42 to remove the "plank" from our own eye before trying to remove a "speck" from someone else's. So often it is much easier to see the mistakes of others than it is to recognize our own flaws. That's why it's important to ask for God's help in launching a self-examination, as David did in Psalm 139:23–24: "Search me, O God, and know my heart; try me, and know my anxieties; and see if there is any wicked way in me, and lead me in the way everlasting" (NKJV).

Nathan Had to Put It Plainly

David had taken a good first step toward the light Nathan was trying to show him, but the king was still in the shadowy territory just outside the full truth. The prophet finally flipped the light switch on with plain-spoken words:

> **2 SAMUEL 12:7–9** *You are the man! Thus says the LORD God of Israel: "I anointed you king over Israel, and I delivered you from the hand of Saul. I gave you your master's house and your master's wives into your keeping, and gave you the house of Israel and Judah. And if that had been too little, I also would have given you much more! Why have you despised the commandment of the LORD, to do evil in His sight? You have killed Uriah the Hittite with the sword; you have taken his wife to be your wife, and have killed him with the sword of the people of Ammon." (NKJV)*

key point

If David had been wondering why Nathan was bothering him with the details of a livestock dispute in a remote corner of the countryside, there was no room for doubt now. The prophet's words could not have been clearer: David had taken Uriah's wife. He had taken Uriah's life. He was the thief in the parable. He had sinned against

God. Because God in His holiness cannot tolerate sin, judgment must surely follow. Nathan spelled out that judgment.

A Promise of Painful Consequences

> 2 SAMUEL 12:10–12 *"Now therefore, the sword shall never depart from your house, because you have despised Me, and have taken the wife of Uriah the Hittite to be your wife." Thus says the LORD: "Behold, I will raise up adversity against you from your own house; and I will take your wives before your eyes and give them to your neighbor, and he shall lie with your wives in the sight of this sun. For you did it secretly, but I will do this thing before all Israel, before the sun." (NKJV)*

David's sin, God said, would yield painful consequences. The peace in the king's household would from then on be disrupted by violence and hardship. Why wouldn't God go easy on David? Couldn't He have let him slide, just this once? After all, David had established a fairly consistent track record of obedience and faithfulness. He had done great things for his nation in God's name. He was respected and loved by his family, friends, and followers. Wouldn't it be in David's best interests for God to look the other way this time, to spare His beloved son from pain and hardship? And wouldn't it be in God's best interests to let this slip-up slide so that His right-hand man wouldn't risk losing the respect and support of His people—especially when things were going so well for the nation? Further, wouldn't it be in God's best interests to let David off the hook so He wouldn't suffer the fallout of the bad press His unpleasant judgment on His right-hand man would certainly bring?

The truth is, God couldn't have cared less about "bad press." And, He couldn't have cared more about David's best interests. In fact, God would have been showing *less* love by withholding His judgment than He did by dispensing it.

what others say

David Robinson

The purpose of God even in judgment is not to hurt and destroy, but to heal and to help. Sometimes severe measures are necessary to accomplish good things. Consider that in . . . hospitals, surgeons are cutting into the bodies of others. The surgeon's kindness will result in pain. But this is not done to harm the patient. Instead, it is done in an attempt to heal disease and save lives. So God in His goodness must judge sin that we may live, not so that we will suffer. Indeed, the only thing God has to do to insure our suffering is leave us alone. Left to our own devices, our doom is certain.[28]

The reference to David's wives being given to the neighbors refers to political turmoil as well as to domestic disorder.

Steven L. McKenzie

The threat here is not to David's wives. Nor is it merely a matter of shaming him. It plays . . . on the notion that to sleep with a member of the harem was to lay claim to the throne itself. David's neighbor could lie with David's wives in full sunlight only if David were deposed. These words threatened nothing less than David's removal as king. . . David's "neighbor" turns out to be his own son![29]

David's Confession

2 SAMUEL 12:13 *So David said to Nathan, "I have sinned against the LORD." And Nathan said to David, "The LORD also has put away your sin; you shall not die." (NKJV)*

key point

David's confession allowed God to forgive—and forget—his sin. It's important to remember that the state of David's heart was far more important than the words he spoke. God always knows the difference between compulsory confession and heartfelt remorse.

Kathy Collard Miller and D. Larry Miller

There isn't anything that can't be forgiven by God, except the "unpardonable sin"—the rejection of God's offer of salvation. Such a merciful God as Jehovah can even forgive adultery and murder. God is motivated to forgive any and every confessed sin.[30]

Francine Rivers

David confessed to God. David waited on God. David worshiped God. David believed God for the future. These steps lead to a restored relationship with God.[31]

Newfound Joy in a Bundle of Boy

> **2 SAMUEL 12:14–15; 24–25** *"However, because by this deed you have given great occasion to the enemies of the LORD to blaspheme, the child also who is born to you shall surely die." Then Nathan departed to his house. And the LORD struck the child that Uriah's wife bore to David, and it became ill. . . . Then David comforted Bathsheba his wife, and went in to her and lay with her. So she bore a son, and he called his name Solomon. Now, the LORD loved him, and He sent word by the hand of Nathan the prophet: So he called his name Jedidiah, because of the LORD. (NKJV)*

Once God forgave David's sin, David's relationship with the Lord was restored. God spared David's life; however, He did require David to suffer the consequences of his sin. One of the first painful penalties came when David and Bathsheba's firstborn son became ill and died. But when the king went to comfort his wife, who was understandably heartbroken over the tragic loss, their intimacy that night produced a second son, Solomon.

The death of a child. Nothing compares to the heartbreaking sorrow of losing one's son or daughter. And yet nothing compares to the joy brought by the birth of a child, either. God wasted no time in demonstrating His tender mercy when he allowed the grieving couple to conceive a child in the darkest night of their sorrow. This situation puts a different slant on Solomon's words in Proverbs 10:1: "A wise son [Solomon] makes a glad father" (NKJV).

what others say

Judy Bodmer

David and Bathsheba dealt with their grief by not withholding sex from each other. Oftentimes, a grieving wife will think her husband is insensitive if he wants to have sex after they experience the loss of a child. She may think he just wants to have pleasure. But for a man, sex is sometimes the only way he knows how to express closeness. An understanding wife will welcome his desire to draw close to her in that way—especially since he may not be able to express his grief as an emotion of sadness.[32]

strengthen your family

Solomon
1 Chronicles
22:7–10

Jedidiah
2 Samuel 12:25

what others say

Matthew Henry

God had removed one son from them, but now gave them another instead of him, like Seth instead of Abel. Thus God often balances the griefs of his people with comforts in the same thing wherein he hath afflicted them, setting the one over-against the other.[33]

Judy Bodmer

The customary penalty for adultery and murder was death. The Lord showed great mercy in allowing David to live and continue to rule over Israel. David and Bathsheba experienced great mercy at the hands of God.[34]

Named Before He Was Born

No matter how much planning—or lack of planning—a couple makes, it's important to remember that there is no such thing as an unexpected pregnancy in God's book. David expressed this clearly in Psalm 139:16: "Your eyes saw my substance, being yet unformed. And in Your book they all were written, the days fashioned for me, when as yet there were none of them" (NKJV).

Many years later, when Solomon was a young man, David would tell his son that his birth indeed had not come as a surprise—neither to God nor to David. The king had been expecting his son's arrival because God had told him he would have a son named Solomon.

what others say

Henry Morris

God had, therefore, even chosen Solomon's name before he was born, a name which means "peaceful." Actually, when Solomon was born, God also gave him another name as well. Jedidiah means "beloved of the Lord."[35]

Richard D. Phillips

"Jedidiah" means "beloved of the Lord," and this name parallels David's own name, which in the Hebrew language also means "beloved."[36]

Back on the Battlefield

> **2 SAMUEL 12:26–31** *Now Joab fought against Rabbah of the people of Ammon, and took the royal city. And Joab sent messengers to David, and said, "I have fought against Rabbah, and I have taken the city's water supply. Now therefore, gather the rest of the people together and encamp against the city and take it, lest I take the city and it be called after my name." So David gathered all the people together and went to Rabbah, fought against it, and took it. Then he took their king's crown from his head. Its weight was a talent of gold, with precious stones. And it was set on David's head. Also he brought out the spoil of the city in great abundance. And he brought out the people who were in it, and put them to work with saws and iron picks and iron axes, and made them cross over to the brick works. So he did to all the cities of the people of Ammon. Then David and all the people returned to Jerusalem. (NKJV)*

This dramatic episode in David's life ended in much the same way as it had begun: The king was at the palace and his men were out on the battlefield wrapping up the war against the Ammonites that had been started in 2 Samuel 10. Joab, on the brink of completely vanquishing Rabbah, invited the king to join him there to ensure that David would receive the credit for the success. David did so and, while there, secured great wealth—including the Ammonite king's seventy-five-pound gold crown—and made slave laborers of the Ammonite survivors.

While David's relationship with God had hung in the balance, so had the outcome of the Israelites' conflict with the Ammonites. However, once David's relationship with God was restored, God blessed David and the Israelites with victory.

Chapter Wrap-Up

- Solomon's father, David, had been set apart by God when he was a young boy to become Israel's second king. After a long and winding journey to the nation's throne, he set up his new government in Jerusalem, which quickly became the political, economic, and religious center of the nation.

- Solomon's mother, Bathsheba, was bathing one evening when King David—having uncharacteristically stayed behind when all his soldiers had gone to battle—spied her from his rooftop patio. He summoned her and had sex with her. She happened to be married to Uriah, one of his highly esteemed soldiers.

- Bathsheba became pregnant, and David had Uriah killed on the battlefield so he could marry the woman to cover up their crime.

- Nathan confronted David with the truth about the king's sin. When David finally understood what the prophet was trying to tell him, he confessed his sin and repented.

- God forgave David, but predicted dire consequences that would deeply affect his household.

- Part of the consequences for David's sin was the death of his and Bathsheba's infant son.

- In their grief, David and Bathsheba conceived another son, Solomon, who God said would become David's heir to the throne.

Study Questions

1. What were some possible factors that put David at risk for sinning with Bathsheba?

2. How did David initially attempt to deal with his sin?

3. How did David respond to Nathan's parable?

4. What was a consequence of David's sin?

5. How did God show mercy and kindness to David and Bathsheba after the death of their infant son?

2 Samuel 13-19; 1 Kings 1; 2 Chronicles 1: The Man After the Man After God's Own Heart

Chapter Highlights:
- Innocent Daughter, Corrupt Son
- Amnon and Absalom
- Absalom and David
- Adonijah's Power Grab

Let's Get Started

No doubt about it: God had chosen Solomon to become Israel's next king. He had told David as much in His words to the king recorded in 1 Chronicles 22:7–10. But David's son by Bathsheba wouldn't take his place on the throne before God's promise of <u>consequences</u> for his sin came to pass.

David and Bathsheba already had endured the unspeakable pain of losing a child. But that was just the beginning of a string of events that would bring sorrow, violence, and unrest to David's family and, consequently, to the entire nation before Israel's leadership would change hands. The young Prince Solomon's earliest few years, while enjoyed in luxurious surroundings with all the privileges of a member of a royal family, were hardly spent in an idyllic setting. The little boy grew up in a home life jarred by rape, incest, murder, mind games, and estrangement. David's family had become what would certainly be called in today's terminology a dysfunctional family.

go to

consequences
2 Samuel 12:14

Amnon
David's firstborn son, whose mother was Ahinoam

Tamar
David's daughter by his wife Maacah

Innocent Daughter, Corrupt Son

2 SAMUEL 13:1–2, 14–15 *After this Absalom the son of David had a lovely sister, whose name was Tamar; and Amnon the son of David loved her. Amnon was so distressed over his sister Tamar that he became sick; for she was a virgin. And it was improper for Amnon to do anything to her. . . . Being stronger than she, he forced her and lay with her. Then Amnon hated her exceedingly, so that the hatred with which he hated her was greater than the love with which he had loved her. (NKJV)*

The first incident that touched off turmoil in David's home began when David's firstborn son, **Amnon**, consumed with desire for his beautiful half sister, **Tamar**, raped her. Before the crime, Tamar begged Amnon to stop, but he was determined to satisfy his sick lust. Afterward, devastated by what had happened, Tamar pleaded

go to

divorce
Deuteronomy
24:1–3

discipline
Proverbs 29:15, 17

Absalom
brother of Tamar,
who shared David's
wife Maacah as a
mother with her

with him not to send her away. Despite her pleas, he refused to have anything further to do with her, compounding her shame and misery.

Tamar's brother, **Absalom**, was incensed about what had happened. He told his sister to keep quiet and invited her to live with him. David was also furious about the crime that had taken place under his own roof, but he did little more than rant and rave. Tamar's life, in essence, was ruined. Although Amnon had not killed her, he had destroyed her chances of ever marrying and having a family because he had stolen her virginity. She would live in disgrace for the rest of her life.

Man Power

The culture and customs of a patriarchal society governed by Old Testament Law strongly favored men over women.

- A woman was identified by her father or her husband.
- A woman depended upon men for a place to live, because the law restricted her ability to own property.
- A woman had virtually no say with respect to whom she would marry.
- A woman had no way of initiating a <u>divorce</u>, as did men in certain circumstances.

These restrictions, as well as many others, placed women in vulnerable positions. They were frequently regarded as little more than property, and their value stemmed from their ability to produce sons for their husbands. Women who were not virgins were considered "damaged goods" and could never hope to marry. When Tamar was raped, she could no longer even entertain the dream cherished by all women in her time and place: That she might one day marry and have children of her own.

David: A Deadbeat Dad?

key point

How could David let his mean-hearted son get away with ruining his innocent daughter's life? Perhaps he was paralyzed by lingering guilt over his own sexual sins. It's important for parents to refuse to let their own shortcomings rob them of their authority and responsibility to teach and <u>discipline</u> their children.

Beth Moore

David allowed his own failure to disable him to lead his household in justice and righteousness. He had been forgiven by God but he had not chosen to live like a forgiven person. He allowed his own sense of guilt to handicap him as a parent.[1]

They Did as He Did

Setting the right kind of example for children to follow can be among the most daunting responsibilities of parenting. As tough as it can be to toe the line, it's important to try to live lives worthy of imitation, because imitation is precisely what kids do best. Clearly, while David had been busy marrying multiple wives against God's wishes, and while he had contrived a way to take Bathsheba for himself, he wasn't aware that he had an audience. But he did. His sons had been watching his every move.

apply it

Beth Moore

Like his father, Amnon saw something beautiful and determined to have it. He gave no consideration to the other party involved. Only his lust mattered. He literally became sin-sick to the point of stopping at nothing to satisfy his appetite. Tamar pled with him to spare her disgrace and his reputation, but he "refused to listen."[2]

Judy Bodmer

Whether we want to believe it or not, we are the most important role models our children have. Everything we do and are affects them deeply.[3]

The tragedy of this episode springs from the fact that Tamar was an innocent victim whose life was destroyed because of the sin of her brother.

The Birds and the Bees

It sounds like a plot for a weeknight situation-comedy: A man known for having made many blunders in the department of sexual fidelity sits down at the kitchen table with his teenage sons to try to impart his "wisdom" on the topic. The father makes little headway in telling his boys how they "should" act because they constantly interrupt his pointers with the remark: "But that's not what you did, Dad."

It's true: Actions often do speak louder than words. So it's no surprise, given David's passion for accumulating wives, that he pretty much blew his chances for raising sons who would have a clear understanding of God's good plan for sexual relationships.

Dennis Rainey, executive director of FamilyLife Today, offers parents the following tips for talking with kids about sex:

- **God created sex.** Genesis 1:27 tells us, "And God created man in His own image, in the image of God He created him; male and female He created them." The Creator of the universe stamped and embedded His image within us in a way that is somehow mysteriously tied to our sexuality.

- **Sex is for procreation in marriage.** God created sex so that we can reproduce after our own kind.

- **Sex is for intimacy in marriage.** Genesis 4:1 says, "Now the man had relations with his wife Eve, and she conceived." God intended us to become one flesh to draw us together. It's a wonderful aspect of sex.

- **Sex is for pleasure in marriage.** God approves of appropriate gestures of love, romance, and pleasure within marriage. He also wrote an entire book of the Bible about sexual love in marriage, The Song of Solomon. God is not down on sexual pleasure in marriage.

- **Sex was created to be enjoyed by a man and a woman in marriage.** [However,] you will need to share with your child that there is a radical homosexual element in our culture saying, "You're going to see us kissing on television and in movies. We want to become acceptable."

- **Sex outside of marriage is a sin.** But when God forbids something, it is for our own good.[4]

strengthen your family

Amnon: Another Name for "Fool"

When Tamar was pleading with Amnon to spare her, she appealed to his sense of honor: "No, my brother, do not force me, for no such thing should be done in Israel. Do not do this disgraceful thing! And I, where could I take my shame? And as for you, you would be like one of the fools in Israel. Now therefore, please speak to the king; for he will not withhold me from you" (2 Samuel 13:12–13 NKJV). Her pleas fell on deaf ears, however, because Amnon's heart didn't harbor a shred of honor. Tamar wisely stated what Amnon would be if he were to give in to his lust and commit incest with his own sister: He would be a fool. Funny, that she happened to call him that.

It's an understatement to say that Amnon's younger brother, Solomon, grew up to become a prolific and insightful writer. In the book of Proverbs, Solomon repeatedly emphasized the contrast between a wise person and a fool. According to the following proverbs, Tamar was spot-on in classifying her brother Amnon as a fool. He:

- Refused to listen to sound advice (Proverbs 10:8; 12:15).
- Made a sport of evil (Proverbs 10:23).
- Based his actions on his emotions (Proverbs 14:16; 28:26; 29:11).
- Was arrogant (Proverbs 14:16).

what others say

Sue and Larry Richards

Tamar was a lovely and innocent young woman whose life was destroyed by Amnon's brutal rape. Her hope of recovery was thwarted by Absalom and David's failures to deal honestly with the crime. Yet, what a future we might have projected for Tamar. Her recorded words to Amnon suggest a high moral quality and sensitivity like that displayed by Abigail when she first met David. But unlike David, Amnon refused to be persuaded to take the right course.[5]

Amnon and Absalom

2 SAMUEL 13:28–29 *Now Absalom had commanded his servants, saying, "Watch now, when Amnon's heart is merry with wine, and when I say to you, 'Strike Amnon!' then kill him. Do not be afraid. Have I not commanded you? Be courageous and*

go to

Talmai
2 Samuel 13:37

Jonadab
David's nephew and
the son of David's
brother Shimeah

Geshur
city northeast of the
Sea of Galilee

Talmai
Absalom's grand-
father; Maacah's
mother

*valiant." So the servants of Absalom did to Amnon as Absalom
had commanded. Then all the king's sons arose, and each one got
on his mule and fled. (NKJV)*

Absalom may have remained silent, but he wasn't indifferent to
the crime that had been committed against his sister. Quite the
opposite. Absalom had allowed his anger over the incident to sim-
mer for two years, which he spent waiting for the opportunity to
have Amnon killed to avenge his sister's rape. David's nephew
Jonadab confirmed the slow burn with his words: "For by the command of Absalom this has been determined *from the day that he
forced his sister Tamar*" (2 Samuel 13:32 NKJV, italics added). Clearly,
Absalom belonged in the same category as Amnon: "foolish."
Solomon also had much to say about anger and how it relates to
foolishness:

- Do not hasten in your spirit to be angry, for anger rests in
  the bosom of fools. (Ecclesiastes 7:9 NKJV)

- A wrathful man stirs up strife, but he who is slow to anger
  allays contention. (Proverbs 15:18 NKJV)

- He who is slow to anger is better than the mighty, and he
  who rules his spirit than he who takes a city. (Proverbs 16:32
  NKJV)

- The discretion of a man makes him slow to anger, and his
  glory is to overlook a transgression. (Proverbs 19:11 NKJV)

It's noted in the book on the life of David in this series that
"Absalom was furious, but rather than dealing promptly with his
anger or dealing with the crime through legal channels, he, as seen
in the next passage, let his emotions crackle and spark for two full
years before he took action. By that time, his fury had lit the fire of
murderous rage."[6]

key point

Absalom and David

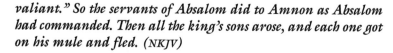

the big picture

2 Samuel 13:34–14:33

Absalom's murder of Amnon led to a lengthy estrangement
from David. Absalom spent three years in **Geshur**, where he
stayed with his grandfather **Talmai**, who was the father of David's
wife Maacah. David spent that time grieving—first, over the

death of Amnon and second, after his sorrow over Amnon had subsided, over his separation from Absalom. Joab, David's general, knew David was yearning for reconciliation, so he contrived an elaborate scheme to reunite father and son. David invited Absalom to return home, but refused to see him in person. After Absalom had been in Jerusalem for another two years, he finally convinced Joab to arrange a personal meeting with the king. David greeted his son with a kiss.

NKJV Study Bible

The kiss was the symbol of their reconciliation. Although David and Absalom were reconciled, the seeds of bitterness that had been sown would soon bear the fruit of conspiracy and rebellion. David's protracted delay in coming to terms with his son ultimately led to disaster.[7]

Absalom's Angle

Although he had patched up the rift with his father, a residue of resentment must have lingered in Absalom's heart. He probably resented the fact that David had done little more than shrug and say, "Oh, well," when his sister was raped. And he probably felt slighted when, after he took it upon himself to avenge the crime, his father didn't say, "Thanks," or "I owe you one." Instead, David was angry at Absalom's refusal to let Amnon slide.

Richard D. Phillips

While Absalom was eager to return to David's court, it is clear that he neither loved nor respected his father. His resentment surely originated with David's failure to act after Tamar's rape, and his attitude eventually ripened into contempt and rebellion. Indeed, it was not long before the unemployed prince began to seek out work for himself.[8]

Absalom's Revenge

2 SAMUEL 15:1–6 *After this it happened that Absalom provided himself with chariots and horses, and fifty men to run before him. Now Absalom would rise early and stand beside the*

way to the gate. So it was, whenever anyone who had a lawsuit came to the king for a decision, that Absalom would call to him and say, "What city are you from?" And he would say, "Your servant is from such and such a tribe of Israel." Then Absalom would say to him, "Look, your case is good and right; but there is no deputy of the king to hear you." Moreover Absalom would say, "Oh, that I were made judge in the land, and everyone who has any suit or cause would come to me; then I would give him justice." And so it was, whenever anyone came near to bow down to him, that he would put out his hand and take him and kiss him. In this manner Absalom acted toward all Israel who came to the king for judgment. So Absalom stole the hearts of the men of Israel. (NKJV)

Word of the animosity between the king and his son began to spread, and Absalom seized the opportunity to capitalize on the nation's unrest by trying to wrangle power from David. His first part of a three-pronged strategy involved hitting the pavement, much like today's politicians, to "steal the hearts" of the public. He listened to citizens' complaints, never missing a chance to sling mud at his father for not being there to take care of the people's problems. And he made a showy claim to the throne with a flashy chariot and a sizable entourage.

key point

what others say

Richard D. Phillips

Notice that it is the administration of justice that Absalom especially picks at. David's glaring failure to do right in his own family was apparently mirrored in his failure to establish an effective system for dealing with grievances among the people. How easy it was, then, for Absalom to draw frustrated claimants to his cause, probably sinning over both sides in every case.[9]

Working His Plan

2 SAMUEL 15:7–9 *Now it came to pass after forty years that Absalom said to the king, "Please, let me go to Hebron and pay the vow which I made to the LORD. For your servant took a vow while I dwelt at Geshur in Syria, saying, 'If the LORD indeed brings me back to Jerusalem, then I will serve the LORD.'" And the king said to him, "Go in peace." So he arose and went to Hebron. (NKJV)*

The second prong of Absalom's strategy involved a cross-country trip. He traveled to Hebron, the heart of David's dynasty, to establish a foothold of support there.

2 SAMUEL 15:10–12 *Then Absalom sent spies throughout all the tribes of Israel, saying, "As soon as you hear the sound of the trumpet, then you shall say, 'Absalom reigns in Hebron!'" And with Absalom went two hundred men invited from Jerusalem, and they went along innocently and did not know anything. Then Absalom sent for Ahithophel the Gilonite, David's counselor, from his city—from Giloh—while he offered sacrifices. And the conspiracy grew strong, for the people with Absalom continually increased in number.* (NKJV)

The third and final prong in Absalom's strategy was announcing his intention to take power from his father. A full-blown coup was under way. First, David's infant son had died. Then, his son Amnon had raped his daughter Tamar. Next, another son, Absalom, had murdered Amnon. Now, Absalom was launching a rebellion against him. Nathan's prophecy of trouble in David's family was certainly coming to pass. *God always* keeps His word. He keeps His promises of judgment just as surely as He keeps His promises of blessings.

David Fled Jerusalem

go to

concubines
Genesis 25:6; 35:22;
Judges 19:1;
2 Samuel 3:7; 5:13,
16:21;
1 Kings 11:3;
1 Chronicles 1:32;
Esther 2:14

Question: Why did David leave Jerusalem? He was, after all, the king of Israel, and his well-fortified palace was in the capital city of Jerusalem. During a rebellion such as this, it would seem to make more sense for David to stay put, safe inside the walls of the great city, than to flee. Looks like running away would have left both David and his city all the more vulnerable to attack.

Answer: David knew that if Absalom were indeed moving in on him, his son's first move would be to take the city. The king didn't want to put his people and the city he loved through the risks involved in a potentially devastating military assault.

David didn't leave Jerusalem solo. He was accompanied by an entourage that included his numerous wives, all but ten of his **concubines**, his officials, and some of his army.

what others say

Zondervan NIV Bible Commentary

By any reckoning David has a sizable and dependable military force to protect him from whatever contingency might arise from Absalom's delusions of grandeur.[11]

David is believed to have written Psalm 3 when he fled from Jerusalem. The short psalm can be divided into four parts:

1. David's Cry

PSALM 3:1–2 *Lord, how they have increased who trouble me! Many are they who rise up against me. Many are they who say of me, "There is no help for him in God." Selah.* (NKJV)

David's opening lament describes his predicament: "Many"— including his son Absalom and all those who have chosen to follow Absalom rather than David—had turned on him and made it their goal to destroy him.

2. David's Confidence

PSALM 3:3–4 *But You, O Lord, are a shield for me, my glory and the One who lifts up my head. I cried to the Lord with my voice, and He heard me from His holy hill. Selah.* (NKJV)

concubines
female slaves or
mistresses

Selah
a term for musical
direction used in
the Psalms

With two words, "But You," David's pleading lament blossomed into a confident confession of his trust in the Lord, who had rescued David from his enemies in the past and whom David could count on to do the same on this day and in the future.

never stop praying
1 Thessalonians 5:17

3. David's Demonstration

PSALM 3:5–6 *I lay down and slept; I awoke, for the LORD sustained me. I will not be afraid of ten thousands of people who have set themselves against me all around. (NKJV)*

Usually when we're worried or frightened, a good night's sleep is hard to come by. Questions of "What if?" and "What next?" keep us tossing and turning for hours on end. In verses 3 and 4, David had expressed his confidence in God's care; in verses 5 and 6 he shows that he meant it. He demonstrated his assurance by deliberately shoving aside worry and fear. Apparently, he was so successful in doing that, he was able to get in a full eight hours of shut-eye—a rare commodity for a man on the run!

what others say

H. A. Ironside

Here is David fleeing from Absalom, not knowing what moment the army will be coming over the hill; but night has fallen, and he has committed himself to God, and so he wraps his robe around him and lies down and goes to sleep! He is safe, for he has handed everything over to God.[12]

4. David's Continuing Plea

PSALM 3:7–8 *Arise, O LORD; save me, O my God! For You have struck all my enemies on the cheekbone; You have broken the teeth of the ungodly. Salvation belongs to the LORD. Your blessing is upon Your people. Selah. (NKJV)*

Although he remained confident of God's care, David continued to pray, a reminder of the New Testament instruction to <u>never stop praying</u>.

anointed
2 Samuel 5:1–5

go to

what others say

H. A. Ironside

David, the true king, was rejected and Absalom, the usurper, was reigning; and that is the condition of things now. Our Lord Jesus, the true King, is rejected and an usurper is on the throne; so we can expect suffering and sorrow. David's experience pictures in a very wonderful way what the people of God will go through during the day of the Lord's rejection.[13]

Jerusalem's Special History

Why was Jerusalem so special to David that he would rather leave than see it destroyed? After he had been <u>anointed</u> as king of Israel, David had hand-picked Jerusalem as his capital. The city was at the top of his list of suitable sites because of its central location, easy access, and abundant water supplies. Further, it was located in a politically neutral territory.

what others say

Richard D. Phillips

Jerusalem had long been on David's mind. It was not only a prominent and strategically vital location right in the heart of Israel but its ability to hold out against the Israelites was a centuries-old symbol of their failure, faithlessness, and mediocrity. Other brave men had tried to take Jerusalem . . . and they had ultimately shrunk back from the task. Jerusalem was the ideal defensive position . . . So to take Jerusalem would be more than a coup, it would be the kind of success around which a new identity is forged. For Israel, a future in Jerusalem meant the fulfillment of its past and the promises such fulfillment held for tomorrow.[14]

Alfred J. Kolatch

Jewish history and Jewish tradition is linked to Jerusalem more than to any other place on earth. From about 1000 B.C.E., when David captured the city from the Jebusites (of whom there is no longer any trace) and set it up as his capital, Jerusalem has been sacred to Jews. When Solomon built the first temple there, it became a holy city, often called "the Eternal City." Jews lived in Jerusalem and prayed for its well-being for 1,000 years before there were Christians on the face of the earth, and for 1,600 years before Islamic nations came into being.[15]

Rose Book of Bible Charts, Maps and Timelines

The City of David Archaeological Project uncovered much of the buried remains of David's city of Jerusalem between 1978–1985. Archaeologists have uncovered remains of that city, including evidence of David's conquest and a palace that may have belonged to David himself.[16]

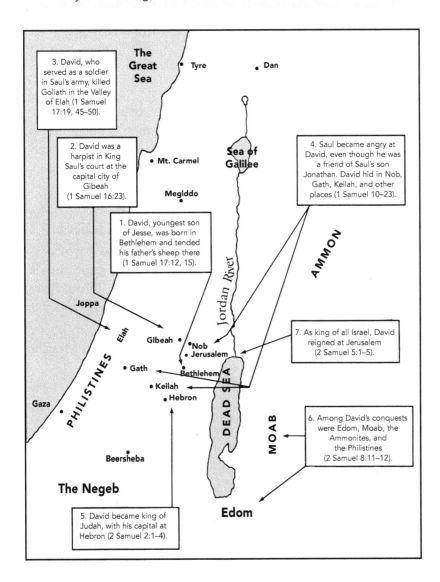

The Life of David
This map shows major events in the life of David, keyed to the actual locations at which they took place.

3. David, who served as a soldier in Saul's army, killed Goliath in the Valley of Elah (1 Samuel 17:19, 45–50).

2. David was a harpist in King Saul's court at the capital city of Gibeah (1 Samuel 16:23).

4. Saul became angry at David, even though he was a friend of Saul's son Jonathan. David hid in Nob, Gath, Keilah, and other places (1 Samuel 10–23).

1. David, youngest son of Jesse, was born in Bethlehem and tended his father's sheep there (1 Samuel 17:12, 15).

7. As king of all Israel, David reigned at Jerusalem (2 Samuel 5:1–5).

6. Among David's conquests were Edom, Moab, the Ammonites, and the Philistines (2 Samuel 8:11–12).

5. David became king of Judah, with his capital at Hebron (2 Samuel 2:1–4).

The Great Sea • Tyre • Dan • Mt. Carmel Sea of Galilee Megiddo AMMON Jordan River Joppa Elah Gibeah • • Nob • Jerusalem PHILISTINES • Gath Bethlehem • Keilah • Hebron DEAD SEA MOAB Gaza • Beersheba The Negeb Edom

go to

brought the ark into battle
1 Samuel 4:3–4

inscribed
Exodus 32:15–16

dry ground
Joshua 3:15–17

walls came tumbling down
Joshua 6:3–20

ark of God
1 Samuel 3:3

ark of the covenant
Joshua 3:6;
Hebrews 9:4

ark of the testimony
Exodus 25:22

Moses
great prophet and lawgiver who led the Israelites from Egyptian bondage

Ten Commandments
God's laws for life

Canaan
the land God promised Abraham and his descendants, the Israelites

Jericho
site of Israel's first great victory in the land God had promised them

On Second Thought . . .

Why did David change his mind about bringing the ark along on his flight from Jerusalem? There are a couple of possible reasons. He might have wanted to make it clear that he did not regard the ark as a good luck charm, as the Israelites had done many years before, when they had <u>brought the ark into battle</u> against the Philistines. Or, he might have been sticking to his resolve to keep worship—symbolized by the ark—in the nation's capital where it belonged.

The Ark's Holy History

The Hebrew word used for ark, *aron*, is a common name for any kind of a chest. But the ark of the covenant didn't contain linens, pottery, or clothing, however. It served a sacred purpose. As the centerpiece of Israel's worship, it was a reminder of God's continuing protection and provision.

- God had told **Moses** to build a special box for the tablets upon which the **Ten Commandments** were <u>inscribed</u>.
- The Israelites had taken the ark with them as a symbol of God's presence as they wandered in the wilderness, and the priests had carried the ark into the bed of the Jordan River, which God parted in order for the Israelites to cross into **Canaan** on <u>dry ground</u>.
- The ark had been carried in the procession around **Jericho** before the <u>walls came tumbling down</u>.

Three Names

The ark of the covenant is referred to in Scripture by three terms. The "<u>ark of God</u>" reflects its relationship to God; the "<u>ark of the covenant</u>" alludes to the promises God made the Israelites when He gave Moses the Law. And the "<u>ark of the testimony</u>" highlights the stone tablets containing the Ten Commandments, which are sometimes called the "testimony."

Divine Design

At about four feet long and a little more than two feet wide and tall, the ark of the covenant compared to the size and shape of a modern-day cedar chest. It was built and embellished according to a set of underlined instructions God gave Moses. Part of those instructions called for portability. Because the vessel would need to be moved from place to place along with the tabernacle, its design included gold rings through which golden poles could be inserted in order to carry it. It also featured a solid gold lid, called the mercy seat because it was where God positioned Himself within the most holy place. Atop the mercy seat, two **cherubim** faced each other, with their wings spanning over the mercy seat, or the throne of God.

In addition to the two tablets of stone on which God had inscribed the Ten Commandments, the ark contained other unique artifacts: the pot of **manna** God had provided the Israelites as sustenance while they wandered in the wilderness and **Aaron**'s rod that budded when God appointed him as Israel's first high priest.

God was as specific in providing instructions for the way the ark should be handled as He was for the way it should be built. Because it was such a sacred object, no one was allowed to touch it. Any time it was moved, members of a special family of priests were to carry the ark on their shoulders using the rings and poles under a purple canopy ahead of the rest of the travelers.

go to

detailed instructions
Exodus 25:10–22

tablets of stone
Deuteronomy 31:24–26

manna
Exodus 16:12–36

rod that budded
Numbers 17:8, 10

carry the ark
Numbers 4:5; 6;
10:33–36;
Psalm 132:8

cherubim
type of angels that guard the throne of God

manna
nourishing food God miraculously provided each morning

Aaron
Moses' brother and the first high priest

Handle with Care!

the big picture

2 Samuel 6:3–8; 1 Chronicles 13:5–12

When David first tried to move the ark into Jerusalem, he failed to insist that it be handled with appropriate care. He allowed it to be placed on a cart—sidestepping God's directions that it be carried with poles—and allowed unqualified men to supervise the operation. When the cart rolled across a bump in the road the oxen pulling the cart stumbled, the cart tipped, and the ark began to slide toward the edge. One of the "ark movers," Uzza, reached out to steady the ark and prevent it from crashing to the ground, violating the sanctity of the vessel. He was instantly struck dead.

Mount of Olives
Zechariah 14:4;
1 Kings 11:7;
2 Kings 23:13;
Nehemiah 8:15;
Ezekiel 11:23;
Matthew 21:1; 24:3;
26:30, 39

Mount of Olives
mountain east of
Jerusalem

what others say

The Bible Almanac

During the wanderings in the wilderness and in the conquest of the Promised Land, the ark always went before the enemies of Israel. This was to symbolize God's active presence with His people.[17]

He Wanted to Worship

the big picture

2 Samuel 15:30–37

On his way out of town, David made an important stop: He led the people who were with him up the **Mount of Olives** to worship and pray. While he was there, David prayed that God would confound the advice of the usually wise Ahithophel. Then he recruited his friend Hushai to go to Jerusalem and get into the court as a counselor in order to contradict Ahithophel's advice to Absalom, and to serve as a spy.

what others say

Steven L. McKenzie

[Ahithophel] may have borne a personal grudge against David because of the Bathsheba affair. Bathsheba was the daughter of Eliam (2 Samuel 11:5), and Ahithophel had a son named Eliam, who was among David's best warriors (2 Samuel 15:12; 23:34). If these two Eliams were the same person, then Bathsheba was Ahithophel's granddaughter and Ahithophel may have acted against David as revenge for Uriah's death and the humiliation of Bathsheba.[18]

Ziba's News Flash

2 SAMUEL 16:1–4 *When David was a little past the top of the mountain, there was Ziba the servant of Mephibosheth, who met him with a couple of saddled donkeys, and on them two hundred loaves of bread, one hundred clusters of raisins, one hundred summer fruits, and a skin of wine. And the king said to Ziba, "What do you mean to do with these?" So Ziba said, "The donkeys are for the king's household to ride on, the bread and summer fruit for the young men to eat, and the wine for those who* *are faint in the wilderness to drink." Then the king said, "And where is your master's son?" And Ziba said to the king, "Indeed he is staying in Jerusalem, for he said, 'Today the house of Israel will restore the kingdom of my father to me.'" So the king said to Ziba, "Here, all that belongs to Mephibosheth is yours." And Ziba said, "I humbly bow before you, that I may find favor in your sight, my lord, O king!" (NKJV)*

While David was fleeing Jerusalem after stopping to worship and pray on the Mount of Olives, he met a man named Ziba. Ziba was the servant of Mephibosheth, the son of David's dear friend **Jonathan**, who had <u>died in battle</u> about the same time as his father, King Saul. To honor a <u>covenant of friendship</u> David had made with Jonathan many years earlier, David had welcomed the lame boy, **Mephibosheth**, into his own home. He had given him a standing invitation to eat dinner at the king's table, a provision that also included a lifetime pension, to put it in modern terms. Plus, he had restored to Mephibosheth the land and property he had lost when his grandfather had died.

Now, as Ziba greeted David and his party with provisions for their flight from Jerusalem, the servant offered some startling news. He said his master had turned against the king in the hope of claiming his dead grandfather's throne. In an on-the-spot judgment, David took away Mephibosheth's pension and handed it all over to Ziba.

This turn of events regarding Mephibosheth's loyalty seems puzzling. At this point in the narrative, it's difficult to explain why Jonathan's son, whom David had treated so kindly and welcomed into his own family, betrayed the king. A glimpse ahead, however, to 2 Samuel 19:24–30, indicates that Ziba wasn't on the up-and-up. The way David ultimately handled the matter is a plot that will continue into the beginning days of Solomon's reign.

Stoned by Shimei

2 SAMUEL 16:5–6 *Now when King David came to* **Bahurim**, *there was a man from the family of the house of Saul, whose name was* **Shimei** *the son of Gera, coming from there. He came out, cursing continuously as he came. And he threw stones at David and at all the servants of King David.* (NKJV)

died in battle
1 Samuel 31:2

covenant of friendship
1 Samuel 20

Mephibosheth
2 Samuel 4:4–6;
9:1–13

Jonathan
oldest son of King
Saul and close friend
of David

Mephibosheth
a son of Jonathan
and grandson of
Saul

Bahurim
a city near
Jerusalem, east of
the Mount of Olives

Shimei
a distant relative of
Saul

Mahanaim
the well-fortified,
former capital of
Israel

After encountering Ziba, David proceeded eastward toward
Bahurim. There, one of Saul's distant relatives, Shimei, approached
him, all the while spewing curses and hurling rocks. Although cursing the king was a capital offense, David refused to allow Abishai, his
bodyguard and nephew, to execute Shimei (see 2 Samuel 16:9–13).

Cursing: More Than a Foul Mouth

When the Bible says Shimei was cursing, it doesn't necessarily
mean he was using four-letter words. It was much more serious than
that. He was calling upon God to destroy David. Since God Himself
had ordained David to be His anointed king, the words were blas-
phemous and, under the Law, uttering them was a crime that carried
the death penalty.

Joab Murdered Absalom

the big picture

2 Samuel 16–18

David continued to flee eastward; meanwhile, Absalom went
to Jerusalem where Hushai, David's spy friend, pretended to
remain loyal to Absalom. Ahithophel urged Absalom to sleep
with his father's concubines to make a clear statement to the
effect that he was assuming power. Absalom chose Hushai's
counsel to wait over Ahithophel's advice to attack. Ahithophel
was so offended by the slight that he committed suicide. The
interval gave David and his men time to travel all the way to
Mahanaim. At Mahanaim, David gathered support and provisions and regrouped. Before launching a fresh attack he issued
an explicit order that Absalom should be kept from harm in the
battle. Absalom tried to escape from David's soldiers on the
back of a mule, but was stopped in his tracks when his long,
thick hair got tangled in the branches of a tree in the thick forest
of Ephraim. Joab killed Absalom right then and there. The news
of his son's death sent David into inconsolable grief.

Thomas L. Constable

Absalom was never Yahweh's choice to succeed David (cf. 12:24–25; 1 Chronicles 22:9–10). Therefore his attempt to dethrone the Lord's anointed was contrary to God's will and doomed to fail from the beginning.[19]

"Absalom! Absalom!"

> 2 SAMUEL 19:1–4 *And Joab was told, "Behold, the king is weeping and mourning for Absalom." So the victory that day was turned into mourning for all the people. For the people heard it said that day, "The king is grieved for his son." And the people stole back into the city that day, as people who are ashamed steal away when they flee in battle. But the king covered his face, and the king cried out with a loud voice, "O my son Absalom! O Absalom, my son, my son!"* (NKJV)

David's grief over Absalom's death almost paralyzed him. Even though his troops had stopped the revolt, he appeared to be in no hurry to retake his rightful place on the throne of Israel. He remained cloistered away at his chambers in Mahanaim, crying pitifully.

The king, it seemed, couldn't have cared less about politics at the moment. But his right-hand man, Joab, couldn't have cared more. He clearly saw what was going on in the nation, and he didn't like the looks of things. Even though David had secured victory over Absalom and his troops, the Israelites remained uncertain about their future. Some had promised loyalty to Absalom, a leader who was now dead. Others had faithfully stood by David—but he was nowhere to be seen. They expected their victorious leader to be out in the city **gate** doing a little public relations work, thanking his loyal followers and honoring his soldiers for their valor.

If David didn't do something—*anything*—soon, even more political turmoil was likely to erupt. Joab knew all of this, and he minced no words in giving David a piece of his mind about the situation:

> 2 SAMUEL 19:5–7 *Then Joab came into the house to the king, and said, "Today you have disgraced all your servants who today have saved your life, the lives of your sons and daughters, the lives of your wives and the lives of your concubines, in that you love your enemies and hate your friends. For you have declared*

go to

gate
Deuteronomy 21:19; 22:24;
Joshua 20:4;
Ruth 4:1;
2 Kings 7:1

gate
place where public affairs were handled

today that you regard neither princes nor servants; for today I perceive that if Absalom had lived and all of us had died today, then it would have pleased you well. Now therefore, arise, go out and speak comfort to your servants. For I swear by the LORD, if you do not go out, not one will stay with you this night. And that will be worse for you than all the evil that has befallen you from your youth until now." (NKJV)

the big picture

2 Samuel 19:8–18

Joab's words worked; the king complied. As David sat in the gate to greet and thank his people, he devised a plan for strengthening the national government's shaky underpinnings. He would start by appealing to the elders of his own tribe, Judah, for their help in returning him to his rightful place on the throne. After naming **Amasa** of Judah—Absalom's general and David's own nephew—to replace Joab, David—escorted by the men of Judah—set out on the journey back home to Jerusalem.

Adonijah's Power Grab

1 KINGS 1:1–4 *Now King David was old, advanced in years; and they put covers on him, but he could not get warm. Therefore his servants said to him, "Let a young woman, a virgin, be sought for our lord the king, and let her stand before the king, and let her care for him; and let her lie in your bosom, that our lord the king may be warm." So they sought for a lovely young woman throughout all the territory of Israel, and found Abishag the Shunamite, and brought her to the king. The young woman was very lovely; and she cared for the king, and served him; but the king did not know her.* (NKJV)

After Absalom's revolt, Israel enjoyed a long period of peace. During these peaceful years, Solomon was still quite young (although no one knows his exact age). Scripture indicates that he spent much time by his father's side as David devoted himself to making plans for the temple. When his father was about seventy years old, Solomon would have been old enough to see that his father's health had begun to deteriorate. David's strong, sturdy body became weak and delicate, and he felt a constant chill. Anxious to provide their master some comfort, David's servants brought their bedridden king an attractive young virgin from Shunam named

Abishag. She cared for David and slept with him (although many scholars note that the relationship was not intimate) in order to keep him warm at night.

what others say

NKJV Study Bible

Using a healthy person's body warmth to care for a sick person is a medical procedure noted by the second-century Greek physician Galen and the Jewish historian Josephus.[20]

Robert Alter

David, lying in bed with this desirable virgin, but now beyond any thought of capacity of sexual consummation, is of course a sad image of infirm old age. At the same time, this . . . is a pointed reversal of the Bathsheba story that brought down God's curse on the house of David, triggering all the subsequent troubles of dynastic succession.[21]

Getting His Game On

1 KINGS 1:5–6 Then Adonijah the son of Haggith exalted himself, saying, "I will be king"; and he prepared for himself chariots and horsemen, and fifty men to run before him. (And his father had not rebuked him at any time by saying, "Why have you done so?" He was also very good-looking. His mother had borne him after Absalom.) (NKJV)

Adonijah, David's son with **Haggith** and born in Hebron, was Absalom's younger half brother. As David's oldest surviving son, he assumed he was next in line for the throne and saw his father's physical decline as his chance to announce his intention of becoming Israel's next king.

*1 KINGS 1:7–10 Then he conferred with Joab the son of Zeruiah and with **Abiathar** the priest, and they followed and helped Adonijah. But **Zadok** the priest, **Benaiah** the son of Jehoiada, Nathan the prophet, Shimei, Rei, and the mighty men who belonged to David were not with Adonijah. And Adonijah sacrificed sheep and oxen and fattened cattle by the stone of Zoheleth, which is by En Rogel; he also invited all his brothers, the king's sons, and all the men of Judah, the king's servants. But he did not invite Nathan the prophet, Benaiah, the mighty men, or Solomon his brother. (NKJV)*

Abishag
Shunamite virgin hired to care for the elderly David

Haggith
one of David's wives

Abiathar
a chief priest in David's court

Zadok
high priest in David's court

Benaiah
commander of David's guard

In putting together a high-powered transition team, Adonijah recruited Joab, the commander of David's army, and Abiathar, the priest. He didn't, however, succeed at winning over Zadok the priest; Benaiah, one of David's highest-ranking soldiers; Nathan the prophet; or Shimei and Rei, the king's special guards. With great flourish, Adonijah staged a great feast near En Rogel, just southeast of Jerusalem. The fact that he incorporated the ceremony of making sacrifices into the festivities signaled that he considered this a God-ordained inauguration.

Adonijah's Arrogance

The Bible doesn't have a whole lot to say about Adonijah, but the few words devoted to David's oldest living son paint a disturbing portrait of Solomon's oldest living brother:

- *He was arrogant.* "Then Adonijah the son of Haggith exalted himself" (1 Kings 1:5 NKJV). The word used for "exalted" has to do with "lifting up," or "raising." To put it bluntly, Adonijah put himself on a pedestal. Jesus warned people who presume to raise themselves up in the eyes of others that it's an exercise in futility: "For whoever exalts himself will be humbled, and he who humbles himself will be exalted" (Luke 14:11 NKJV). Adonijah and David serve as living proof of this principle: In raising himself up, Adonijah would ultimately be knocked down; in remaining humble, David was ultimately given high honors.

- *He wasn't concerned with God's plans.* "I will be king," Adonijah said in 1 Kings 1:5 (NKJV). It's not clear whether he was unaware that Solomon was going to be Israel's next king, or whether he simply chose to ignore what he had heard. Either way, had he consulted the Lord about such a significant claim, he would have discovered for himself that his name wasn't to be the next one inscribed over the door of the throne room. But Adonijah wasn't the kind of man to bother with formalities. He saw his dad's decline as a job opening, and he made a beeline to elbow his way to the front of the line.

Notice how Adonijah's words echo those of the fallen angel Lucifer in Isaiah 14:13–14, whose five "I will" statements express the essence of self-centered arrogance:

1. "I will ascend into heaven" (NKJV).

2. "I will exalt my throne above the stars of God" (NKJV).

3. "I will also sit on the mount of the congregation" (NKJV).

4. "I will ascend above the heights" (NKJV).

5. "I will be like the Most High" (NKJV).

Adonijah wasn't alone in believing that he was the one who would replace David as Israel's king. It's likely that most of the people of Israel thought so as well. As Adonijah would later tell Bathsheba, "You know that the kingdom was mine, and all Israel had set their expectations on me, that I should reign" (1 Kings 2:15 NKJV). Israel might have expected him to become king based on what they saw in the other nations around them. It was customary for a king's oldest living son to succeed his father.

How typical of the people of Israel, that they would once again focus on how the other nations operated rather than looking to God for His way of working things out! The nation had made a similar move when they demanded that God give them another arrogant young man, Saul, as a king. They kept forgetting that, as God's people, they weren't supposed to follow the pattern set by the rest of the world. God had said He alone reserved the right to name the king of His nation Israel (see Deuteronomy 17:15).

key point

handsome
1 Kings 1:6

Absalom's play for control
1 Kings 1:5

rod
Proverbs 29:15

- He was the "spitting image" of his older brother (and that's not a compliment!). Even though he was physically <u>handsome</u> like Absalom (no surprise there; they shared the same mother, who was drop-dead gorgeous), he apparently lacked either the brains or the originality to think up his own publicity stunts. In gathering chariots and horsemen, plus fifty runners, baby brother was simply copying the behavior of his big brother <u>Absalom's play for control</u>.

- He was spoiled. First Kings 1:6 states that David had never rebuked his son. Apparently David had continued his pattern of passive parenting with Adonijah, upon whom David apparently continually "spared the <u>rod</u>" when he had demonstrated bad behavior.

what others say

J. Vernon McGee

[Adonijah] was a very proud young man with a high regard for himself. He was conceited, and you can detect in him some of the traits of his half brother Absalom who had led a rebellion against David. Adonijah, had something not been done, would also have led a rebellion against his father. David never had a reputation of disciplining his family. . . . Adonijah took full advantage of the situation. David never rebuked him. When he did wrong, I think David just smiled over his boy as an old indulgent man would do.[23]

More important than the names Adonijah included on his guest list for the feast were the names he did *not* include: Nathan, Benaiah, Shimei, Rei, and Solomon. Had these people eaten at Adonijah's table he would have been obliged not to harm them. Their absence from the guest list was a clear signal of his intentions: He meant to kill them.

what others say

Ryrie Study Bible, NIV

As a prelude to taking over the throne, Adonijah held a feast but did not invite Nathan and Solomon. He apparently was planning to kill them, for had they eaten together, he would have been obliged to protect them.[24]

Nathan Intervened

1 KINGS 1:11 So Nathan spoke to Bathsheba the mother of Solomon, saying, "Have you not heard that Adonijah the son of Haggith has become king, and David our lord does not know it?" (NKJV)

Nathan knew what God wanted done concerning David's succession. He knew because <u>God had told him</u>. The prophet could not sit by and watch an egotistical young man take the helm of the great nation of Israel against God's will. But, how to stop him? He had to get word to the king. Nathan had certainly approached David before. He had been the one to tell David that God didn't intend for him to build the <u>temple</u>, and he had been the one to <u>confront David</u> with the harsh reality of his sin with Bathsheba.

When Nathan had talked to David about Bathsheba, he had approached the king by way of a parable. This time, he would approach the king by way of Bathsheba. As David's beloved wife, she had access to the king's chambers. And as Solomon's mother, the woman whose life God had so tenderly knit to David's following the devastation of the couple's sin, she had access to the king's heart.

go to

God had told him
2 Samuel 12:1, 25

temple
1 Chronicles 17

confront David
2 Samuel 12:1–12

what others say

Thomas L. Constable

Adonijah had become king (v. 11) only in the sense that he was the people's choice at that moment. Perhaps Nathan was trying to shock Bathsheba and David by referring to Adonijah as the king.[25]

Richard D. Phillips

It is fascinating to see who these loyalists turned to in their bid to save the day. It was Bathsheba, Solomon's mother, who now stepped forth as the most prominent among David's wives and the key support for her husband.[26]

1 KINGS 1:12–14 Come, please, let me now give you advice, that you may save your own life and the life of your son Solomon. Go immediately to King David and say to him, "Did you not, my lord, O king, swear to your maidservant, saying, 'Assuredly your son Solomon shall reign after me, and he shall sit on my throne'? Why then has Adonijah become king?" Then, while you are still talking there with the king, I also will come in after you and confirm your words. (NKJV)

restoration
Acts 3:21;
Revelation 21:1–5

Nathan told Bathsheba to tell David what was going on, and to remind him of his pledge that Solomon would be his successor. She did so, and Nathan, as he had planned, also visited the king to confirm Bathsheba's words.

Adultery + Pregnancy + Murder + Grief: _Not_ the Recipe for a Happy Marriage

David had married Bathsheba to cover up their sin of adultery that had resulted in her pregnancy. Bathsheba had come into the marriage grieving the loss of her first husband, whom her second husband had, in essence, murdered. So the marriage of convenience for David and Bathsheba had been built on a shaky foundation of deceit, manipulation, criminal activity, and grief. In many cases, a relationship like that might be destined for divorce court. But when God is involved, things don't always turn out as people might expect. God is in the business of restoration, and He was able to transform the rubble of the once-unholy alliance into a loving, long-lasting relationship based on mutual trust in God and respect for one another. That's evident in this passage, which shows that Bathsheba—one of many wives in David's household—didn't have to take a number to get a royal audience. Obviously she had ready access to the king.

Where Was Solomon?

Solomon knew he was supposed to become king. So why wasn't he busy sticking out his foot to trip up his brother's sprint for the throne? In one of only two psalms attributed to Solomon (the other is Psalm 72), he offers a clue:

> **PSALM 127:1–2** _Unless the_ LORD _builds the house, they labor in vain who build it; unless the_ LORD _guards the city, the watchman stays awake in vain. It is vain for you to rise up early, to sit up late, to eat the bread of sorrows, for so He gives His beloved sleep._ (NKJV)

Apparently, taking his position on the throne was a "house" Solomon was resolved to let the Lord build. He was content to let God orchestrate the transition of power—and he was wise enough to know that God didn't need his mortal meddling.

Matthew Henry

Solomon, it is likely, knew of it, but was as a deaf man that heard not. Though he had years, and wisdom above his years, yet we do not find that he stirred to oppose Adonijah, but quietly composed himself and left it to God and his friends to order the matter.[27]

Awakened into Action

1 KINGS 1:20–21 *And as for you, my lord, O king, the eyes of all Israel are on you, that you should tell them who will sit on the throne of my lord the king after him. Otherwise it will happen, when my lord the king rests with his fathers, that I and my son Solomon will be counted as offenders.* (NKJV)

Hints of Bathsheba's maturing faith are beginning to surface. A boldness she lacked in her encounter with David the night he summoned her to his chambers now resonates in her words to the king. She confidently reminded David it was his duty as king to publicly settle the matter of his successor, and it was his duty as her husband to protect the lives of her and of their son—both would be at risk should Adonijah succeed.

key point

Thomas L. Constable

Normally in the ancient Near East a new king would purge his political enemies when he came to power (cf. 2:13–46). This was the basis for Bathsheba's fear (v. 21).[28]

Solomon, King of Israel

the big picture

1 Kings 1:22–48

The words revitalized David's weak body. He got out of bed and took charge. Vowing that Solomon would indeed become his successor, he issued detailed orders: Zadok, Nathan, and Benaiah—the highest-ranking priest, prophet, and soldier, respectively—would accompany Solomon to Gihon. The young man was to ride on David's mule, a clear indication to anyone watching that Solomon was the appointed successor to the

go to

deliverer of Israel
Psalm 2:2;
Daniel 9:25–26

**Christ was anointed
with the Holy Spirit**
Isaiah 61:1;
John 1:41;
Acts 9:22; 17:2–3;
18:4, 28;
John 1:32–33;
Acts 4:27; 10:38

> throne. After they arrived Zadok and Nathan anointed Solomon, blew the trumpet to announce the occasion, and shouted, "Long live King Solomon!"

The Bible makes one fact clear: Solomon became king that day. This is emphasized by the fact that Solomon's crowning is described three different times:

1. *David Gives Directions* (verses 32–36). David issued detailed instructions for making Solomon king.

2. *David's Men Deliver* (verses 37–40). David's men faithfully and swiftly carried out his instructions.

3. *Adonijah Is Informed* (verses 43–48). Jonathan, Abiathar's son, offered Adonijah a clear report of how David's succession had been settled.

About Anointing

Solomon's anointing held deeply religious and prophetic significance. Anointing someone, which means pouring or sprinkling oil on them (usually olive oil), was a common practice in the Hebrew culture. The Bible mentions anointing in several situations. For example, a hospitable host would often rub oil on a guest's head to soothe his sun-parched scalp. Anointing was used most frequently in the inauguration of prophets, priests, and kings. The oil symbolized God's guidance and power on the anointed person's life. Thus an oil anointing assured the king that he was:

- Set apart for God's holy work.

- Designated as an authorized agent of God who would apply God's wisdom to the administration of His people.

- Empowered to ensure peace and provide military security.

A More Powerful Power

The Messiah, whose name means "anointed one," was the promised <u>deliverer of Israel</u>. <u>Christ was anointed with the Holy Spirit</u> rather than with physical oil.

A More Powerful Power

Christians are anointed with the Holy Spirit when they put their faith in God:

1 JOHN 2:27 *But the anointing which you have received from Him abides in you, and you do not need that anyone teach you.* (*NKJV*)

Benefits of having the Holy Spirit with us include:

- Experiencing the constant presence of God (1 Corinthians 6:19)
- Receiving courage in the face of fear (2 Timothy 1:7)
- Having the ability to understand the things of God (John 14:26; 1 Corinthians 2:11–12)
- Having One to intercede on our behalf (Romans 8:26–27)

what others say

Billy Graham

What makes Christians different from everyone else is that God Himself lives within them by His Holy Spirit. When we come to Christ and give our lives to Him, God actually takes up residence within us. We may not always feel different or be aware of His presence, but Jesus' promise to His disciples has already been fulfilled: "I will ask the Father, and he will give you another Counselor to be with you forever—the Spirit of truth" (John 14:16–17).[29]

Paper or Plastic? Glass or Horn?

The story that begins in the Bible with the birth of the prophet Samuel and then outlines the reigns of Kings Saul, David, and Solomon is called by Bible scholars the "Succession Narratives." In these passages, three people were anointed as king: Saul, a man the people chose as king; David, a man God chose as king; and Solomon, another man God chose as king. Interestingly, the containers used to dispense the oil in each anointing carried great significance:

- Saul was anointed with oil dispensed from a fragile clay flask that was small and breakable, offering an apt illustration of

go to

Christians are anointed
2 Corinthians 1:21

the reign of the king whose strength and power was limited by his fragile faith in God.

- David and Solomon were anointed with oil dispensed from sturdy horns, larger and much more durable vessels that symbolized the strength of God that underlay their reigns.

Adonijah: Afraid for His Life

1 KINGS 1:49–53 So all the guests who were with Adonijah were afraid, and arose, and each one went his way. Now Adonijah was afraid of Solomon; so he arose, and went and took hold of the horns of the altar. And it was told Solomon, saying, "Indeed Adonijah is afraid of King Solomon; for look, he has taken hold of the horns of the altar, saying, 'Let King Solomon swear to me today that he will not put his servant to death with the sword.'" Then Solomon said, "If he proves himself a worthy man, not one hair of him shall fall to the earth; but if wickedness is found in him, he shall die." So King Solomon sent them to bring him down from the altar. And he came and fell down before King Solomon; and Solomon said to him, "Go to your house." (NKJV)

Finally, Solomon had taken his place on David's throne. The Israelites responded to the news with great celebration. The merriment was so spirited, in fact, that their music and dancing literally shook the ground. Meanwhile, across the river at Adonijah's self-proclaimed inaugural ball, the guests scattered when they received the news that Solomon was now king. They were afraid they might be charged with conspiring against the newly anointed monarch. Within moments, Adonijah's head-swelling high dissipated into run-for-your-life fear. He headed straight for the altar, where he grabbed onto its horn-shaped knobs in an appeal for his life to be spared for having plotted against the king. When Solomon heard his brother was so frightened, he promised to let him live on the condition that he behaved himself. If he didn't, Solomon reserved the option of putting him to death.

what others say

Peter Leithart

Ironically, Adonijah means "Yah is master." In spite of his efforts to make himself master, Adonijah's life history demonstrates that Yah is indeed Master.[30]

Words of Promise

The horns of the altar, as well as the altar itself, were considered places of absolute safety. The person who grabbed the horns was appealing to the pardoning power and grace of God. For New Testament Christians, the cross of Jesus Christ is our refuge. Because God sacrificed His Son on the altar of the cross, we are assured that all our sins are forgiven. As we cling to Jesus in childlike faith, looking to Him as the beginner and fulfiller, the author and perfecter of our faith, no one can harm us. We are in absolute safety.[31]

Chapter Wrap-Up

- David's firstborn son, Amnon, raped his half sister, Tamar—effectively ruining her life by stealing her virginity, and sparking a seething fury in her brother, Absalom. After fuming for two years, Absalom arranged to have Amnon killed.

- Absalom's murder of Amnon led to a three-year estrangement from David. The two finally reconciled after Joab intervened.

- Absalom quietly and with cunning staged a coup, prompting David to flee Jerusalem with an entourage of wives, concubines, officials, and army members. However, after gathering support and provisions, David and his men were able to turn the tables. Against the king's explicit orders, Absalom was killed at the hands of Joab as he tried to escape the ensuing battle.

- When David became old and feeble, his oldest living son, Adonijah, set his eyes on the throne. Bathsheba got wind of his plans through Nathan and told David, who knew that Solomon, not Adonijah, was God's choice for Israel's next king.

- David arose from his sick bed with newfound energy to thwart the coup. Solomon was anointed king.

Study Questions

1. What impact did Amnon's rape of Tamar have on her? On the whole family?

2. What might have caused Absalom to become so bitter and resentful toward David—to the point that he attempted to seize the throne from his father?

3. As David was fleeing Jerusalem in the wake of his son's attempted coup, what significant stop did he make on his way out of town?

4. Why did Nathan approach Bathsheba with the news of Adonijah's attempted power play?

5. What did Adonijah do when he discovered his plot against the king had failed and that Solomon had been anointed?

2 Samuel 23:1-7; 1 Kings 2:1-12: David's Death

Let's Get Started

The question of David's successor was settled. Solomon had been anointed as the one who would eventually replace his father as Israel's king. But for the time being, the two men likely served as co-regents. It's generally assumed that David probably still called the shots during this time, with Solomon watching carefully—much like an apprentice, or a "king-in-training."

Meanwhile, David's health had been declining. (That was made clear when the human heating pad named <u>Abishag</u> was brought in!) Although illness and frailty slowed his steps, David's mind must have raced ahead as he saw and felt the signals that the time he had left on this earth was limited. Clearly, the king had much to say to his nation, and the father had much to say to his son. The royal scribes must have strained to hear and record every word as, voice weak and heart full, the beloved king of Israel issued his final public statements to Israel and uttered his last private words to Solomon. The Bible records two sets of David's "last" words:

Abishag
1 Kings 1:3–4

anointed Saul
1 Samuel 10:1

1. His last words to the nation are recorded in 2 Samuel 23:1–7.

2. His last words to his son are recorded in 1 Kings 2:1–9.

The Times, They Are A-Changin' . . . Again

Change was the one thing—in addition to God's presence—that had remained a permanent fixture in Israel's history. Most recent changes had centered on the structure of the nation's government.

Israel's government had undergone a radical makeover when it shifted from a theocracy—a nation led by God—to a monarchy—a nation led by a king—when Samuel had <u>anointed Saul</u> as the nation's first king. This set in motion huge changes. In preparing the nation for the transformation, Samuel outlined what Israel could expect:

- *A New Army*—A standing army would be drafted and trained, replacing the former system that relied on volunteers. Further, Israelite soldiers would be responsible for building and maintaining an inventory of supplies and equipment.

- *A New Palace*—A king, after all, must have a suitable place to live. Building, maintaining, and staffing a palace for the king and his leaders didn't come without a price. Israelite families not only would have to see their sons drafted into military service; they would have to allow their daughters to be drafted into domestic service at the royal home.

- *New Taxes*—The cost of living in ancient Israel increased dramatically as families were required to pay taxes to fund the operations of the new government.

- *New Restrictions*—The Israelites, accustomed to freedom and independence, would have to adjust to the rule of a king who might or might not have their best interests in mind.

Change #2: From Saul to David

Next, Israel had been transformed from a monarchy led by the people's choice of a king into one led by God's choice. Not much is said in the Bible about Saul's accomplishments during his reign, other than that he organized an army and led several successful military campaigns.

key point

However, the few strides Saul made as he pioneered his nation's new form of government were overshadowed by his disobedience to God, the dark spirit that settled over him when he refused to follow God's directions, and his destructive designs against David. When David finally became king of Israel, he established a secure and thriving capital in the city of Jerusalem, organized a formidable military, expanded the nation's borders, subdued its enemies, collected great wealth—treasures accumulated from the spoils of war and gifts given him by kings of neighboring allies—and restored worship of God as the nation's center of focus.

Change #3: From David to Solomon

Now it was time for the old regime under David to give way to a new one that would be led by Solomon. It was important to David to make sure that the nation and his son understood both where they were coming from *and* where they were going as God's chosen nation. David wanted to make sure the people of Israel recognized God's sovereignty in their history and their future.

It's important to look both directions when considering God's work in our lives:

purpose
Psalm 20:4

greater purposes
Exodus 9:16;
Psalm 33:11;
Proverbs 19:21

- Looking back, it's helpful to evaluate the circumstances God has placed us in that have helped shape and direct us, and to learn from the people He has placed in our lives to counsel us by their examples and their words.

- Looking forward, it's good to remember that God has a distinct purpose for our lives. More important, He wants to use us for His greater purposes. Let's not be shy about holding Him to the promises He has given concerning our future!

David's First Last Words

The words referred to by the historians who put together the early versions of the Bible as "David's last words" were a formal address to the nation of Israel. Their position in Scripture is significant because they immediately follow David's passionate song of praise in 2 Samuel 22. The praise song, featured in an "encore" presentation in Psalm 18, seemed to have three goals:

1. Highlighting what God had done for David;

2. Emphasizing the nature of God, particularly His just-ness; and

3. Reminding Israel of the covenant God had made with David regarding its future (more on that a bit later).

A Powerful Preface

2 SAMUEL 23:1 Now these are the last words of David. Thus says David the son of Jesse; thus says the man raised up on high, the anointed of the God of Jacob, and the sweet psalmist of Israel. (NKJV)

birth in a manger
Luke 2:7, 12, 16

Some scholars attribute this passage to David. They say these words are autobiographical—his signature line, in a sense. Others claim the court scribes recording David's address inserted these words at the beginning of his speech as if they were an editor's note identifying the speaker. Either way—whether they came from David's mind or off the pen of an ancient court reporter—the words hold great significance.

- ***These are the last words of David***. The last words of anyone—grandparent, friend, mentor, pastor, mother, or father—are special. But the last words of a widely known public figure such as a president, prime minister, or king can hold added weight. Prefacing the subsequent remarks with this phrase gives readers and listeners a cue: "Pay attention! Historic words ahead!"

what others say

Charles H. Spurgeon

It is well to hear saints' words when they are near heaven—when they stand upon the banks of Jordan. But here is a special case, for these be the last words of David. They are something more than human utterances; for we are told that the Spirit of the Lord spake by him, and his word was in his tongue.[1]

key point

- ***Thus says David the son of Jesse***. This phrase refers to David's roots, which were very modest. The youngest of eight sons of a farmer named Jesse who lived in Bethlehem, nothing about his origin indicated that he was destined for more than a life of shepherding in the areas surrounding his village.

- ***Thus says the man raised up on high***. These words acknowledge the fact that David hadn't pulled himself up by his bootstraps, worked his way up the ladder, or won enough friends and influenced enough people to earn the office with the big windows on the top floor. Very much the opposite: God had done all the work. He had swept up David from his lowly position as a shepherd boy and elevated him to a place of prominence within the nation. This theme—raising a humble man to a high place—foreshadows Jesus' life. His humble beginnings included <u>birth in a manger</u> to poor parents of low social standing; He was "raised up" when He arose from death and ascended into heaven.

David's attitude is a reminder that the proper response to our accomplishments is to direct the credit where it belongs: to God. It is by His hands—not by our handiwork—that we, like David, are lifted up to whatever successes in life we may enjoy. David emphasized that thought in Psalm 34:2, "My soul shall make its boast in the LORD; the humble shall hear of it and be glad" (NKJV); and years later the prophet Jeremiah echoed the sentiment: "Let not the wise man glory in his wisdom, let not the mighty man glory in his might, nor let the rich man glory in his riches; but let him who glories glory in this, that he understands and knows Me" (Jeremiah 9:23–24 NKJV).

- **The anointed.** Wearing a crown doesn't make a person a king; it's the anointing by God that sets a ruler apart. And the "anointing" is much more than a religious ritual. It signifies the fact that God has singled out a person—via the power and presence of His Holy Spirit—to rule. Anointing speaks of empowering and equipping someone to act with God's authority and blessing. When Saul was still Israel's official ruler, he had become mentally unstable and insanely jealous of David. He developed a hatred for David so intense that, before long, he was spending much more time and energy trying to find and kill David than in governing the nation. At least twice, David caught Saul in a vulnerable spot. He could have easily killed the king each time, yet David refused. He insisted that he would spare Saul's life. That was because he recognized and respected the sanctity of Saul's position as God's anointed. David refused to "stretch out" his "hand against the LORD's anointed" (1 Samuel 26:11 NKJV). He was content to wait for God to work out the details of Saul's demise.

- **Of the God of Jacob.** The phrase "the God of Jacob" sets David in his historical context. It reminds readers that David was picking up the baton handed down from the patriarchs Abraham, Isaac, and Jacob.

arose from death
Matthew 28:1–15;
Mark 16:1–8;
Luke 24:1–12;
John 20:1–10

ascended into heaven
Mark 16:19–20;
Luke 24:50–51;
Acts 1:9

mentally unstable
1 Samuel 16:14;
18:10; 19:9

jealous
1 Samuel 18:7–8

kill David
1 Samuel 18:10–16;
19:1–24; 20:1–42

spare Saul's life
1 Samuel 24, 26

go to

psalmist
1 Chronicles 16:4–5,
7, 9;
Amos 6:5

what others say

Bob Deffinbaugh

David is . . . the offspring of Jacob, or Israel. . . . This notation does link David with the Abrahamic Covenant (Genesis 12:1–3, etc.) and with the promise to Jacob that through his son Judah, the Messiah (anointed one) would come (Genesis 49:8–10).[2]

- *And the sweet __psalmist__ of Israel.* Long before Saul started chasing David, the king had capitalized on the young man's gift for making music that would soothe the king's tormented spirit. Apparently, David's flair for music was matched by a gift for poetry; through the years David's poems of praise and prayer—many composed during or following key incidents in his life—were incorporated into oral tradition and then were recorded in the book of Psalms. Of the 150 psalms, in fact, 73 are credited to David.

Psalms of Prayer and Prophecy

Psalms are Hebrew poetry, even though they don't follow the patterns of rhythm and rhyme (at least, not in English) modern readers are accustomed to seeing in poetry. The word *psalms* is taken from a Hebrew word meaning "praises," and most of David's praise poems fall into two categories:

1. *Prayers for help.* In many of David's psalms, he asked God for help during times of trouble. For example, Psalm 59 records David's plea for deliverance after Saul sent his men to murder him.

what others say

H. A. Ironside

Many of these Psalms were the prayers of Jesus. It has been said, "The strings of David's harps are the chords of the heart of Jesus."[3]

2. *Prayers of Prophecy.* The Psalms include at least 23 prophecies about Christ alone that were fulfilled in the New Testament.

H. A. Ironside

Many do not realize that David was a prophet, but the Psalms are all prophetic, and that in a most marvelous way.[4]

The prayer psalms David prayed came "full circle" in that they were inspired by God, prayed by David, and then repeated by Jesus Christ Himself on many occasions when He lived on earth.

Alton H. McEachern

Jesus' own devotional life was nourished on the Psalms.[5]

Nelson's NKJV Study Bible

Many psalms . . . point forward to Jesus Christ. Some psalms are directly prophetic (Ps. 2; 110). Others prophetically foreshadow events related to Christ (compare the description of a wedding of a King in Ps. 45 with Hebrews 1:8, 9; Rev. 19:6–8). But almost all the psalms point forward in some way to the coming Messiah and His eternal reign of righteousness.[6]

God's Portrait of a King

2 SAMUEL 23:2–4 *The Spirit of the LORD spoke by me, and His word was on my tongue. The God of Israel said, The Rock of Israel spoke to me: "He who rules over men must be just, ruling in the fear of God. And he shall be like the light of the morning when the sun rises, a morning without clouds, like the tender grass springing out of the earth, by clear shining after rain."* (NKJV)

Before he went any farther, David related the seal of God's authority on his words, echoing his words of Psalm 139:4: "For there is not a word on my tongue, but behold, O LORD, You know it altogether" (NKJV). Then he went on to detail God's definition of an ideal king—one who would exemplify just-ness and who would revere God. David described the land of such a ruler as one characterized by sunshine, brightness, and fertility.

Not "Just" a King; a "Just" King!

Justice was critical for the well-being of Israelites living during Old Testament times. Many of God's laws for His people described how justice should be carried out for those who might be considered the "underdogs" of society. People who were orphans, widows, or poor, without someone making sure justice was served, might not have survived were it not for just men in place to properly administer God's laws on their behalf.

Injustice in Action

First Samuel 8:3 speaks of "perverted justice" (NKJV) in describing Samuel's sons, Joel and Abijah. They used their authority to administer justice in a skewed way to accomplish their own personal gain, practicing the very behavior condemned in Proverbs 17:23: "A wicked man accepts a bribe behind the back to pervert the ways of justice" (NKJV).

The only One who can treat everyone on earth with absolute justice is God, who, according to Psalm 103:6, "executes righteousness and justice for all who are oppressed" (NKJV).

key point

what others say

Charles H. Spurgeon

Whatever earthly courts may do, heaven's throne ministers judgment in uprightness. Partiality and respect of persons are things unknown in the dealings of the Holy One of Israel. How the prospect of appearing before the impartial tribunal of the Great King should act as a check to us when tempted to sin, and as a comfort when we are slandered or oppressed.[7]

Nelson's Student Bible Dictionary

Justice (or "judgment," KJV) specifies what is right, not only as measured by a code of law, but also by what makes for right relationships as well as harmony and peace.[8]

Jacob A. O. Preus

Standing against all human accomplishment or claim on God is the righteousness of God that comes through faith. This is a justice, first of all, which is God's very own. . . . The righteousness that justifies is precisely God's very own justice. He gives it to us by declaring us, as a Judge would, "Not guilty." Absolute justice does not enable unfit sinners to enjoy the provision, protection and presence of a Holy God. So, remarkably, God allowed His Son Jesus to suffer tremendous injustice on our behalf.[9]

A God-Fearing King

Demonstrating justice is a natural by-product of knowing who's really in charge. Rather than lording his authority over those who are under one's leadership, a truly great leader recognizes that authority comes from God alone, and that God is worthy of much respect.

God: Friendly or Frightening?

David stressed that the ideal king will fear God. That phrasing may sound strange to ears more accustomed to hearing the friendlier refrains stating "God is love" than the fearsome warning that "God is frightening." But in truth, because God is a just source of justice as described above, He is also to be feared. As Jonathan Edwards explained in a sermon called "Sinners in the Hands of an Angry God" in 1741, "[God] is not only able to cast wicked men into hell, but he can most easily do it." He also warned that "there are the black clouds of God's wrath now hanging directly over your heads, full of the dreadful storm, and big with thunder; and were it not for the restraining hand of God, it would immediately burst forth upon you." Indeed, God is an awesome—and at times, frightening—God, as noted in the following verses:

- Isaiah 59:18 states that God will "repay, fury to His adversaries" (NKJV).

- Isaiah 66:15 warns, "The LORD will come with fire and with His chariots, like a whirlwind, to render His anger with fury, and His rebuke with flames of fire" (NKJV).

- Revelation 19:15 speaks of "the winepress of the fierceness and wrath of Almighty God" (NKJV).

go to

everlasting kingdom.
2 Samuel 7:12–13;
1 Kings 2:4;
Matthew 1:1, 3–6;
Luke 1:32;
Romans 1:3

what others say

NKJV Study Bible

The use of this word does not imply that one needs to be afraid of God, but it does demand the appropriate recognition and respect for God's fearsome qualities, such as His righteous wrath (see Psalm 5:4–7). The fear of God—that is, the proper respect of God—compels us to abandon our evil ways (Proverbs 16:6) and teaches us wisdom (Proverbs 9:10). Perhaps somewhat ironically, fear of God leads to confidence in this life, for if we have submitted to the Almighty we do not have to fear any other power in this world.[10]

David's Model of Leadership Works Today

apply it

Bookstore shelves are lined with hundreds of titles promising to provide the secrets of how to be a good leader. But no advice concerning leadership skills could possibly be as valuable as the challenge David presented to Solomon and, in turn, to those who are living today: a good leader is one who is God-fearing and just. Everyone is a leader, in a sense. We hold all sorts of leadership positions, whether it's within our families, within our professions, or even among our peers. Armed with a willingness to serve out those positions of leadership with justice and a reverence for God, we can enjoy the protection and provision God promises.

A Notable, Personal Exception

After enthusiastically describing the kind of king who would rate a perfect score of 10, imagine David's voice quieting into a sigh as he shifted the spotlight to himself and spoke the next words:

2 SAMUEL 23:5 *Although my house is not so with God, yet He has made with me an everlasting covenant, ordered in all things and secure. For this is all my salvation and all my desire; will He not make it increase? (NKJV)*

David acknowledged that his kingdom was merely an example—a flawed one, at that—of a coming, perfect kingdom. But while his own reign fell far short of ideal, he asserted that he could depend on God to honor His promise of an everlasting kingdom.

The "everlasting covenant" David referred to is called the Davidic covenant. It reaffirmed God's promise of land to Israel; it assured David that he was the first in a long dynasty of kings; and it assured David that his kingdom would never end because of the work of a coming Messiah, a Savior who would enter the history of human-kind through the lineage of David and the tribe of Judah.

David didn't fully measure up to the caliber of the kind of "ideal king" described in his last words; neither did his descendents fulfill that ideal. But God's promise that David's house would endure for-ever was—and is—fulfilled in Jesus Christ:

what others say

Robbie Castleman

In Jesus Christ, the son of David, is found the fulfillment of the everlasting covenant of salvation, life, and peace between God and his people.[11]

Tim LaHaye

Over a period of 500 years, the promise that the Davidic line would continue forever was repeated many times: to David himself, to Solomon, in the Psalms, and by the prophets Isaiah, Jeremiah, Amos, Micah and Zechariah. While individ-ual kings were chastised for disobedience, the covenant was never **abrogated**. From David a direct line of descent contin-ued for over one thousand years, until Jesus, the Son of Abraham, the Son of David, was born.[12]

A Word About the Worthless Wicked

2 SAMUEL 23:6–7 *But the sons of rebellion shall all be as thorns thrust away, because they cannot be taken with hands. But the man who touches them must be armed with iron and the shaft of a spear, and they shall be utterly burned with fire in their place.* (NKJV)

David had vividly described the land governed by leaders who fear the Lord as a fertile landscape bathed in sunlight and blanketed by lush grass. On the other hand, he likened leaders who reject God to thorns—worthless plants that are cast aside and burned.

abrogated
abolished

David's Second Last Words

The second group of passages called David's last words dramatically differs in setting and tone. The scene shifts from a king's public address to his nation to a father's private audience with his son. Most notably, David is no longer referred to in the biblical text as "king" because his age and infirmity make it clear that it was time for Solomon to take full charge of the affairs of the nation.

The emotions in the room during this father-son meeting must have been almost palpable: As David eyed his son, probably as handsome as Bathsheba was beautiful, his heart was surely full. So much to say, yet such little time left in which to say it. Weighing and measuring each word carefully, he described—probably not for the first time, but most likely for the last—the spiritual foundation upon which he wanted his son to continue building the nation. And he offered some practical political advice as well.

Solomon, still very young, must have known this day would be coming soon. After all, he had seen the young woman brought in to warm his dad's chilled body. He had noticed the signs of his father's declining health. And he had heard his father's once-vibrant voice take on a thinner quality with each passing day. Yet now, as Solomon sat beside his father, any faintness in the older man's voice would have done little to dilute the power of the words he was speaking.

> **1 KINGS 2:1–4** *Now the days of David drew near that he should die, and he charged Solomon his son, saying: "I go the way of all the earth; be strong, therefore, and prove yourself a man. And keep the charge of the LORD your God: to walk in His ways, to keep His statutes, His commandments, His judgments, and His testimonies, as it is written in the Law of Moses, that you may prosper in all that you do and wherever you turn; that the LORD may fulfill His word which He spoke concerning me, saying, 'If your sons take heed to their way, to walk before Me in truth with all their heart and with all their soul,' He said, 'you shall not lack a man on the throne of Israel.'"* (NKJV)

key point

David was a deeply spiritual man with a close relationship to God. Unlike many people who tend to separate business and politics from spiritual matters, there was no disconnect between David's public life and his spiritual life. Quite the contrary. Whether he was living as a shepherd, a fugitive, a musician, a warrior, or a king, David was all about one thing and one thing only—loving God. It's no surprise that David's first order of business in sharing some final words with his son was to direct Solomon's focus onto his spiritual life. David encouraged Solomon to be strong. He explained that his son could find true strength only in faithfully keeping God's word.

The Secret for Success

In so many words, David was telling Solomon that his success would hinge on his willingness to submit to God's authority. It can be difficult for anyone in authority—whether he or she is a political leader, a business executive, a teacher, or a parent—to recognize and submit to anyone else's command, either on earth or in heaven. Yet that posture of submission—first to earthly "superiors" and ultimately to the will of God—is an important ingredient of success.

apply it

what others say

Tedd Tripp

God calls His creatures to live under authority. He is our authority and has vested authority in people within the institutions he has established (home, church, state, business).[13]

Richard D. Phillips

Imagine all the advice David might have given: details regarding military tactics, financial secrets, pointers on handling the neighboring kings. Instead he offered something so much more precious; he pointed his son in the direction of true strength.[14]

People Problems

David then turned his attention to some more practical matters concerning people in his and Solomon's lives. He gave his son specific advice about Joab, his commander; Barzillai, the man who had helped David when he had fled Jerusalem during Absalom's coup; and Shimei, the man who had cursed and stoned David. (Details about David's directions concerning some of these people, and how Solomon carried them out are discussed in the next chapter.)

As a seasoned leader, David had proven himself to be an excellent "people person." He had enjoyed the benefits of close, loyal friendships (think Jonathan and the mighty men), and he had also learned

something to ponder

a thing or two about how to deal with difficult people (cases in point: King Saul and David's older brother, Eliab). But Solomon's life had been very different from David's. David had been exposed to a wide variety of people, from farmers and villagers to warriors and kings. His son had led a sheltered existence. As a prince, Solomon's relationships would have been largely limited to those formed within the walls of the royal palace. Perhaps it's because David was wise enough to understand these differences that he believed it necessary to give Solomon a bit of a head start in figuring out how to deal with the people who were likely to be involved in Solomon's most pressing concerns after David's death.

apply it

Some of our greatest challenges have nothing to do with policies or procedures and everything to do with people and personal relationships. Although people can certainly color our lives with love, friendship, and blessing, they can also test our patience, betray our trust, ignite our tempers, upset our plans, disturb our peace, and threaten our well-being! Just as David left Solomon with specific, practical advice for dealing with certain people, God has given His followers very specific, practical advice for dealing with people as well. He urges us, among many other things, to:

- Love our enemies (Matthew 5:44; Romans 12:14)
- Love one another (John 15:12; Romans 13:8)
- Bear one another's burdens (Romans 12:15)
- Put the needs of others first (Romans 12:10)
- Submit to authority (Romans 13:1)
- Honor and obey one's parents (Exodus 20:12; Ephesians 6:1; Colossians 3:20)
- Respect one's elders (1 Timothy 5:1–2)
- Keep unity (Ephesians 4:1–3)
- Show hospitality (Romans 12:13)
- Repay evil with good (Romans 12:17)
- Refrain from retaliation (Matthew 5:39)
- Behave peaceably (Romans 12:18)

David's Death

1 KINGS 2:10–12 So David rested with his fathers, and was buried in the City of David. The period that David reigned over Israel was forty years; seven years he reigned in Hebron, and in Jerusalem he reigned thirty-three years. Then Solomon sat on the throne of his father David; and his kingdom was firmly established. (NKJV)

The life of the man after God's own heart ended with little biblical fanfare. After ruling over Israel for forty years, David simply died and was buried in the city that bore his name. But as God had promised, David's story wouldn't end with his death. While he went on to receive his heart's deepest desire, to "dwell in the house of the LORD" forever (Psalm 27:4 NKJV), his story would continue to unfold as Solomon picked up where he left off in the grand job of leading God's chosen people.

Chapter Wrap-Up

- King David's last words to the people of Israel highlighted what God had done for David; emphasized the nature of God; and reminded Israel of God's promises to the nation.

- His words also painted a vivid portrait of an "ideal" king as one who dispenses justice and fears the Lord.

- He acknowledged that his service as king fell far short of the ideal, but emphasized his trust in God to honor the promises he had made to himself and to Israel.

- David's last words to Solomon focused on the younger man's spiritual life. He urged his son to be strong—with the kind of strength that springs from obedience to God and submission to His authority.

- David also gave Solomon specific instructions on how to deal with Joab, his commander; Barzillai, the man who had helped David following Absalom's coup; and Shimei, the man who had cursed and stoned David.

- David died after ruling over Israel for forty years, leaving his nation and his son a strong spiritual legacy.

Study Questions

1. To whom were David's two sets of "last words" directed?

2. In David's formal address to Israel, what kind of traits did he stress as being essential in an ideal king?

3. Did David assert that his kingdom was ideal?

4. In David's final words to his son, what did he say was the key to success?

5. What very practical words of advice did David have for Solomon?

Part Two
Wisdom & Wealth: Building God's Kingdom

1 Kings 2:13-46: Politics and Power

Chapter Highlights:
- Adonijah's at It Again
- A Simple Request
- A Royal Audience
- A Time to Kill
- Kind King or Merciless Monarch?

Let's Get Started

"The eyes of Israel are upon you" is basically what Bathsheba said to David when Adonijah tried to take the throne from Solomon. The people of Israel no doubt were studying the new king with extreme scrutiny. Their eyes were upon Solomon, and they were watching him closely to learn the answer to one very big question: Did this son of David really have what it took to follow in his father's enormous footsteps?

Practically speaking, Solomon's transition into taking full charge of the nation after his father's death should have gone smoothly for many reasons:

- *Destined to Be King.* Solomon had grown up knowing he would one day become king, so in a sense for his entire life he had been in training for the day he would replace his father. While his brothers had been busy sparring with each other for the crown, Solomon had remained ringside. He had been content to let God work out the details of his father's succession while he concentrated on soaking up all the instruction he could from his mother, his father, and the many others who were living in David's household.

- *A Legacy of Success.* Because of the political alliances David had formed, the military victories he had accumulated, the administrative innovations he had put in motion, and the spiritual leadership he had provided, he had left Solomon the keys to a kingdom that was strong on all fronts. Israel was politically secure, militarily strong, economically flourishing, and religiously united.

- *A High-Powered Endorsement.* Solomon's father had widely broadcast his opinion of Solomon's transition into his new office. Israel's beloved king had publicly endorsed his son's leadership, saying to the people, in essence, "You can trust him because God chose him."

go to

young and inexperienced
1 Chronicles 29:1

• *Man-to-Man Mentoring.* Solomon had received plenty of personal, spiritual, and practical advice from his father. David, fully aware of the impact all the responsibility of leading the nation would have on a man who, at around age twenty or so, was <u>young and inexperienced</u>, and had probably taken advantage of many opportunities to counsel his son about what to do when the nation was in his hands.

what others say

Mark Matlock

Imagine the pressure Solomon must have felt. Not only did he have to follow a legend, but the nation was struggling to hold itself together in the wake of David's death. Several powerful national leaders had supported Solomon's older, better-known brother. And, after 40 years of following the same king, everyone was watching to see how young Solomon would lead the people.[1]

Adonijah's at It Again

Even though David had done all he could to ensure a smooth start for Solomon, the young king ran into trouble from the word *go*. His older brother, Adonijah, took his dad's death as a nod to resume his malicious play for power. This time, instead of grandstanding by arranging his own inaugural party, he took a shrewder approach.

1 KINGS 2:13–14 *Now Adonijah the son of Haggith came to Bathsheba the mother of Solomon. So she said, "Do you come peaceably?" And he said, "Peaceably." Moreover he said, "I have something to say to you." And she said, "Say it."* (NKJV)

The last mention of Adonijah—in 1 Kings 1:50–52—found him clinging to the horns of the altar, trembling in fright at the thought of what the newly crowned King Solomon might do to punish him for his political treachery. Solomon, however, showed mercy and promised his half brother he would spare his life on one condition: that he prove to be a "worthy" man. Otherwise, Solomon had made an ominous vow: ". . . if wickedness is found in him, he shall die" (1 Kings 1:52 NKJV).

How quickly Adonijah had shed his fear and resumed his personal political agenda! To his plan to reclaim power into motion,

Solomon's conniving older brother marched straight to a person he guessed would be a soft touch and his best ally: Bathsheba.

Why did Adonijah go to the queen instead of to a former cohort, such as Joab?

go to
no one is worthy
Romans 3:9–23

- He figured that because her own son's seat on the throne was secured, Bathsheba might be willing to show the first-runner-up a little sympathy.

- He understood Bathsheba's power of influence—not only as queen mother, but as a woman who seemed to have an especially close relationship with her son Solomon.

He remembered well that Solomon had spared his life on the condition that he refrained from demonstrating wickedness in any way. A visit to the queen was not likely to be construed as a "wicked" move. On the other hand, anyone who happened to spot Adonijah in a political huddle with Joab & Co. might raise more than an eyebrow.

Worth vs. Wickedness

Solomon's proposition for Adonijah—that he would live if he proved worthy but would die if he was found to be wicked—is the same offer that's in front of every human on the planet. If we prove worthy, we can enjoy eternal life with the Lord; if we don't, we will experience everlasting death. Sounds simple enough; anyone in his right mind would choose "worthiness" over "wickedness"! But here's the catch: Because of human sin, <u>no one is worthy</u> on his own. No one is even capable of *becoming* "worthy" on his or her own. No amount of self-control, good intentions, outstanding accomplishments, impeccable manners, or cash donations to good causes can ever add up to the kind of "worthiness" it takes to be fit to live in God's holy presence. The good news—and that's exactly what it's called in the Bible, the "Good News"—is that Christ stepped in to help us solve the problem of our unworthiness: "But God demonstrates His own love toward us, in that while we were still sinners, Christ died for us" (Romans 5:8 NKJV).

apply it

Larry Richards

At the cross an amazing transaction took place. Jesus took our sins on himself; his death took the penalty that our sins deserved. And, wonder of wonders, God then credited the righteousness of Jesus to us![2]

Shaking in His Sandals?

Adonijah must have been nervous when Bathsheba seemed suspicious of his motives by asking whether he came in peace (in verse 13). He mustered a controlled reply, then probably stifled a sigh of relief when she appeared to accept his answer as an honest one when she invited him to state his mind.

Roger Hahn

As queen mother Bathsheba was an extremely powerful figure in Israelite culture. She directed all domestic matters relating to the royal family. In particular she had "say-so" over every other woman in the palace. It is true that she would provide privileged access to Solomon, but only regarding matters of the royal household. Thus the fact that Adonijah came to Bathsheba shows that his intention is to either gain favor in or intrude into the royal family structure.[3]

A Simple Request

1 KINGS 2:15–17 Then he said, "You know that the kingdom was mine, and all Israel had set their expectations on me, that I should reign. However, the kingdom has been turned over, and has become my brother's; for it was his from the LORD. Now I ask one petition of you; do not deny me." And she said to him, "Say it." Then he said, "Please speak to King Solomon, for he will not refuse you, that he may give me Abishag the Shunammite as wife." (NKJV)

something to ponder

Jesus pointed out in Matthew 12:34 and Luke 6:45 that "out of the abundance of the heart the mouth speaks" (NKJV). Adonijah's words may have sounded innocent enough, but each phrase exposed an abundance of evil attitudes and deceitful intentions spilling from his heart:

key point

- *"You know that the kingdom was mine"* (v. 15 NKJV). Adonijah stated this as if it were true, but it was really wishful thinking. The kingdom never had been his, even though he had tried to make it so. He never let go of his attitude of entitlement to the throne. Notice the vast contrast between Adonijah's proud "I deserve it" attitude and David's humble "Who am I?" posture!

- *"All Israel had set their expectations on me, that I should reign"* (v. 15 NKJV). In other words, "I wasn't the *only* one who thought I should be king; the people wanted me as well." Adonijah was trying to turn the issue of David's succession into an after-the-fact popularity contest. In Saul, Israel had already learned firsthand the tragic results that can follow the coronation of a "popular" king. *No thanks, Adonijah! We'll have what God's having!*

- *"The kingdom has been turned over, and has become my brother's"* (v. 15 NKJV). Adonijah had this backward. The kingdom wasn't "turned over" at all when the kingship went from David to Solomon; it had only appeared to be "turned over" for the brief time when it seemed like the kingship might pass from David to Adonijah. This skewed perspective is a characteristic of the <u>spiritual confusion</u> of ungodly people.

- *"It was his from the LORD"* (v. 15 NKJV). Adonijah attempted to cover up his manipulation with the sugary frosting of nice-sounding religious words. Everything he had said up to this point indicates that he didn't really believe God had set Solomon apart for the job but because it sounded like a good thing to say, he said it.

what others say

Thomas L. Constable

There is no evidence that Adonijah was ever sincerely interested in what the Lord wanted. But there is much evidence that he was interested in what Adonijah wanted![4]

Matthew Henry

[Adonijah] pretends to be well pleased with Solomon's accession to the throne, when he is doing all he can to give him disturbance. *His words were smoother than butter, but war was in his heart.*[5]

go to

spiritual confusion
Isaiah 5:20

lineage of Jesus Christ
Matthew 1:6

• *"Please speak to King Solomon, for he will not refuse you, that he may give me Abishag the Shunammite as wife"* (v. 17 NKJV). Adonijah paved the path to his request with blatant flattery, then dropped the bomb: He wanted to take his father's concubine as his wife. (Although Abishag and David probably had not been sexually intimate, she still would have been considered part of David's harem.)

A Royal Audience

1 KINGS 2:18–20 *So Bathsheba said, "Very well, I will speak for you to the king." Bathsheba therefore went to King Solomon, to speak to him for Adonijah. And the king rose up to meet her and bowed down to her, and sat down on his throne and had a throne set for the king's mother; so she sat at his right hand. Then she said, "I desire one small petition of you; do not refuse me." And the king said to her, "Ask it, my mother, for I will not refuse you." (NKJV)*

Unable to thwart Adonijah's malicious plans herself, Bathsheba abruptly ended the conversation by assuring her stepson—possibly with her tongue parked firmly inside her cheek—that she would speak with Solomon. Oh, she would speak with Solomon, all right. All she had to do was relay Adonijah's message to her son, and he would be glad to take it from there.

Keen on the Queen

Note the height to which Bathsheba has risen! At one of her lowest points, she found herself widowed and pregnant by a man who wasn't her husband. In another valley, she mourned the death of her firstborn son. Those had been dismal days indeed. But the Lord had rescued her, drawing her into the light of His love and care. He had raised her from the depths of guilt, fear, and sorrow to a lofty position of honor. Her son, the king of Israel, now not only bowed before her, he also placed a throne for her beside his very own.

The Lord greatly honored Bathsheba by allowing her to become David's queen and Solomon's mother. But His most remarkable tribute to her placed her in the <u>lineage of Jesus Christ</u>.

A person's lineage was extremely important to ancient Jews—it provided a historical record of things like a family's real estate holdings and social status. Plus, it detailed a family's tribal affiliation. The Levites, for example, were the tribe set apart to serve in the priesthood. Typically, family trees recorded only the men in a person's genealogy. Interestingly, the first page of Jesus' story—which outlines His family tree in great detail—includes the names of four women. In addition to Bathsheba, Tamar, Rahab, and Ruth were also included. These women, by most standards, would have been considered highly unworthy to be ancestors of the Messiah.

- <u>Tamar</u>, the woman who pretended to be a harlot and slept with her father-in-law.
- <u>Rahab</u>, the Gentile prostitute who hid two Hebrew spies, helping them to escape.
- <u>Ruth</u>, a Gentile from Moab.

what others say

Sue and Larry Richards

Put bluntly, few would be proud to have these four women emphasized in his or her family line.[6]

By placing these unlikely women—characterized by words such as *adulterer*, *prostitute*, and *Gentile*—in Jesus' earthly bloodline, God emphasized several points:

- He can use anyone to accomplish His plans.
- His Son, Jesus Christ, was in every way—right down to His lineage populated by flawed people—fully human as much as He was fully God.

what others say

Jane Kopas

Women have a heritage of influence and action in relation to the Kingdom of God even when their power is limited both as women and as outsiders. Each of these "outsiders" moved in a world where men doubly dictated the terms of power. Men dominated both as men and as keepers of the religious tradition. Each of the women finds a way to deal with this dominance and to benefit others.[7]

Tamar
Genesis 38

Rahab
Joshua 2:1–21;
6:17–25

Ruth
The Book of Ruth

The Answer Bathsheba Expected?

1 KINGS 2:21–22 So she said, "Let Abishag the Shunammite be given to Adonijah your brother as wife." And King Solomon answered and said to his mother, "Now why do you ask Abishag the Shunammite for Adonijah? Ask for him the kingdom also—for he is my older brother—for him, and for Abiathar the priest, and for Joab the son of Zeruiah." (NKJV)

Some scholars believe Bathsheba was nothing more than a well-meaning, meddling matchmaker. They hold that she was completely unaware of the treachery his request implied, and that she believed she was doing nothing more than helping a young man who was down on his luck and love-struck over a beautiful woman. If this was the case, Solomon's words in verse 22 were appropriately stern. She would have deserved this verbal splash of cold water to wake her up from her ignorance.

However, others find it difficult to believe Bathsheba could have been that dense. After all, she had been a member of the royal court for many years. She should have been very familiar with the nuances of politics and power. Remember, she had taken an active role in putting a stop to Adonijah's first attempt to seize the throne and in seeing her son named king. So "smart and savvy" appear to be better terms to describe her than "naive."

Bathsheba may have been sensitive to Adonijah's plight up to a point. But if she had been smiling and leaning forward to indicate her willingness to grant Adonijah his petition, his request for Abishag would have erased her smile, set her shoulders erect, and sent a shiver down her spine. She would have known as well as Adonijah that this wasn't an innocent plea for a consolation prize; it was a blatant proclamation of the young man's intentions to continue pursuing the crown. If this indeed was the case, then it's easy to perceive a tone of witty banter in Solomon's words: "You might as well have asked me to turn over the kingdom, too."

Tradition holds that Solomon wrote Proverbs 31, which describes the "ideal woman," in honor of his mother. If that were true, these would be the most descriptive words in Bathsheba's personality profile:

- virtuous (v. 10)
- valuable (v. 10)

- trustworthy (v. 11)
- kind (vv. 12, 26)
- enterprising (vv. 13–14)
- hardworking (vv. 13, 18, 22, 27)
- a family provider (vv. 14, 21, 27)
- energetic (vv. 15, 18)
- business-minded (vv. 16, 24)
- strong (v. 17)
- productive (vv. 18, 22)
- generous (v. 20)
- attractive (v. 22)
- forward-thinking (v. 21)
- confident (vv. 21, 25)
- wise (v. 26)

A Time to Kill

1 KINGS 2:23–25 *Then King Solomon swore by the LORD, saying, "May God do so to me, and more also, if Adonijah has not spoken this word against his own life! Now therefore, as the LORD lives, who has confirmed me and set me on the throne of David my father, and who has established a house for me, as He promised, Adonijah shall be put to death today!" So King Solomon sent by the hand of Benaiah the son of Jehoiada; and he struck him down, and he died. (NKJV)*

Enough was enough: Solomon had shown Adonijah mercy once, but he wouldn't do it again. In revolting against Solomon, Adonijah was really rebelling against the Lord. That was something Solomon would not—could not—tolerate. He took action immediately by having his traitorous half brother killed.

Benaiah: A Faithful Friend

Solomon dispatched **Benaiah** to carry out the execution. Benaiah was David's friend and one of the "mightiest" of his mighty men. In David's chief counselor, Solomon had inherited a loyal supporter

Benaiah
one of David's closest, most trusted counselors

who had taken no part in Adonijah's revolt and who was later hand-picked by David to <u>proclaim Solomon king</u> over Israel.

proclaim Solomon king
1 Kings 1:28–35

Eli
1 Samuel 1–4; 14:3

massacre
1 Samuel 22:6–23

cave of Adullum
1 Samuel 22:20–23; 23:6

high priest
1 Chronicles 15:11; 1 Kings 2:26

king's companion
1 Chronicles 27:34

Eli
high priest during the period of the judges

Nob
priestly community

cave of Adullam
cave near the city of Adullam, about sixteen miles southwest of Jerusalem

Old Prophecy Fulfilled

> 1 KINGS 2:26–27 *And to Abiathar the priest the king said, "Go to Anathoth, to your own fields, for you are deserving of death; but I will not put you to death at this time, because you carried the ark of the Lord GOD before my father David, and because you were afflicted every time my father was afflicted." So Solomon removed Abiathar from being priest to the LORD, that he might fulfill the word of the LORD which He spoke concerning the house of Eli at Shiloh. (NKJV)*

After issuing the orders for Adonijah's execution, Solomon quickly turned his attention to purging the palace of any other traitors who might remain. As his eyes searched the chambers and halls of the royal complex, his gaze fell on the priest who had supported Adonijah's rebellion: Abiathar. Their families had shared a history at several points:

- Abiathar was the great-great-grandson of **Eli**. Eli had raised and mentored Samuel, the much-loved prophet who had anointed Solomon's father.

- Abiathar had been the only person to escape from the city of **Nob** when Saul had murdered his father, Ahimelech, and eighty-eight other priests during a <u>massacre</u> to punish them for what the king had mistakenly believed, in his enraged paranoia, to be a conspiracy against him.

- After Abiathar had escaped Nob, he had joined David in the **cave of Adullam**. He had remained with David, and eventually was named <u>high priest</u> and the <u>king's companion</u>.

In recognition of Abiathar's former faithful service to his father, Solomon refused to have the priest executed. He did, however, remove him from his office and exile him to his homeland of Anathoth.

Curse Against Eli's Family Fulfilled

In banishing Abiathar and removing him from service as a priest, Solomon referred to a "word of the Lord" concerning "the house of

Eli." He was recalling the time when God, through an unnamed messenger, had <u>rebuked Eli</u> for raising disobedient, dishonorable sons, **Hophni and Phinehas**. The pair had failed miserably at carrying out their duties in the tabernacle. God had told Eli that, because he had allowed his sons to corrupt the tabernacle, his descendants would die young. Further, He said he would eventually end their tenure as priests. That prophecy was fulfilled when Hophni and Phinehas <u>died in battle</u>. Eli then died of a heart attack when he heard the news of their deaths, and that the Philistines had captured the ark of the covenant. Further, Ahimelech, Abiathar's father, had been murdered by Saul.

rebuked Eli
1 Samuel 2:27–34

died in battle
1 Samuel 4:17

occupation of Jerusalem
1 Chronicles 11:4–9

census
1 Chronicles 21:1–3

Hophni and Phinehas
Eli's disobedient sons

Joab: Too Little, Too Late

1 KINGS 2:28–30 *Then news came to Joab, for Joab had defected to Adonijah, though he had not defected to Absalom. So Joab fled to the tabernacle of the LORD, and took hold of the horns of the altar. And King Solomon was told, "Joab has fled to the tabernacle of the LORD; there he is, by the altar." Then Solomon sent Benaiah the son of Jehoiada, saying, "Go, strike him down." So Benaiah went to the tabernacle of the LORD, and said to him, "Thus says the king, 'Come out!'" And he said, "No, but I will die here." And Benaiah brought back word to the king, saying, "Thus said Joab, and thus he answered me." (NKJV)*

Joab held an impressive track record in Israel's military service. Solomon's cousin—the son of David's sister, Zeruiah—had been commander of Israel's military for many years, first serving under David and now under the current king. Throughout his tenure he had demonstrated the kind of courage and cunning that would earn modern-day soldiers a lapel full of medals. In addition to leading one successful military campaign after another against Israel's enemies, he masterminded the <u>occupation of Jerusalem</u>.

Off the battlefield, Joab had a worthy résumé as a perceptive counselor as well. On many occasions he had given the king solid advice. For example, it had been Joab who had urged David not to count the people of Israel when David lost confidence in God's promise to be Israel's protector and provider and placed undue confidence in the numbers of his subjects and the strength of his army by ordering a <u>census</u>. (David didn't follow Joab's advice and paid dearly for his

The Divided Kingdom
Unfortunately, the children of Israel had already divided themselves into two separate kingdoms prior to Solomon's ascension to the throne—"Israel" to the north and "Judah" to the south.

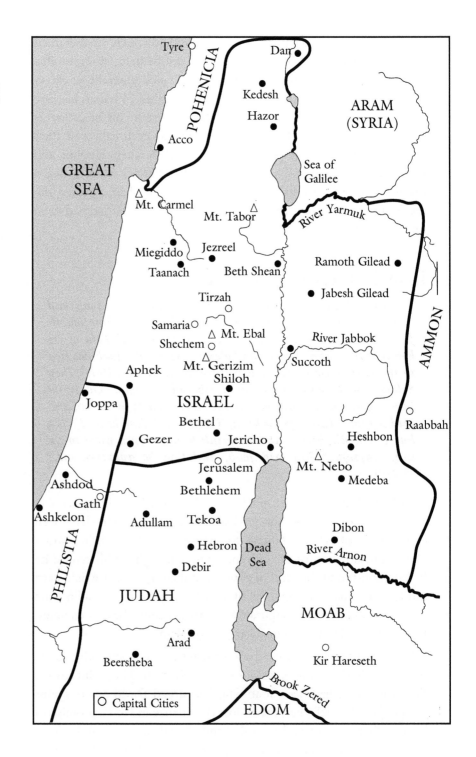

Tyre

Dan

Kedesh

Hazor

POHENICIA

ARAM (SYRIA)

Acco

GREAT SEA

Sea of Galilee

Mt. Carmel

Mt. Tabor

River Yarmuk

Miegiddo

Jezreel

Taanach

Beth Shean

Ramoth Gilead

Jabesh Gilead

Tirzah

Samaria

Mt. Ebal

Shechem

River Jabbok

Mt. Gerizim

Succoth

Shiloh

Aphek

ISRAEL

AMMON

Joppa

Bethel

Gezer

Jericho

Heshbon

Raabbah

Jerusalem

Mt. Nebo

Ashdod

Bethlehem

Medeba

Gath

Adullam

Tekoa

Ashkelon

Dibon

Hebron

Dead Sea

River Arnon

Debir

PHILISTIA

JUDAH

MOAB

Arad

Kir Hareseth

Beersheba

Brook Zered

○ Capital Cities

EDOM

sin! For more details on how that episode in David's life played out, read 2 Samuel 24 and 1 Chronicles 21.) Joab was the one who reconciled David with his estranged son, Absalom, following Absalom's murder of Amnon (see 2 Samuel 14:1–24). And Joab had also given David the wake-up call to stop weeping and wailing about Absalom's death and get back to the business of running the country (see 2 Samuel 19:1–8).

Even so, although Joab had been a success in some areas, he had been a miserable failure in others. He fell far short of the mark in issues of godly character and integrity—issues that mattered greatly to David and Solomon because they matter greatly to God.

Joab was:

- **Vindictive.** While the Lord clearly states that <u>vengeance</u>, or punishing people for wrongs they have done, is *His* job, Joab gave his vengeful nature free rein when he conspired against and <u>killed **Abner**</u> to retaliate for Abner's killing of Joab's brother during warfare.

- **Murderous.** A man of war was expected to have blood on his hands, but Joab had crossed the boundaries of the law when he had killed Abner.

- **Disobedient.** In God's <u>rejection of Saul as king</u>, He powerfully condemned disobedience, putting it on par with practicing witchcraft. Disobedience, however, was one of Joab's worst faults. He defied David's strict orders to protect Absalom's life during the struggle for the succession. Not only did he fail to protect Absalom from harm; he was the one to issue the execution orders when the young man was found alive, caught in a tree by his hair as he had tried to escape to safety. (See 2 Samuel 18:1–33.)

- **Traitorous.** When David had reached the point that he could no longer trust his nephew as commanding general, he had <u>replaced Joab</u> with his cousin, Amasa. Joab, using treachery and deceit, had <u>killed Amasa</u> and resumed control of David's army. Then, of course, he had been counted among Adonijah's supporters during the <u>attempted coup</u>.

go to

vengeance
Leviticus 19:18;
Deuteronomy 32:35;
Romans 12:19

killed Abner
2 Samuel 3:22–30

rejection of Saul as king
1 Samuel 15:22–23

replaced Joab
2 Samuel 17:25;
19:13

killed Amasa
2 Samuel 20:8–13;
1 Kings 2:5

attempted coup
1 Kings 1

Abner
commander-in-chief
of Saul's army

Robert Alter

With Adonijah dead and Abiathar banished, Joab realizes that all who remain from the recent anti-Solomon alliance have been isolated and cut off. This relentlessly political general recognizes that he has no power base left to protect him against the resolute young king. He has only the desperate last remedy of seeking sanctuary at the altar.[8]

Rose Book of Bible Charts, Maps and Timelines

The Old Testament speaks of horned incense altars at least 20 times. . . . Excavations have turned up some excellent examples of horned altars. Horned altars made of stone have been found at places like Dan and Beersheba.[9]

Joab's Death

1 KINGS 2:31–35 *Then the king said to him, "Do as he has said, and strike him down and bury him, that you may take away from me and from the house of my father the innocent blood which Joab shed." . . . So Benaiah the son of Jehoiada went up and struck and killed him; and he was buried in his own house in the wilderness. The king put Benaiah the son of Jehoiada in his place over the army, and the king put Zadok the priest in the place of Abiathar. (NKJV)*

Joab, the commander of David's armies, had at times served David well with his fierce loyalty, his outspoken counsel, and his military prowess. However, he had disobeyed David's orders not to kill Absalom; further, he had killed both Abner and Amasa, Absalom's field commander, in acts of treachery. His latest betrayal had occurred when he supported Adonijah's efforts to seize the throne. Because Joab was clearly guilty of murder, justice must be carried out; David had instructed his son to put him to death and Solomon was ready to comply. Remember: Administering justice was part of the "ideal" king's essential traits David outlined in 2 Samuel 23.

Shimei

Shimei, a bitter relative of King Saul, believed the throne of Israel rightfully belonged to his family, not to David's. So when David fled Jerusalem during Absalom's revolt, Shimei had hurled both rocks and curses at David. Unfortunately for Shimei, the attack against the king was, in effect, an attack against God Himself because He was the One who selected and anointed the line through which He would bring blessing to the world. Shimei's crime, therefore, had been nothing short of blasphemy. By law, he could have been put to death. However, when David had put down Absalom's revolt and was making his way back to Jerusalem, the hotheaded Shimei had approached the king. He had apologized—profusely—for his behavior, and begged David's mercy. David complied.

As the king neared the time of his death, he apparently began to question his own judgment. Did Shimei really deserve a pardon for his behavior? David was concerned that Shimei's apology had been insincere. If Shimei still believed his family had a right to the throne, he might rally support from his people and stir up all kinds of trouble for Solomon. So just before he died, David had urged Solomon to deal wisely with the man: "Therefore," David had said, "do not hold him guiltless, for you are a wise man and know what you ought to do to him; but bring his gray hair down to the grave with blood" (1 Kings 2:9 NKJV). Now Shimei's fate rested not so securely in Solomon's hands.

key point

what others say

David H. Roper

To speak evil of the king is to speak evil of God and his program of salvation because it was God's intention to bring salvation to the world through the kings of Judah. That is part of the promise that was given to David at the very beginning. In fact, even farther back, God promised to Abraham that he would bless the world through the nation of Israel and that through the tribe of Judah he would bring the King, Messiah, who would be the source of blessing to the whole world. So, when Shimei speaks out against the king, he is speaking out against God and his program to bring salvation to the world. He is rejecting God—and that is a serious thing.[10]

House Arrest

1 KINGS 2:36–38 *Then the king sent and called for Shimei, and said to him, "Build yourself a house in Jerusalem and dwell there, and do not go out from there anywhere. For it shall be, on the day you go out and cross the Brook Kidron, know for certain you shall surely die; your blood shall be on your own*

head." And Shimei said to the king, "The saying is good. As my lord the king has said, so your servant will do." So Shimei dwelt in Jerusalem many days. (NKJV)

Solomon decided to continue to show mercy to Shimei as his father had done. But because he couldn't be sure of what the man might do, he placed Shimei under a form of house arrest, instructing him not to cross designated boundaries. Solomon sure didn't need the volatile guy roaming the countryside, crossing borders and stirring his relatives into an uprising. Shimei, grateful for the stay of execution, seemed eager to comply. He managed to stay put for quite some time.

From House Arrest to AWOL

the big picture

1 Kings 2:39–46

Shimei complied with the house arrest until he got word that a couple of his slaves had run away to Gath. He then traveled there to retrieve them, directly disobeying the king's orders to stay inside the boundaries Solomon had marked. When Solomon got word that Shimei had misbehaved he summoned the man, gave him a sound scolding, reminded him of his past offense against David, and ordered him executed in a final act of diplomatic "housekeeping" that swept away the last potential troublemaker. Now the kingdom was firmly established in Solomon's hands, and the king enjoyed the blessing of God's favor: "Now Solomon the son of David was strengthened in his kingdom, and the LORD his God was with him and exalted him exceedingly" (2 Chronicles 1:1 NKJV).

what others say

Zondervan NIV Bible Commentary

[Shimei] had already been the recipient of a gracious pardon from David. But now Solomon was going to mete out justice on the exact terms of the oath. Shimei had taken grace lightly and demonstrated his unrepentant heart.[11]

Solomon: Kind King or Merciless Monarch?

Modern Western sensibilities make it difficult to understand why the incoming king dealt so harshly with Abiathar, Joab, and Shimei. In today's world, news watchers are accustomed to major—even dramatic—administrative changes when a new president steps into office. Many people lose their jobs as key positions are filled with new faces. A flood of information is unleashed as old policies are eliminated and new ones implemented.

key point

But a bloody purge the likes of which Solomon orchestrated sends the modern mind reeling. Why not a simple demotion to punish Joab for his disobedience? After all, his overall track record demonstrated as much or more valor than venom. And about Abiathar: Couldn't Solomon cut the guy a little slack? He was a simple man of the cloth, possibly more misguided than malicious. Finally, "poor" Shimei was no more or less than an ancient protestor. Today his type might be wearing a T-shirt with a pointed slogan, causing quite a spectacle during an elected official's speech. Not the most pleasant guy to be around, but he was entitled to his opinion . . . wasn't he?

The fact is, not even a remote comparison can be made between modern American democracy and tenth-century Israeli monarchy. Foreign relations were forged more by aggression than by diplomacy, and violence—even grisly brutality—was often an integral part of the justice system.

It's also important to remember that the heart of the Hebrew monarchy was God's sovereignty. David had reminded Solomon that God's ideal king would be just, ruling in the fear of God. With that instruction came the responsibility to remove from the picture anyone who violated God's Law or who didn't show proper fear of the Lord. David himself had practiced this kind of righteousness and integrity; in Psalm 26 he stated, "I have walked in my integrity. . . . I have walked in Your truth. I have not sat with idolatrous mortals, nor will I go in with hypocrites. I have hated the assembly of evildoers, and will not sit with the wicked" (Psalm 26:1–5 NKJV).

something to ponder

Sue and Larry Richards

While other monarchs of the ancient world were absolute rulers, Hebrew kings were to be ruled by God and to remain conscious of His sovereignty.[12]

No Tolerance

God's anointed king needed to rid the kingdom of the evil these men represented before his peaceful reign could be securely established. Believers—those whom God has anointed with His Holy Spirit—have been given a similar charge. Only when we rid our lives of disobedience, pride, etc., can we hope to enjoy the peace that God promises those who trust in Him.

Dorothy Russell

The principle behind Solomon's purge is that the enemies of God must and will be destroyed. Adonijah and his supporters wanted to go against God's will, and to set themselves up in the place where God's chosen one was to be. This is exactly what Satan tries to do and make people do. . . . Satan would have us believe that God is no longer in control, and that man can bring about a better world by his own efforts.[13]

Chapter Wrap-Up

- Adonijah took his dad's death as an impetus to resume his pursuit of the throne. He approached Bathsheba and asked her to speak with David about giving him one of David's concubines.

- Probably well aware of how Solomon would react to Adonijah's bold and threatening move, Bathsheba spoke to her son, who understood that the request was indeed an indication that Adonijah could not be trusted.

- Solomon instructed his faithful friend Benaiah to execute Adonijah.

- Solomon turned his attention to tying up the loose ends with people David had pointed out to him. First, he removed from service and banished Abiathar, the priest, for supporting Adonijah's rebellion.

- Solomon also had his general, Joab, executed for his treason in supporting Adonijah.

- Solomon then placed Shimei under a form of house arrest. Shimei was the man who had cursed David when he fled Jerusalem during Absalom's coup. Shimei had apologized and pledged loyalty to David, but Solomon wasn't sure of his sincerity. After Shimei broke the condition of his confinement, Solomon had him executed as well.

- The way Solomon handled these men may seem harsh, but the purge was necessary in order for the king to secure the kind of peace God intended for the nation.

Study Questions

1. What were some of the possible reasons why Adonijah took his request to Bathsheba rather than to Solomon himself?

2. How did his remarks betray his true feelings about Solomon's position as king?

3. How did Solomon respond to the request Bathsheba brought him on behalf of Adonijah?

4. Why did Solomon have Abiathar banished, rather than executed, for his act of treason?

5. Why was Joab so frightened that he clung to the horns of the altar, hoping for protection?

6. What did Shimei do to deserve execution?

7. Why was it necessary for Solomon to carry out these harsh acts of justice?

1 Kings 3; 2 Chronicles 1:2-13: Foreign Relations and a Famous Request

Let's Get Started

Tying up loose ends by carrying out his father's deathbed instructions had been at the top of Solomon's list of things to do in the previous chapter. When he had checked off all the items by getting his challengers out of the way and securing his kingdom, he could get down to the everyday business of being king.

First Kings 3 opens with two pivotal events in Solomon's life: his marriage to an Egyptian princess and his appeal to God for wisdom. Each circumstance offers an opportunity for much speculation and debate about the true state of the king's heart in the earliest days of his reign.

Foreign Relations

1 KINGS 3:1 *Now Solomon made a treaty with Pharaoh king of Egypt, and married Pharaoh's daughter; then he brought her to the City of David until he had finished building his own house, and the house of the LORD, and the wall all around Jerusalem.* (NKJV)

Solomon was a consummate politician; his gaze constantly swept across the landscape as he looked for ways to strengthen his nation and improve its economy. As he eyed the eastern border of his land, he saw a good opportunity for forging a friendship with his powerful neighbor, Pharaoh, the king of Egypt. Such a move would offer clear advantages:

- It would fortify Israel against invading enemies.
- It would expand Israel's political sphere of influence.
- It would improve Israel's trade potential.

From Pharaoh's vantage point, an alliance with Israel would be beneficial, too. It would give the Egyptians—who, incidentally, were experiencing a decline in power—safe passage through Israel. That a faltering Egypt would seek friendship with a flourishing Israel was quite a turnaround from the days when Israelites had been enslaved by the Egyptians, but nonetheless the change was real.

In ancient days, it was customary for a king to give a daughter in marriage to another king as a way of sealing treaties. That's how Solomon's father had accumulated many of his wives. In this case, Solomon cemented the advantageous alliance with Egypt by marrying the pharaoh's daughter. This unnamed princess would become Solomon's second wife; his first wife was a Shulamite, whom most scholars believe to be the unnamed love of the Song of Solomon.

There is also speculation that the Shulamite was <u>Abishag</u>, the beautiful virgin who had been hired to warm his father's bed. For a closer look at the Song of Solomon, see a later chapter in this book.

Is She or Isn't She?

The million-dollar question about how Solomon's marriage to the pharaoh's daughter affected Solomon's life isn't how much wealth her **dowry** deposited into his treasure chests. (However, 1 Kings 9:16 states that he received an entire town—Gezer—as a wedding gift, if that's any indication of the size of the bounty she brought with her.) Nor is it how much political and commercial power Solomon gained by calling the king of Egypt his father-in-law. Instead, the key question to ask about the royal union is this: Was the Egyptian princess a God-fearing woman or a pagan? The answer is all-important for one very big reason: God's Law instructed the Israelites not to marry foreigners. He had warned that doing so would tempt His people to turn away from God and worship foreign gods:

Abishag
1 Kings 1:1–4

dowry
money or goods given to a bride's husband at their marriage

DEUTERONOMY 7:3–4 Nor shall you make marriages with them. You shall not give your daughter to their son, nor take their daughter for your son. For they will turn your sons away from following Me, to serve other gods; so the anger of the LORD will be aroused against you and destroy you suddenly. (NKJV)

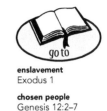

go to

enslavement
Exodus 1

chosen people
Genesis 12:2–7

what others say

James Burton Coffman

It was unlawful for an Israelite to marry a foreign woman unless she changed her religion to that of her husband's nation. Even then, the permission to marry foreign women was usually related to captives taken in war. But, at the same time, it was permitted only when the foreign wives renounced their idolatry and confessed their faith in Jehovah. It was only then that such marriages were in accordance with the spirit of God's law.[2]

What's So Evil About Egypt?

Egypt was renowned for its commerce, wealth, art, literature, live-stock, and fine linens. But God warned Israel against intermarriage with Egyptians, among other foreign people, and remarks about the sinfulness of that nation appear often throughout Scripture. Here are a few of the Egyptians' offensive practices and attitudes noted in the Bible:

The Nature of the Egyptians

The Egyptians Were . . .	Reference
Idolatrous	Exodus 12:12; Numbers 33:4; Isaiah 19:1; Ezekiel 30:13
Practicers of magic	Exodus 7:11, 12, 22; 8:7
Proud and arrogant	Ezekiel 29:3; 30:6
Pompous	Ezekiel 32:12
Ambitious	Jeremiah 46:8
Treacherous	Isaiah 36:6
Superstitious	Isaiah 19:3

And that doesn't even mention the brutal treatment Egypt inflicted on the Israelites during their <u>enslavement</u> there! God set apart the people of Israel, who eventually became known as the Jews, as His <u>chosen people</u>. One glance at the chart above illustrates why He advised His children against intermarrying with Egyptians. Many of the actions and attitudes they embraced clearly opposed the actions and attitudes God expected from His followers.

In the New Testament, God makes it clear that *all* people—regardless of their nationality or formal religious affiliation—are <u>set apart</u> as His chosen people if they believe that Jesus Christ is Savior. And just as God instructed the Israelites to refrain from marrying foreign wives, He warns His followers against marrying unbelievers: "Do not be unequally yoked together with unbelievers. For what fellowship has righteousness with lawlessness? And what communion has light with darkness?" (2 Corinthians 6:14 NKJV). Had Solomon kept away from such mismatches, his story might have turned out quite differently! (For a more in-depth discussion of Solomon's marital mistakes, see the chapter entitled, "The Godly King Does Ungodly Things.")

"May I Check Your Bags Please?"

If the Egyptian princess worshipped the God of Abraham, Isaac, and Jacob, then Solomon wouldn't be in hot water. However, if the young woman packed idols of her Egyptian gods into her bridal trousseau, Solomon could rest assured that trouble would eventually come knocking at his door.

So what is the verdict? Scholars have debated this issue for ages. Some say that because Solomon was known to be a God-fearing man, at least in these early years of his reign, it can safely be assumed that the Egyptian princess was a **convert** to the faith of the Israelites. Others, however, see no reason to make that assumption.

set apart
1 Peter 2:9

convert
someone who renounces his or her faith system to join another

proselyte
new convert to a religion

what others say

Adam Clarke Commentary
We have no evidence that the daughter of Pharaoh was a **proselyte**, no more than that her father was a true believer.[3]

The best assistance in settling the debate doesn't come from Bible scholars or ancient historical records; it comes from the pages of the Bible itself:

NEHEMIAH 13:26 *Did not Solomon king of Israel sin by these things? Yet among many nations there was no king like him, who was beloved of his God; and God made him king over all Israel. Nevertheless pagan women caused even him to sin.* (NKJV)

palace
1 Kings 7:8

1 KINGS 11:1–2 *But King Solomon loved many foreign women, as well as the daughter of Pharaoh: women of the Moabites, Ammonites, Edomites, Sidonians, and Hittites—from the nations of whom the LORD had said to the children of Israel, "You shall not intermarry with them, nor they with you. Surely they will turn away your hearts after their gods." Solomon clung to these in love.* (NKJV)

Each passage points to Solomon's relationships with pagan and foreign women as an element of his sin, and the second specifically names the pharaoh's daughter in its indictment. That's enough evidence to say with confidence that while marrying the Egyptian princess might have bolstered Solomon's relationship with Pharaoh, it didn't do anything to strengthen his relationship with God. It seems to have been a first step—albeit a small one, and one that God doesn't explicitly censure in this passage—in the wrong direction.

key point

The Honeymooners' Home

The Bible mentions that Solomon moved his bride into temporary quarters in Jerusalem while he completed several of his building projects, including his palace, the temple, and other structures. After that, he built her a palace of her own.

Worshipping the Right God in the Wrong Places

1 KINGS 3:2–3 *Meanwhile the people sacrificed at the high places, because there was no house built for the name of the LORD until those days. And Solomon loved the LORD, walking in the statutes of his father David, except that he sacrificed and burned incense at the high places.* (NKJV)

On the heels of the verse about Solomon's questionable decision to take a foreign wife comes a "by the way" description of the

go to

built an altar
Genesis 12:7–8

destroy the pagan altars
Exodus 34:13;
Deuteronomy 7:5;
12:2–3

refuse to worship Him
Leviticus 17:3–4;
Deuteronomy
12:11–14;
Jeremiah 7:31;
Ezekiel 6:3–4;
Hosea 10:8

Promised Land
land God gave the
Israelites as part of
His covenant with
them

nation's religious practices. Readers are told that the people of Israel were making sacrifices at the high places.

The Low-Down on the High Places

High places were simply altars, or piles of stones, erected on mountaintops or other elevated sites, where people would make sacrifices. The thinking was that the high places positioned the worshippers above the commotion and distractions of day-to-day life in the nearby villages, and placed them closer to the heavens. These were places where, in a sense, heaven met earth.

High places weren't inherently bad. For example, Abraham had built an altar on a mountain east of Bethel after the Lord called him to be the leader of His people. However, not everyone used high places to worship the one true God. Pagans—in particular, the Canaanites—used these sites to offer sacrifices to their false gods. After the Israelites entered the **Promised Land**, God told His people to destroy the pagan altars and said they should refuse to worship Him in such spots.

what others say

King James Study Bible for Women

The basic problem with the high places was that they too easily became spots where the religious practices of Canaan could creep into Israel's worship experience.[4]

Beth Moore

The high places were elevated on hilltop sites dedicated to worship of pagan gods. Alarming, isn't it? The thought of the people of God building shrines to other gods is almost unthinkable, yet they did it over and over. God warned His people constantly not to take on the practices of the Canaanite pagans. He told them he would not share His glory with another, and that such practices would surely lead them into captivity.[5]

God Selected the Spot

Forbidding the Israelites to worship at the high places, God had offered a sanctioned alternative, a site of worship He designed just for them: "But you shall seek the place where the LORD your God chooses, out of all your tribes, to put His name for His dwelling place; and there you shall go" (Deuteronomy 12:5 NKJV). During their wilderness years and continuing through the reign of David, the site the Lord chose for them was the movable tabernacle. During the reign of Solomon His chosen site became the glorious temple in Jerusalem that Solomon built for Him.

go to

law the Israelites broke
2 Kings 14:4; 15:17–18

Repeat Offenders

God's prohibition against the high places was one <u>law the Israelites broke</u> consistently. In this case, they seemed to have a reasonable excuse for their transgression: "because there was no house built for the name of the LORD until those days" (1 Kings 3:2 NKJV).

Was that an acceptable excuse? Commentators differ in their views. Some hold that worshippers should have refrained from offering sacrifices at the high places until they could make the trip to the tabernacle, which at this time was at Gibeon. Others say that worship at the high places should have been—and was in fact—tolerated because it was extremely impractical to follow the tabernacle around as it was moved from place to place.

something to ponder

what others say

Adam Clarke Commentary

Could there be any sin in this, or was it unlawful till after the temple was built? For prophets, judges, the kings who preceded Solomon, and Solomon himself, sacrificed on high places, such as Gibeon, Gilgal, Shiloh, Hebron, Kirjath-jearim. . . . The explanation appears to be this: as the *ark* and *tabernacle* were still in being, it was not right to offer sacrifices but where they were; and wherever they were, whether on a high place or a plain, there sacrifices might be lawfully offered, previously to the building of the temple. And the tabernacle was now at Gibeon.[6]

Jamieson, Fausset, Brown

But, so long as the tabernacle was migratory and the means for the national worship were merely provisional, the worship on those high places was tolerated. Hence, as accounting for their continuance, it is expressly stated (1 Kings 3:2) that God had not yet chosen a permanent and exclusive place for his worship.[7]

A Notable "Except"-ion

Once again, Scripture itself can help settle the debate. First Kings 3:3 notes that Solomon loved God and obeyed the Law just as his father had. But there's an exception: "EXCEPT that he sacrificed and burned incense at the high places" (NKJV, emphasis added). Clearly this counterpoint to Solomon's otherwise worthy behavior labels worship at the high places "unacceptable"—even though the criticism of Solomon is nearly hidden in the applause for his good traits.

> **2 CHRONICLES 1:2–3** *And Solomon spoke to all Israel, to the captains of thousands and of hundreds, to the judges, and to every leader in all Israel, the heads of the fathers' houses. Then Solomon, and all the assembly with him, went to the high place that was at Gibeon; for the tabernacle of meeting with God was there, which Moses the servant of the LORD had made in the wilderness. (NKJV)*

key point

Just imagine the grandeur! As the caravan of the mighty young king of Israel rolled into town, the people of Gibeon must have stared openmouthed at the procession of ox-drawn carts loaded down with magnificent tents, skins of fine wines, and baskets of breads, grains, and fruits. Camels and donkeys steadily trudged behind, their packs bulging with enough utensils and provisions to feed and house a small army. In fact, a small army is a good way to describe this group; the king's entourage included all of the most powerful military leaders and political heavyweights in Israel.

Solomon may have offered sacrifices at off-limits altars on occasion, but Bible scholars generally agree that the wording here indicates it was Solomon's regular practice to make this pilgrimage to God's sanctioned place of worship at Gibeon, about five miles north of Jerusalem. (See also 1 Kings 3:4—this parallel passage refers to this as the "great high place" [NKJV].)

This was one of two tabernacles in operation at the time. The other one was in Jerusalem; David had built it to house the ark of the covenant when he brought it to the nation's capital.

NKJV Study Notes

The high place at Gibeon was the location of the Mosaic tabernacle after Saul destroyed Nob (1 Sam. 22:19). It seems that the Israelites moved the tabernacle to Nob after they had stopped using Shiloh as the religious center of Israel (1 Sam. 4:21; 22; Jer. 7:12). The tabernacle remained in Gibeon together with the great bronze altar throughout David's reign.[8]

Off to a Good Start

One detail set this trip apart from others Solomon may have made to Gibeon. This was likely his first journey there as Israel's king. That's significant because it shows that he was walking in his father's footsteps of faith; he was putting God first. Poised at the very beginning of the assignment of a lifetime, Solomon didn't want to go an inch further until he had drawn aside to spend time with the Lord. He would use the "spiritual retreat," which could have lasted as long as thirty days, to pray, worship, rest, feast, and fellowship with the leaders in his administration. Most important, he would take time to contemplate the words of advice his earthly father had left him and to seek further guidance in the words his heavenly Father might have to offer.

David Guzik

This was an important event marking the "ceremonial" beginning of Solomon's reign.[9]

Spending time with God is the ideal way to kick off any endeavor!

apply it

A Thousand Sacrifices

2 CHRONICLES 1:6 *And Solomon went up there to the bronze altar before the LORD, which was at the tabernacle of meeting, and offered a thousand burnt offerings on it. (NKJV)*

Offerings and sacrifices were an integral part of worship. While based on a simple concept—the death of a substitute in payment for

sacrifice
Romans 6:10;
Hebrews 10:10–12,
14

sin—the system of offerings and sacrifices was quite complex. It is detailed in Leviticus 1–7. Each type of sacrifice held distinct meaning. For example:

- A burnt offering of an animal or bird symbolized commitment to God (Leviticus 1; 6:8–12).

- A grain offering, called the "meal" offering, symbolized devotion to God (Leviticus 2; 6:14–23).

- A fellowship offering of an unblemished herd or flock animal, called the "peace" offering, symbolized thanksgiving (Leviticus 3; 7:11–36).

- A sin offering of an animal atoned for sin or uncleanness (Leviticus 4:1–5:13; 6:24–30; 12:6–8; 14:12–14).

- A guilt offering of a valuable ram or lamb atoned for sins that violated others' rights; or uncleanness (Leviticus 5:14–6:7; 7:1–6; 14:12–18).

The Once-and-for-All Sacrifice

Jesus Christ died on the cross as the perfect <u>sacrifice</u> whose blood paid for all the sins we have ever committed and for all the sins we have yet to commit. Because of that, those who follow God are no longer required to perform the ritual of sacrifices. However, Romans 12:1 says we should offer our own bodies as "living" sacrifices (NKJV) to God. That means yielding every part of our lives—from our time and money to our decisions and dreams—to use for God's plans.

That's a Lot of Meat!

Of course Solomon would be offering sacrifices on this visit to Gibeon; that's why he went there. But it wasn't small change dropped into the offering plate. The king presented the Lord a staggering one thousand burnt offerings.

What compelled Solomon to make this journey and then offer not three, or ten, or even fifty burnt offerings—but a *thousand*? Why such excess? Scripture doesn't explain, but here are some possibilities that offer food for thought:

- *The weight of wealth.* Solomon had inherited a vast amount of wealth from his father. Many of these were the treasures that David had gained from the coffers of defeated foes following his many victories. And, there were the extravagant gifts he had received from his many friends in high places. A large part of this wealth also included <u>flocks and livestock</u>. While a thousand sacrifices might seem extreme, this might have been simply an appropriate portion for a man of Solomon's affluence to offer. In a way, it's a practical example of the spiritual principle taught by Jesus: "For everyone to whom much is given, from him much will be required; and to whom much has been committed, of him they will ask the more" (Luke 12:48 NKJV).

- *The sting of guilt.* Solomon may have earned favor with God, but he was not without sin. At this point he had already married an off-limits bride and had taken up questionable religious practices. Could these sins have been bothering him so much that he longed to make an over-the-top sacrifice of **atonement**?

go to

flocks and livestock
1 Chronicles 27:29, 31

atonement
restoration of harmony between God and humans

burnt offerings
payment for sins

what others say

Henry Morris

It may be that these matters were weighing heavily on his mind and heart, as he decided to offer a thousand **burnt offerings** at the altar at the tabernacle in Gibeon, perhaps seeking cleansing from whatever sinful actions he felt guilty about.[10]

- *Extraordinary situation, extraordinary worship.* King of Israel: The responsibilities were staggering; the expectations placed on him were possibly paralyzing. This man was to lead a nation whose history had been defined by tests, turmoil, and trauma. Was he up for the job? His father had told him time after time that the key to his success would be his relationship with God, above all else. What better way to nourish that relationship than by offering sacrifices? One after another, after another . . . Solomon handed over an excessive number of sacrifices to show his excessive devotion to God.

Rick Killian

The kingdom his father built now lay upon him to rule, judge, and prosper—and Solomon knew the task was too great to handle alone. To rule wisely and justly, he needed God's counsel above all else, and so he had offered a thousand sacrifices and prayed. This costly act of worship would truly mark his kingship and be the foundation of his reign over Israel. God first, no sacrifice too great in His cause, and nothing more important in his heart.[11]

Ray Bentley

As soon as the caravan arrived, the work began. The shrieks of slaughtered livestock rose above the hurried orders; quickly, the blood was thrown onto the bronze altar, while the animals were gutted. His congregation watched as Solomon gave animal after animal to the consuming fire, their praise and adoration rising with each surge of flames.[12]

David Guzik

This almost grotesque amount of sacrifice demonstrated both Solomon's great wealth and his heart to use it to glorify God.[13]

Even Better Than Sacrifice?

While God Himself established the sacrificial system, He stresses that He is far more interested in the motive behind the ritual of offering sacrifices. For example:

- When the prophet Samuel scolded King Saul for disobeying God, he said, "Has the LORD as great delight in burnt offerings and sacrifices, as in obeying the voice of the LORD? Behold, to obey is better than sacrifice, and to heed than the fat of rams" (1 Samuel 15:22 NKJV).

- In God's indictment of the Israelites through the mouth of the prophet Isaiah, He said, "To what purpose is the multitude of your sacrifices to Me? . . . I have had enough of burnt offerings of rams and the fat of fed cattle. I do not delight in the blood of bulls, or of lambs or goats. When you come to appear before Me, who has required this from your hand, to trample My courts? Bring no more futile sacrifices" (Isaiah 1:11–13 NKJV).

- In talking with a tax collector, Jesus said, "But go and learn what this means: 'I desire mercy and not sacrifice'" (Matthew 9:13 NKJV), to point out that God is more concerned about the contents of a person's heart than in the rituals they perform.

A Blank Check from God

> 1 KINGS 3:5 *At Gibeon the LORD appeared to Solomon in a dream by night; and God said, "Ask! What shall I give you?"* (NKJV)

Before Solomon made his famous request for wisdom, God made an amazing inquiry of the king: He wanted to know what *He* could do for *Solomon*. (See also 2 Chronicles 1:7.)

Don't miss the significance of this! The God who spoke the world into existence didn't wait for Solomon to tug Him on the sleeve to ask for something he needed or wanted. Instead, God Himself made the first move. *He* was the One who tugged Solomon on the sleeve—through a middle-of-the-night vision—to find out how He could serve His servant.

key point

Had there been any question about the sincerity of Solomon's motives in offering a thousand sacrifices, this puts all doubts to rest. God, who judges solely on the basis of what's in a person's heart, might not have been impressed with the number of sacrifices Solomon had made. But He apparently had been impressed with what He had seen inside Solomon's heart while he had been making those sacrifices. Impressed, and pleased. Pleased enough, in fact, that He approached the king with a mind-boggling offer.

what others say

Mark Matlock

Now God is no genie in a bottle. He loves to give his children good gifts, but we don't know of anyone else but Solomon who was presented with a blank check and told "fill in whatever you want."[14]

It Wasn't Too Good to Be True

David might have told his son many times in person what he permanently recorded for the public in Psalm 37:4: "Delight yourself also in the LORD, and He shall give you the desires of your heart" (NKJV). This is a perfect case in point. Solomon had delighted himself in the Lord; therefore, it's logical to assume that, considering the challenges before him, heavenly assistance for the task before him was his deepest desire.

Psalm 37:4 may be one of the most enticing verses in the whole Bible! It sounds almost too good to be true. Thoughts of sports cars and Caribbean cruises, sparkling diamonds and custom-built homes race through our minds as we imagine what we stand to get from God . . . "IF."

"If" what?

"If" we "delight ourselves in the Lord."

The English word *delight* is translated from the Hebrew word *anag*, which suggests being "soft" or "pliable." So a reasonable paraphrase of that verse might read like this: "If we allow ourselves to be shaped by the Lord, He'll give us our hearts' desires." Interestingly, allowing the Lord to mold, stretch, and tweak us makes us more like Him. Our "shape" begins to more closely resemble His shape. And as we become more like Him, our hearts' desires will come closer and closer to matching His perfect will until, at some point, the two will collide. It's when those two elements align that we'll hear a resounding "yes" from the Lord to our deepest desires.

> **what others say**
>
> **Cameron Lawrence**
>
> If we walk closely with God, and delight in His presence, we are transformed over time: heart, soul, mind and body—and that includes our desires. The difficult thing is being willing to let our desires go, and humbly rest in the care of our Lord. It's His will that matters, not ours.[15]

A Powerful Prelude

1 KINGS 3:6–8 *And Solomon said: "You have shown great mercy to Your servant David my father, because he walked*

before You in truth, in righteousness, and in uprightness of heart with You; You have continued this great kindness for him, and You have given him a son to sit on his throne, as it is this day. Now, O LORD my God, You have made Your servant king instead of my father David, but I am a little child; I do not know how to go out or come in. And Your servant is in the midst of Your people whom You have chosen, a great people, too numerous to be numbered or counted. (NKJV)

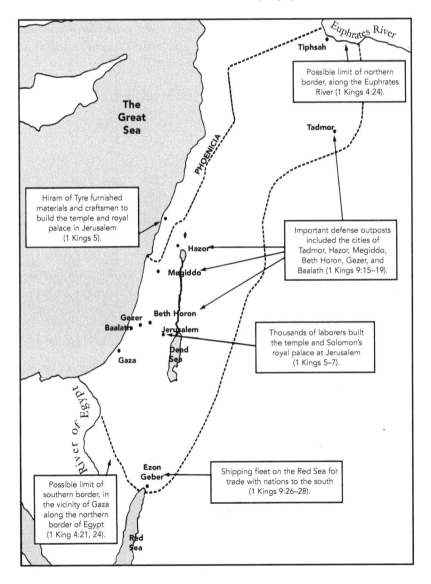

Solomon's Empire
This map shows the location of some of the shipping and construction projects Solomon undertook during his reign.

Possible limit of northern border, along the Euphrates River (1 Kings 4:24).

Hiram of Tyre furnished materials and craftsmen to build the temple and royal palace in Jerusalem (1 Kings 5).

Important defense outposts included the cities of Tadmor, Hazor, Megiddo, Beth Horon, Gezer, and Baalath (1 Kings 9:15–19).

Thousands of laborers built the temple and Solomon's royal palace at Jerusalem (1 Kings 5–7).

Possible limit of southern border, in the vicinity of Gaza along the northern border of Egypt (1 King 4:21, 24).

Shipping fleet on the Red Sea for trade with nations to the south (1 Kings 9:26–28).

In a powerful prelude to his request, Solomon:

1. Reviewed God's mercy, kindness, and commitment to his father.

2. Related his father's legacy of truth, righteousness, and "uprightness of heart."

3. Admitted he was a rookie, owning up to not yet having the benefit of a long history with God or any particular wisdom to lean on to guide his decisions. The term "little child" refers to both his youth and his inexperience.

4. Explained that he understood the magnitude of the responsibility ahead of him.

Imagine the Possibilities!

Solomon had a blank check, and he needed to think carefully before filling it in. After he concluded his remarks to the Lord, he considered his choices. His options boiled down to two:

1. He could build his reign on the shifting sands of the world's version of success by asking for things like wealth, power, influence, romance, success, excitement, victory, strength, or talent.

2. He could build his reign on the bedrock of God's wisdom.

key point

The decision that Solomon faced is the same decision that faces each person on earth: whether to choose the way of the world or the way of the Lord. (See also 2 Chronicles 1:8–10.)

He Chose Wisdom

1 KINGS 3:9 *Therefore give to Your servant an understanding heart to judge Your people, that I may discern between good and evil. For who is able to judge this great people of Yours?* (NKJV)

Peter Leithart

Solomon asks for wisdom, more specifically for "discernment of good and evil" (3:9), using a phrase similar to that found in Genesis 2–3 to describe the tree in the garden, a tree that gives wisdom. Solomon's request can thus be described as a request for access to the tree forbidden to Adam.[16]

"I'm So Glad You Asked That"

1 KINGS 3:10–13 *The speech pleased the Lord, that Solomon had asked this thing. Then God said to him: "Because you have asked this thing, and have not asked long life for yourself, nor have asked riches for yourself, nor have asked the life of your enemies, but have asked for yourself understanding to discern justice, behold, I have done according to your words; see, I have given you a wise and understanding heart, so that there has not been anyone like you before you, nor shall any like you arise after you. And I have also given you what you have not asked: both riches and honor, so that there shall not be anyone like you among the kings all your days." (NKJV)*

If anyone knows what people want, it's God. After all, He created them and He's the One who hears each prayer, day after day and year after year. When God asked Solomon to submit his request, He knew full well the three most popular desires of most people's hearts: health, wealth, and vengeance.

How pleased God must have been that Solomon wasn't like most people! Much like his father, Solomon refused to pattern his behavior according to the world's example. He insisted on asking for something he knew would have tremendous value, not only to himself but to people he governed as well—wisdom. Solomon's request demonstrated the kind of humility and unselfishness that God longs to see in everyone.

Ray Bentley

A greedier man would have asked for power and wealth. A prouder man would have presumed he could handle it. A less intelligent man would have believed he was smart enough to succeed on his own.[17]

When God Says No

apply it

God *always* answers our prayers. Sometimes He says "yes"; other times He says "wait"; and still other times He says "no." This time, God gave Solomon a resounding "yes." From the phrase "because you have asked this thing" (1 Kings 3:11 NKJV), we can gather that God granted Solomon's request because Solomon asked for the right thing. That raises the question, "What if we don't ask for the right thing?" The New Testament writer James clearly answers: "You ask and do not receive, because you ask amiss, that you may spend it on your pleasures" (James 4:3 NKJV). One way to ensure we don't "ask amiss" is to get to know God better and better each day through prayer, meditation, and Bible study.

He Got to Eat His Cake, Too

God's response to Solomon's request was a resounding yes. But He didn't stop there. He not only promised to give the king the wisdom he needed to rule the people with justice and discernment as he had requested; He gave him <u>wisdom in other areas</u> as well. Further, He promised to make the king the wisest person who would ever live: "so that there has not been anyone like you before you, nor shall any like you arise after you" (1 Kings 3:12 NKJV).

He also promised to give the king what he hadn't asked for: riches and honor, too. Generosity is one of God's most striking characteristics. He loves to lavish on His children even <u>more than they ask</u> of Him. All He asks is that His children <u>put Him first</u>.

go to

wisdom in other areas
1 Kings 4:29–34;
10:1–25

more than they ask
Ephesians 3:20

put Him first
Matthew 6:33

est man, not only in Israel but among all the surrounding nations as well. The book of Proverbs, along with other portions of Scripture, is the record of his wisdom. Knowing the extent of Solomon's wisdom should cause us to open our Bibles to Solomon's writings, especially the book of Proverbs, with regularity. In these pages we find the distillation of the thoughts and reflections of the world's wisest man.[19]

go to

fearing God
Proverbs 1:7

A Wealth of Wisdom

The thing that Solomon asked of God—wisdom—is available to everyone! But it doesn't just come naturally.

what others say

Charles Stanley

We must choose to pursue wisdom. It's up to each of us to determine *how* we will walk through this life. Wisdom is not something a person stumbles into or acquires automatically; it must be sought out and pursued.[20]

Solomon himself gives the starting point for gaining wisdom in the book of Proverbs: <u>fearing God</u>. Equipped with that fear of God, it's a matter of asking:

- "If any of you lacks wisdom, let him ask of God, who gives to all liberally and without reproach, and it will be given to him. But let him ask in faith, with no doubting, for he who doubts is like a wave of the sea driven and tossed by the wind" (James 1:5–6 NKJV).

- "Call to Me, and I will answer you, and show you great and mighty things, which you do not know" (Jeremiah 33:3 NKJV).

what others say

L. B. Cowman

Our work is to lay our petitions before the Lord, and in childlike simplicity to pour out our hearts before Him, saying, "I do not deserve that You should hear me and answer my requests, but for the sake of my precious Lord Jesus; for His sake, answer my prayer. And give me grace to wait patiently until it pleases You to grant my petition. For I believe You will do it in Your own time and way."[21]

go to

two kinds of wisdom
James 3:13–18

Two Kinds of Wisdom

According to the book of James, there are <u>two kinds of wisdom</u>:

1. *Godly wisdom:* The kind of wisdom Solomon asked for and received from God was godly wisdom. The Bible is full of passages that explain this kind of wisdom. Its source is God, and it is demonstrated through attitudes of purity, peace, consideration, submission, productivity, impartiality, and sincerity.

2. *Worldly wisdom.* Much of the world operates according to a system the Bible refers to as worldly wisdom. Its source is demonic and its fruit includes attitudes such as bitterness, envy, and selfish ambition.

One Simple Condition

1 KINGS 3:14 *So if you walk in My ways, to keep My statutes and My commandments, as your father David walked, then I will lengthen your days. (NKJV)*

Thanksgiving Day

1 KINGS 3:15 *Then Solomon awoke; and indeed it had been a dream. And he came to Jerusalem and stood before the ark of the covenant of the LORD, offered up burnt offerings, offered peace offerings, and made a feast for all his servants. (NKJV)*

The event ended much as it began, with Solomon making a journey to offer sacrifices. This time, his journey brings to mind the one **leper** out of ten who returned to thank Jesus for healing him. Likewise, Solomon returned to God's presence to reaffirm his commitment, thank Him for what He had done, and celebrate God's goodness with his servants. This is a good reminder that remembering our manners—<u>giving thanks</u> —should be a vital part of any interaction we have with the Lord.

go to

leper
Luke 17:11–19

giving thanks
1 Chronicles 16:8, 34;
Psalms 6:5; 18:49; 30:4; 75:1; 92:1;
1 Thessalonians 5:18;
Revelation 11:17

leper
one suffering with an incurable skin disease

Chapter Wrap-Up

- Solomon cemented an advantageous alliance with Egypt by marrying the pharaoh's daughter. The unnamed princess became Solomon's second wife; his first wife had been a Shulamite, whom many scholars believe to be the unnamed love of the Song of Solomon.

- Because God had warned Israelites not to intermarry with people of foreign lands, Solomon was breaking God's law by taking the Egyptian wife. This is regarded by many as the faithful king's first step toward unfaithfulness.

- The king allowed the Israelites to continue to worship in the high places because they had no temple yet in which to worship. God had forbidden worship in the high places, instructing His people to worship Him at the tabernacle instead.

- Solomon led his officials to worship the Lord at the tabernacle at Gibeon, where he offered an extraordinary number of sacrifices.

- God approached Solomon and asked the king to tell Him what he wanted. Solomon asked for wisdom, a request that pleased God so much that He not only made the king the wisest man in the world; He gave him unsurpassed riches and honor as well.

- Solomon presented the Lord with yet another offering; this time, it was to give thanks for the great gifts He had given the king.

Study Questions

1. How would an alliance with Egypt benefit Solomon? Pharaoh?

2. What were some of the "evil" influences Egyptians could have brought into Israel?

3. What were the high places, and what did God direct Israel to do concerning them?

4. What significant act did Solomon do at Gibeon?

5. How did Solomon come to receive his remarkable gift of wisdom?

6. How did God give Solomon even more than he asked?

1 Kings 3:16-28; 4: Solomon–Chief Justice and CEO

Let's Get Started

The new king had just been given wisdom the likes of which the world had never known before—and would never know again. That fact alone begs the question: "How wise was he?" The rest of 1 Kings 3 and 1 Kings 4 focuses on answering that question. The passages showcase his wisdom in both the courtroom and the executive office of the nation.

Chief Justice Solomon

Solomon may have barely had time to let the magnitude of God's gift of wisdom sink in before he got the chance to put it into action in a court of law. The item on the docket for this day was "Harlot v. Harlot," and the king's groundbreaking decision in this difficult child custody case would firmly establish his reputation as a man with matchless wisdom. Administering justice and settling disputes was a vital part of an ancient king's duties.

key point

The Plaintiffs

> 1 KINGS 3:16 *Now two women who were harlots came to the king, and stood before him.* (NKJV)

Solomon had every reason to consider these women unworthy of his time or attention. As prostitutes, they were less than nothing in the eyes of the society in which they lived. But he wasn't looking at them through the eyes of an ordinary citizen; he was seeing them with the spiritual vision he had been given by the Lord. Where an ordinary man would have seen two women clothed in condemnation and shame, Solomon saw two women in need of justice.

A Couple of Nobodies

Without husbands to speak up for them, and without the benefit of a good reputation to precede them, these two women were essentially "nobodies." That's a sad statement but a true one. As prostitutes, they held no legal or economic status and certainly no social standing. This is all the more reason why the fact that even these prostitutes—the "lowest" members of society—could benefit from Solomon's wisdom is significant; it offers an apt illustration of the fact that *anyone*—regardless of his or her social, legal, or religious "standing"—can come to Christ for salvation.

The Dispute

1 KINGS 3:17–22 *And one woman said, "O my lord, this woman and I dwell in the same house; and I gave birth while she was in the house. Then it happened, the third day after I had given birth, that this woman also gave birth. And we were together; no one was with us in the house, except the two of us in the house. And this woman's son died in the night, because she lay on him. So she arose in the middle of the night and took my son from my side, while your maidservant slept, and laid him in her bosom, and laid her dead child in my bosom. And when I rose in the morning to nurse my son, there he was, dead. But when I had examined him in the morning, indeed, he was not my son whom I had borne." Then the other woman said, "No! But the living one is my son, and the dead one is your son." And*

the first woman said, "No! But the dead one is your son, and the living one is my son." Thus they spoke before the king. (NKJV)

The two women were roommates, and they had given birth to babies just three days apart. One woman's child had died after she accidentally smothered him in her bed while sleeping, so she secretly switched her dead child for the living one lying with his mother in the next bed. When the mother of the living child awoke to find the dead child in her bed and her own infant in the arms of her roommate, she instantly knew what had happened. The other mother stubbornly stuck to her story, however, stating that hers was the child who remained alive. The quarrel drove the women to an impasse that could only be resolved by a judgment from the king.

This was a particularly daunting case for a couple of reasons:

- *There were no witnesses.* The first woman's testimony revealed that she and her roommate had been the only adults in the house, so there was no one to support or deny either woman's claim.

- *There was no physical evidence.* The same scenario, if it were played out in today's courts, would be much different indeed! Before the women ever set foot in the courtroom, detectives would have called in forensics specialists to extract DNA samples; the conflict over the babies' biological mothers could be sorted out in a laboratory in a matter of time. But none of this was possible in Solomon's day. The dispute pitted one woman's word against the other's; the only "evidence" the king had access to was whatever contents of their hearts he could expose through his insight into human nature.

key point

The Decision

1 KINGS 3:23–27 *And the king said, "The one says, 'This is my son, who lives, and your son is the dead one'; and the other says, 'No! But your son is the dead one, and my son is the living one.'" Then the king said, "Bring me a sword." So they brought a sword before the king. And the king said, "Divide the living child in two, and give half to one, and half to the other." Then the woman whose son was living spoke to the king, for she yearned with compassion for her son; and she said, "O my lord,*

give her the living child, and by no means kill him!" But the other said, "Let him be neither mine nor yours, but divide him." So the king answered and said, "Give the first woman the living child, and by no means kill him; she is his mother." (NKJV)

As stated earlier, Solomon had little in the way of conclusive evidence on which to base his judgment. No legal precedents had been set; no laws prescribed what to do. (Well, there is one law cited in Exodus 21:35 that addressed the dividing of a living ox and a dead one, but that could hardly be applied in this case!)

So Solomon simply restated the women's disagreement, then made a request that might have caused the crowd of gathering spectators to squirm: He asked for his sword. Since it seemed that he wasn't going to be able to determine which woman was the living child's mother, was the king going to kill both women? It might have appeared that way—until he made the chilling proclamation: "Divide the child." Of course, his statement produced the outcome he had sought. The maternal instincts of the child's biological mother prompted her to cry out that she would rather give her child away than see him murdered. Meanwhile, the other woman's calm statement that she would prefer to see the child dismembered spoke her chilling confession of guilt.

what others say

Rick Killian

The glossy veneer of shame hung over both women, yet as Solomon considered these things, he knew that if there was anything pure in either one, it would be that of a mother's love. To find it, he would have to judge with the harshness that these women were used to, not the tenderness he preferred.[3]

God's Mysterious Ways

At first, Solomon's grisly proposal must have seemed preposterous. Surely the king didn't know what he was doing when he demanded that the baby be killed; everyone knew that one of the mothers was clearly at fault! But in time, the mystery of Solomon's intentions became evident. When his strategy elicited each woman's true identity, the people realized that Solomon was a wise man indeed.

At times, the solutions God presents to our problems may seem unbelievable, even preposterous. They don't make sense. They don't fit into our plans. They may seem dangerous, or even terribly unfair. We may begin to wonder "What was God thinking?" while we question His judgment and possibly even begin to doubt our faith. But in time, just as evidence of Solomon's wisdom came to light in that ancient courtroom, we eventually see that God works in our own lives with nothing less than perfect wisdom.

apply it

what others say

David Guzik

Solomon's solution to the problem at first looked foolish—even dangerous. The wisdom of his approach was only understood when the matter was settled. In the same way, the works—even the judgments—of God often first seem strange, dangerous, or even foolish. Time shows them to be perfect wisdom.[4]

The Heart of the Matter

1 KINGS 3:28 *And all Israel heard of the judgment which the king had rendered; and they feared the king, for they saw that the wisdom of God was in him to administer justice. (NKJV)*

The people of Israel were still studying the king in these early days of his administration, to see whether he was worthy to sit on his father's throne. Had he failed to render justice in this tough case, his entire administration might have started off on a sour note. Instead, his conduct earned the immense respect of the people.

Solomon didn't have the divine quality of being able to look inside a person's heart as does the Lord, who is able to "bring to light the hidden things of darkness and reveal the counsels of the hearts" (1 Corinthians 4:5 NKJV). However, he was able to use his God-given wisdom—in this instance, packaged in the form of insight into human nature and an understanding of a woman's maternal instincts—to bring the contents of the women's hearts to the surface, where they would become visible to all. That was one smart move, Judge Solomon!

something to ponder

successor
1 Chronicles
22:7–10

CEO Solomon

It would be a dream job for a creative and energetic MBA craving a challenge: stepping behind the chief executive's desk to lead a thriving organization that had been growing in leaps and bounds under his predecessor. Many complex tasks would fill the agenda: planning ambitious new construction projects, organizing an ever-growing personnel pool, placing qualified leaders in key positions, and financing the expense of this tremendous growth.

Not just anyone could pull it off; clearly, such a position would demand nothing less than the right guy for the job, in every possible way. Of course, Solomon was precisely that person. The king had been hardwired for success in his seat at the helm of the nation of Israel for at least two reasons:

- *His divine appointment.* Leading Israel was his God-ordained destiny. God had said as much when He told Solomon's father, David, that Solomon would become his successor.

- *His divine qualifications.* The king knew the ropes when it came to living the life of royalty; after all, he had seen the inner workings of politics and government from his behind-the-scenes vantage point as a young prince growing up in the palace of his father. In addition, he had a God-fearing father who did his best, it seems, to give his son sound advice concerning his reign. But ruling the nation with the kind of wisdom and justice God expected required Solomon to have even more qualifications than a royal background and a head full of advice from his dad. Solomon needed credentials of a divine nature, and he knew it. That's why he asked for and received wisdom.

The narrative of 1 Kings 4 picks up where 1 Kings 3 left off by continuing to provide evidence of the wisdom he requested, specifically highlighting Solomon's administrative finesse. The chapter is organized into three parts:

1. First Kings 4:1–19 outlines how Solomon organized his administration.

2. First Kings 4:20–28 describes the scope of his kingdom.

3. First Kings 4:29–34 revisits the topic of Solomon's wisdom.

forced labor
foreigners who were
hired to work for the
king

Head of the Entire Nation

1 KINGS 4:1 *So King Solomon was king over all Israel. (NKJV)*

This brief verse brings attention to the immensity of Solomon's reign. When his father, David, had first become king, his rule had extended over only part of the nation—the northern portion known as Judah. He didn't take the helm of the entire nation until seven years later. Solomon, however, was in charge of all of Israel from day one.

Solomon's Chief Officials

the big picture

1 Kings 4:2-6

This passage presents a detailed list of the chief officials in Solomon's administration. Here is the lineup:

- High priest: Azariah
- Scribes: Elihoreph and Ahijah
- Recorder: Jehoshaphat
- Commander-in-chief: Benaiah
- Head of district officers: Azariah (not the one mentioned above)
- Personal adviser to the king: Zabud
- Overseer of the household: Ahishar
- Supervisor of **forced labor**: Adoniram

The list of names in Solomon's cabinet is quite similar to that of David's, as cited in 2 Samuel 8:15–18. The only two significant changes were the addition of two new positions—the head of district officers, or, in some translations, superintendent of tax collectors, and the director of forced labor.

Strength in Numbers

It isn't rocket science; anyone in a position of leadership and authority can see the need for help in order to get the job done. Just as the psalms David wrote give readers a glimpse into his heart, the books of Proverbs, Ecclesiastes, and Song of Solomon offer autobiographical clues about Solomon's methods and motives. In those books—in Proverbs especially—the king had much to say about the necessity of partnering with other people, whom he referred to as "counselors." He described the "ideal position" in the midst of trusted advisers as a safe place where plans are established, goals are accomplished, and work is fruitful:

- "Without counsel, plans go awry, but in the multitude of counselors they are established" (Proverbs 15:22 NKJV).

- "Plans are established by counsel" (Proverbs 20:18 NKJV).

- "Where there is no counsel, the people fall; but in the multitude of counselors there is safety" (Proverbs 11:14 NKJV).

- "For by wise counsel you will wage your own war, and in a multitude of counselors there is safety" (Proverbs 24:6 NKJV).

- "Two are better than one, because they have a good reward for their labor. For if they fall, one will lift up his companion. But woe to him who is alone when he falls, for he has no one to help him up.... Though one may be overpowered by another, two can withstand him. And a threefold cord is not quickly broken" (Ecclesiastes 4:9–10, 12 NKJV).

what others say

Steven K. Scott

In any worthwhile endeavor, it's impossible to be diligent without seeking outside counsel and effectively partnering.[5]

Believing the maxim that "no man is an island" and acting on it are often two different things! Many times, we prefer to go it alone. Whether you call us micromanagers, workaholics, control freaks, or simply "do-it-yourselfers," our issues are often the same. We may not have confidence in our coworkers' ability to get the job done; we may think we can do it better; or we may simply have trouble letting go of control. Regardless of the reasons we keep help at arm's length, Solomon urges us not to. He said there really is more strength in numbers!

The Candidates' Qualifications

Figuring out how to narrow the pool of candidates for key offices down to the list of those who would be the best assets within the king's administration called for extraordinary wisdom on Solomon's part. While 1 Kings merely presents a roster of the leaders Solomon chose to fill the highest official positions, readers can presume from the following proverbs a list of qualifications the king would have required:

- He would have sought men who were <u>wise</u>.

- He would have evaluated each candidate's track record for evidence of <u>integrity</u>.

- He would have weeded out men who had been <u>thieves</u>; who were <u>hot-tempered</u>; and who talked too much or <u>told lies</u>.

wise
Proverbs 13:20; 14:7

integrity
Proverbs 25:19

thieves
Proverbs 29:24

hot-tempered
Proverbs 22:24

told lies
Proverbs 20:19

What Did They Do?

It's not far off the mark to think of these chief officials as similar to members of a presidential cabinet. However, the posts these men held may be unfamiliar to modern readers. Here are the job descriptions of a few of the key positions in the ancient Hebrew monarchy:

- *High priest*—This was the most influential person in the administration; this was also the highest religious position to be filled. The high priest served as the king's spiritual adviser and supervised the nation's worship activities.

- *Scribe*—This position was most comparable to today's secretary or administrative assistant. The scribe prepared official documents and correspondence, kept detailed records concerning Israel's trade, commerce, and military alliances, and preserved all vital information in the archives.

- *Recorder*—This position was a bit similar to today's official spokesperson or press secretary. The recorder relayed public comments and requests to the king, communicated the king's response, and supervised royal ceremonies to make sure that proper protocol was followed in all events.

Walking Like the Egyptians?

When Solomon married the pharaoh's daughter, he effectively threw open the doors of the palace and invited Egyptian influence to come on in and have a seat. Diversity may be a politically and socially sought-after commodity today, but as stated earlier, God desired His people to remain "unto themselves." Azariah, Elihoreph, Jehoshaphat . . . to the modern ear, these names were just, well, names. But Bible scholars say these names reveal much: several are Egyptian, making it clear that Solomon mixed and mingled with Egyptians in management as well as in marriage. Their influence was bound to rub off on him and the rest of the Israelites.

> **what others say**
>
> **Roger Hahn**
>
> Since Egypt was the nearest big government organization, it is not surprising that Solomon would have recruited cabinet members from Egypt.[6]

A Dozen Districts

> **the big picture**
>
> **1 Kings 4:7–19**
>
> Solomon divided the kingdom into twelve districts and appointed a governor over each one.

prophecy

The prophet Samuel had answered Israel's demand for a king with a God-breathed <u>warning</u>. A king, he had said, would draft the Israelites' sons and daughters into service and impose taxes. Now the people were seeing evidence of these predictions of a complex—and taxing—bureaucracy beginning to come to pass.

go to

warning
1 Samuel 8:10–18

- *A Dozen Districts.* Solomon divided the kingdom into twelve districts. Before David had become king of Israel, the nation had operated as a loosely organized system of twelve tribes, or families. Justice was administered and God was worshipped on a tribe-by-tribe basis. However, when David became king he shifted the nation's political and religious focus toward a more centralized system. He did this by establishing Jerusalem as the nation's capital, and by bringing the ark there to make that city the center of worship.

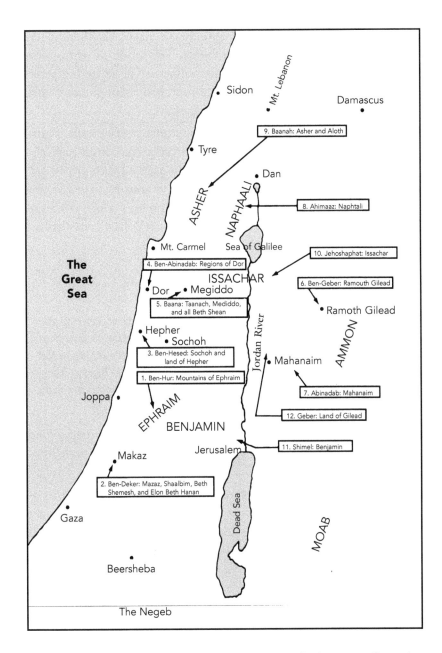

Map labels:

Sidon

Mt. Lebanon

Damascus

9. Baanah: Asher and Aloth

Tyre

Dan

8. Ahimaaz: Naphtali

ASHER

NAPHAALI

Mt. Carmel

Sea of Galilee

10. Jehoshaphat: Issachar

4. Ben-Abinadab: Regions of Dor

The Great Sea

ISSACHAR

6. Ben-Geber: Ramouth Gilead

Dor • Megiddo

5. Baana: Taanach, Mediddo, and all Beth Shean

Ramoth Gilead

AMMON

Hepher
• Sochoh

Jordan River

3. Ben-Hesed: Sochoh and land of Hepher

Mahanaim

1. Ben-Hur: Mountains of Ephraim

7. Abinadab: Mahanaim

Joppa

EPHRAIM

12. Geber: Land of Gilead

BENJAMIN

Jerusalem

11. Shimel: Benjamin

Makaz

2. Ben-Deker: Mazaz, Shaalbim, Beth Shemesh, and Elon Beth Hanan

Dead Sea

Gaza

MOAB

Beersheba

The Negeb

Now, Solomon was moving the nation even farther away from the tribal system. He was making the role of the government in the lives of the Israelites much broader, while making the role of the tribe (or family) of the Israelites much narrower. One evidence of this could be seen in the boundaries he drew around the new districts. They didn't match up with the already established tribal borders. Solomon

Bright and Morning Star
Revelation 22:16

seemed more intent on making the regions equal in size than he did on keeping the tribe's boundaries intact. This made good business sense because it allowed for fairer distribution of taxation, but given the tribal loyalties that undoubtedly prevailed, it might not have been the best way to go from that perspective.

- *A Dozen Governors.* Solomon appointed twelve men as governors, to be responsible for collecting taxes from each district in order to supply the royal household with provisions. This was no small order, as will be seen in the next few verses. Each man would provide Solomon's court with food and supplies for one month out of each year; the men themselves would serve on a rotating basis.

A Blessed Nation

1 KINGS 4:20–21 *Judah and Israel were as numerous as the sand by the sea in multitude, eating and drinking and rejoicing. So Solomon reigned over all kingdoms from the River to the land of the Philistines, as far as the border of Egypt. They brought tribute and served Solomon all the days of his life.* (NKJV)

Centuries before Solomon set foot on Israel's center stage, God had made some staggering predictions to Solomon's ancient forefather, Abram:

- The Lord had told Abram that his descendants would be as numerous as the stars in the sky: "Then [God] brought [Abram] outside and said, 'Look now toward heaven, and count the stars if you are able to number them.' And He said to him, 'So shall your descendants be'" (Genesis 15:5 NKJV). (One of those descendants was to be Jesus Christ, the "Bright and Morning Star"!)

- He identified the borders of the land that He had set aside for Abram's descendants. "On the same day the LORD made a covenant with Abram, saying: 'To your descendants I have given this land, from the river of Egypt to the great river, the River Euphrates'" (Genesis 15:18 NKJV).

- He predicted that Abram's descendants would endure <u>slavery and oppression</u> in Egypt, but that after four generations, they would come back into the Promised Land.

God's words must have seemed unbelievable to Abram, but he chose to believe God, and throughout the following generations his descendants saw the Lord's amazing promises come to pass. Much later, when David was king of Israel, God restated His promise to Abram (by then he was called Abraham) and added the additional promise that David's descendants would reign over Israel for eternity. Those promises are summed up in the following psalm:

> **PSALM 89:28–37** *My mercy I will keep for him forever, and My covenant shall stand firm with him. His seed also I will make to endure forever, and his throne as the days of heaven. "If his sons forsake My law and do not walk in My judgments, if they break My statutes and do not keep My commandments, then I will punish their transgression with the rod, and their iniquity with stripes. Nevertheless My lovingkindness I will not utterly take from him, nor allow My faithfulness to fail. My covenant I will not break, nor alter the word that has gone out of My lips. Once I have sworn by My holiness; I will not lie to David: his seed shall endure forever, and his throne as the sun before Me; it shall be established forever like the moon, even like the faithful witness in the sky." (NKJV)*

How God's words, "as numerous as the stars in the sky," must have resonated in Solomon's heart each time his officials brought the king the new census totals! The nation's population was indeed ever-increasing. And how his faith in God must have been strengthened when he studied the map of Israel that showed its expanded borders: the region in his domain, which some scholars estimate at about fifty thousand square miles, fell along the boundaries God had outlined for Abram all those years before.

what others say

King James Study Bible for Women

The great growth and prosperity of Solomon's kingdom attest the faithfulness of God in carrying out the provisions of the Abrahamic covenant through the line of David.[7]

slavery and
oppression
Exodus 1

William T. James

Some say God's promises to Israel were transferred to the church (all born-again believers of the age of grace) when Israel rejected their Messiah. God, who cannot lie, would be a liar if that were the case. Proof that God's promises to Israel remain in effect today include:

1. The nation was reborn in a single day, just as prophesied in Isaiah 66:6.

2. Israel was scattered and persecuted, and millions were murdered down through the centuries—including the genocide of Hitler's holocaust—yet they are a nation again, with their own unique language.

3. Outnumbered by more than three million to far less than one million, Israel—some believe miraculously—defeated its Arab attackers in 1948, 1956, 1967, and 1973. Israel took back more land God gave the nation through His many promises with each of those succeeding wars in modern times.

4. Old Testament and New Testament prophets, including Jesus Christ, the greatest of all prophets, foretold that Israel will be a nation again just before Christ returns. Zechariah predicted, as given in Zechariah 12:1–3, that Israel will at the time of the end be the center of controversy in the eyes of all nations of the world. Our headlines today attest to the accuracy of that prophecy.[8]

Wealth, Peace, and Prosperity

1 KINGS 4:22–25 *Now Solomon's provision for one day was thirty kors of fine flour, sixty kors of meal, ten fatted oxen, twenty oxen from the pastures, and one hundred sheep, besides deer, gazelles, roebucks, and fatted fowl. For he had dominion over all the region on this side of the River from Tiphsah even to Gaza, namely over all the kings on this side of the River; and he had peace on every side all around him. And Judah and Israel dwelt safely, each man under his vine and his fig tree, from Dan as far as Beersheba, all the days of Solomon.* (NKJV)

The chief officers in Solomon's administration were each responsible for supplying the king with enough provisions to last a month. This passage helps readers grasp how much that entails—consider what had to be provided each day:

- 30 **kors** of fine flour (185 bushels in total), or at least 30 average donkey loads

- 60 kors (375 bushels in total) of meal

- 10 fatted oxen

- 20 oxen (possibly cattle)

- 100 sheep

- unspecified numbers of wild game (deer, gazelles, roebucks, and fowl)

kors
units of measure; 1 kor is approximately 6.25 bushels

Multiply those quantities by thirty (as we have done in the first two listings) and that's what each district officer was responsible for delivering to Solomon's warehouses during their rotation. The contents are as impressive as the quantities; for example, meat wasn't part of an average Israelite's daily diet—but then, Solomon and those who lived in his court weren't your average Israelites!

They Had It All

For Americans of the 1950s, the term "having it all" meant marrying, having two children, and living in a picket-fenced house in the suburbs with a sedan parked in the garage. That was often referred to as the "American Dream." The ancient Israelites used the expression "the vine and the fig tree" to convey a similar idea of "having it all." When they said something about "the vine and the fig tree," they meant they couldn't have asked for anything more.

what others say

Jamieson, Fausset, Brown
This is a common and beautiful metaphor for peace and security (Micah 4:4; Zechariah 3:10), founded on the practice, still common in modern Syria, of training these fruit trees up the walls and stairs of houses, so as to make a shady arbor, beneath which the people sit and relax.[9]

go to

excessive numbers of horses
Deuteronomy 17:16

Horse Rules

1 KINGS 4:26–28 Solomon had forty thousand stalls of horses for his chariots, and twelve thousand horsemen. And these governors, each man in his month, provided food for King Solomon and for all who came to King Solomon's table. There was no lack in their supply. They also brought barley and straw to the proper place, for the horses and steeds, each man according to his charge. (NKJV)

something to ponder

Because the number of Solomon's horses cited in 2 Chronicles 1:14; 9:25; and in 1 Kings 10:26 differs from the number listed here, there's some debate over just how many horses used Solomon's stalls as their stomping grounds. But regardless of how many horses and chariots Solomon owned, the main point is that he owned a whole bunch. Building up his horse holdings was a shrewd move, in that his stables housed an intimidating component of the nation's military defense force. Yet it wasn't an obedient move, in that it was disobedient to God's law stating that kings were not to accumulate <u>excessive numbers of horses</u>.

apply it

David indicated in Psalm 20:7–8 that he preferred to trust in the strength of the Lord rather than in the strength of his military: "Some trust in chariots, and some in horses; but we will remember the name of the LORD our God. They have bowed down and fallen; but we have risen and stand upright" (NKJV). It's easy to rely on physical props such as a bank balance, a powerful job, or influential friends to give us the confidence we need to tackle the challenges life throws our way. But God prefers that we place our trust in Him.

A Walking Encyclopedia

1 KINGS 4:29–34 And God gave Solomon wisdom and exceedingly great understanding, and largeness of heart like the sand on the seashore. Thus Solomon's wisdom excelled the wisdom of all the men of the East and all the wisdom of Egypt. For he was wiser than all men—than Ethan the Ezrahite, and Heman, Chalcol, and Darda, the sons of Mahol; and his fame was in all the surrounding nations. He spoke three thousand proverbs, and his songs were one thousand and five. Also he spoke of trees, from the cedar tree of Lebanon even to the hyssop that springs out of the wall; he spoke also of animals, of birds, of creeping things, and of fish. And men of all nations, from all the kings of the earth who had heard of his wisdom, came to hear the wisdom of Solomon. (NKJV)

Solomon was wise and wealthy beyond imagination. It's as if the words in the above verses are an exclamation point to that statement. They tell of:

- *Solomon's reputation.* The king was known far and wide for his wisdom (verse 34).

- *Solomon's rivals.* Even his most learned colleagues in the East and in the highly developed nation of Egypt couldn't measure up to Solomon's greatness (verses 30–31).

- *Solomon's writings.* The king was a prolific writer; some 3,000 proverbs and 1,005 songs feature his name in their credit lines (verse 32).

- *Solomon's research.* To round off his résumé, Solomon was quite a biologist, zoologist, and botanist as well (verse 33).

what others say

Mark Matlock

Solomon was also a scientist who studied and taught about plants and animals and weather patterns. He had the supernatural ability from God to observe life and come to the right conclusions about it.[10]

Irving L. Jensen

Solomon was an expert in such fields of knowledge as botany and zoology. God used this to His own glory when he inspired Solomon to write books like Proverbs, where spiritual truths are illustrated by the pictures afforded by the physical world.[11]

Chapter Wrap-Up

- As if to answer the question "How wise was Solomon?" the perplexing case of the two harlots claiming the same child came before the king's court. Demonstrating keen insight into human nature and maternal instincts, Solomon solved the case with ease, securing a stellar reputation in the process.

- Solomon's actions prefigured the actions of Jesus, who offers justice to anyone who asks for it—regardless of their social or economic standing.

- The king organized his administration by assigning chief officials to key positions so they could help him effectively conduct the business of the nation.

- He also divided the nation into twelve districts, appointing a governor to oversee each one. Each district was responsible for providing the king with provisions one month out of each year.

- Solomon accumulated an excessive number of horses, in direct disobedience to God's instruction.

- The king earned a wide reputation among the nations for his wisdom, which was evident in his endeavors as a writer, a poet, a botanist, and a zoologist.

Study Questions

1. Why is it surprising that Solomon bothered to give his attention to the two prostitutes?

2. Why was the case an especially tough one to resolve?

3. How did the nation respond to Solomon's judgment?

4. How did Solomon organize his administration?

5. What aspects of his administration marked fulfilled prophecy?

6. What fields did Solomon distinguish himself in besides justice and administration?

Part Three
Building a Temple

1 Kings 5; 2 Chronicles 2: Getting Ready to Build

Chapter Highlights:
• David's Dream House
• Solomon Steps In
• Help from Hiram
• Not an Ordinary Temple
• A Massive Labor Force

Let's Get Started

Solomon came into a stunning inheritance when his father died. Strolling through the nation's storehouses, the young king must have admired the lavish treasures and riches David had accumulated as the bounty of Israel's military victories.

Even so, as Solomon marveled at the gifts that had poured into the royal household when David was establishing the kingdom, he kept coming back to one thought: These items hadn't been treasured by his father because of their monetary value or because they represented an overflowing trust fund for his kids. They had been precious to David because they would be used to fund and furnish the building of his heart's deepest desire: the temple. Solomon was undoubtedly both humbled and honored to know that he was the one God had chosen to bring his father's dream into reality.

But the treasures weren't David's only contribution to the temple project. The king had given his son a running start on the project during the days before his death. This chapter will backtrack just a bit to take a look at David's role in the temple preparations, and the history of the tabernacle, before continuing with the story of the preparations Solomon made for the construction of the magnificent building that was to become the centerpiece of his nation's worship.

David's Dream House

> 2 SAMUEL 7:2–3 *The king said to Nathan the prophet, "See now, I dwell in a house of cedar, but the ark of God dwells inside tent curtains." Then Nathan said to the king, "Go, do all that is in your heart, for the LORD is with you." (NKJV)*

Solomon's father had spent most of his life fighting and fleeing. But at this point in David's career, God had granted him peace and prosperity. As he paused to enjoy the much-needed rest, David had been struck by a shocking incongruity between his lavish surround-

go to

Garden of Eden
Genesis 2:8–9

Adam and Eve
Genesis 2:7–25

disobeyed God's rules
Genesis 3

designs
Exodus 25

Adam and Eve
first man and
woman God created

sin
violation of God's
will

priests
Levites; those who
presided over the
nation's religious life

ings and the modest tabernacle that housed the presence of the Lord. His built-to-last palace seemed far too great for a mere man such as himself, and the portable tent of worship seemed far insufficient for the God of the universe. (See also 1 Chronicles 17:1–2.)

So David decided to do something about it. He would build a house suitable for the Lord. "Surely I will not go into the chamber of my house, or go up to the comfort of my bed; I will not give sleep to my eyes or slumber to my eyelids, until I find a place for the LORD, a dwelling place for the Mighty One of Jacob," he said (Psalm 132:3–5 NKJV). He could barely contain his excitement as he bounced his idea off the prophet Nathan, whose immediate response was enthusiastic approval.

The Tent Called the Tabernacle

The word *tabernacle* means a house or a dwelling place. Its fuller meaning, as used in the Bible, is wrapped up in the history of God's relationship with men and women, and that history tracks all the way back to the <u>Garden of Eden</u>.

The tabernacle wasn't *in* the Garden, but the Garden itself was, in a sense, the first tabernacle. That's because it was where **Adam and Eve** lived in perfect harmony with God before they <u>disobeyed God's rules</u>. When they did, their **sin** separated them from God. He is holy, or perfect, and cannot exist with unholiness, or imperfection.

> **what others say**
>
> ### Joyce L. Gibson
> Once they sinned by disobeying God, the man and woman knew shame and guilt, and their fellowship with God was ruined.[1]

Thankfully, that wasn't the end of the relationship between God and humanity. He designed a way for them to reenter His presence through the system of sacrifices and cleansing. That system was to be administered by **priests** in the tabernacle (and later, the temple). God gave His prophet, Moses, His <u>designs</u> for the tabernacle, just as He later gave David detailed plans for the temple.

what others say

David Jeremiah

The Lord Himself designed the first worship center. He was very specific; it took seven chapters to describe how he wanted it built. He made it portable, and designed it to be a visual aid for the worshipping Israelites. The tabernacle was the center of the encampment of God's people.[2]

A Tour of the Tabernacle

From a distance, the tabernacle David was familiar with would have looked like a large, fancy tent. It featured 7.5-foot-high walls of heavy linen fabric, enclosing a rectangular, 150-foot by 75-foot courtyard that surrounded the 45 by 15 foot tabernacle structure itself. The 30-foot-wide entrance, located directly opposite the building on the eastern side of the courtyard, was flanked by curtains of blue, purple, and scarlet.

Those who came to the tabernacle to worship could only go as far as the outer court, which was separated from the inner court by heavy curtains. That inner area, designated only for **priests**, included two rooms: an inner court, or the holy place, and the holy of holies, also called the most holy place. That was where the **ark of the covenant** was kept. A focal point for the nation of Israel, the ark—which also had been constructed according to very specific instructions from God to Moses—was a reminder of God's protection and provision. God's presence was positioned on the **cherubim** throne of God, the solid gold lid of the ark called the mercy seat.

Ready to Roll

The tabernacle was designed so that it could be easily taken apart and reassembled, making it convenient to move it from camp to camp with the Israelites as they wandered in the wilderness for forty years before entering the **Promised Land**.

what others say

James Strong

In all of these migrations it was taken down piecemeal, carried on vehicles constructed for the purpose and drawn by oxen, in charge of the priests assisted by the Levites, and was re-erected at every stopping place.[3]

priests
Levites; those who presided over the nation's religious life

ark of the covenant
chest containing the two stone tablets on which God had given Moses the Ten Commandments, a pot of manna, and Aaron's rod that budded

cherubim
type of angels that guard the throne of God

Promised Land
the land God promised the descendants of Abraham, Israel

go to

door
John 10:9

sacrifice for sin
Romans 5:6;
Galatians 1:4; 2:20;
1 Timothy 2:5–6;
1 Peter 1:19; 2:24

cleansed
1 John 1:9

light of the world
John 1:9; 8:12;
1 Peter 2:9

lights
Matthew 5:16;
Luke 16:8;
Ephesians 5:8

Bread of Life
John 6:48

fragrance of Christ
2 Corinthians 2:15

High Priest
Hebrews 4:14;
5:9–10; 8:1–2; 10:21

veil was torn
Matthew 27:51;
2 Corinthians
3:14–15

access to God through Christ
Hebrews 10:19–22

Symbolism in the Tabernacle

God's design for the tabernacle featured many highly symbolic details.

Tabernacle Features and Their Meaning

Tabernacle Feature	Meaning for the Israelites	Meaning for Today
Entrance—a single one, through the gate on the eastern wall (Exodus 27:13–16)	A single way to God, through the tabernacle.	A single way to fellowship with God, through Jesus Christ, "the door."
Brazen Altar, or bronze altar (Exodus 27:1–8)	The people brought their animal sacrifices for sin.	Jesus was the perfect, once-and-for-all sacrifice for sin.
Laver, or basin, of brass altar (Exodus 30:18 and 38:8)	The priests washed here to become purified and prepared to enter the tabernacle.	Jesus made it possible for believers to be cleansed by simply believing Him.
Golden Lampstand (Exodus 25:31–40 and Exodus 26:35)	Lit the tabernacle.	Jesus is the light of the world. Christians are called to be lights.
The Table of Showbread (Exodus 25:23–30)	Represented God's continual provision for Israel's 12 tribes.	Jesus is the Bread of Life.
The Altar of Incense (Exodus 30:1–10)	A God-designed recipe of incense was to be burned in the tabernacle constantly.	Believers are called "the fragrance of Christ."
The High Priest (Leviticus 21:10)	Only human pure enough to represent the people before God.	Jesus is our High Priest, who makes it possible for every believer to approach God through Him.
The Veil (Exodus 26:31–33)	Barrier of sin between humans and God.	The veil was torn when Jesus died on the cross, illustrating that while His death did not remove the barrier of sin, it did remove the need for individual blood sacrifices. Those who accept Christ's sacrifice for their sins are forgiven and have access to God through Christ.

The Rose Book of Bible Charts, Maps and Timelines

We study the Tabernacle to understand the steps that the Lord laid out for a sinful people to approach a holy God. The Tabernacle became the place that God dwelt with his people for 400 years: from the Exodus until the time of King Solomon, when the temple was built.[4]

High-Priced Tent

Even though the tabernacle didn't measure up to David's concept of a proper house for the Lord, it actually was quite lavish. According to one scholar the gold and silver in its furnishing, all by themselves, would be worth millions of dollars today:

Lambert Dolphin

The Tabernacle was built by free-will offerings donated by the people in such generous amounts that more than enough materials were available. . . . The total quantity of gold collected was approximately one ton; of silver, 3-¾ tons; and of bronze, 2-½ tons. . . . Hence, the gold and silver used in the Tabernacle of Moses would be worth over $13 million today. The golden lampstand in the tabernacle weighed a talent and would today be worth a half million dollars for its gold alone.[5]

God's Veto

2 Samuel 7:4–17; 1 Chronicles 17:1–15

The night after David declared his intention to build a temple to Nathan, God had given Nathan a message for the king. In the message, God reminded David that He didn't need a house. He stated that He, not David, would ultimately decide whether a temple should be built—and if so, who would build it.

Solomon's Jerusalem
This drawing shows the approximate layout of the city of Jerusalem in Solomon's day.

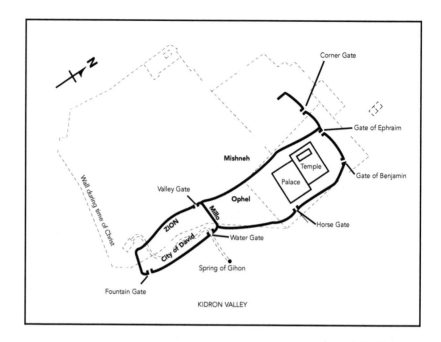

Why would God refuse to let His beloved David build the temple?

It hardly seems reasonable that God refused the one He referred to as the "man after His own heart" the privilege of building this temple. David's had been a heartfelt offer that, as far as anyone knows, sprang from pure motives. But God's no to David is a clear reminder that people can never fully understand the reasons God does the things He does because His ways are higher than our ways. However, sometimes a look back can reveal many possible reasons He sees fit to say "no." For example, sometimes a "no" from God stretches and increases believers' faith. Other times it refines their character, making His followers more Christlike. And often it paves the way for a much bigger "yes" that will better serve God's plans for His people and for His kingdom.[6]

Clean Hands and Bigger Plans

His ways are higher
Isaiah 55:9

There are many times when people who pray don't receive any explanation of God's answers to their requests. But in David's case, Scripture points out a couple of reasons God refused David's proposal:

1. God wanted the temple to be built by a <u>man associated with peace, not war</u>. God had said as much to David:

go to

man associated with peace, not war
1 Chronicles 22:7–10

1 CHRONICLES 22:7–10 *And David said to Solomon: "My son, as for me, it was in my mind to build a house to the name of the LORD my God; but the word of the LORD came to me, saying, 'You have shed much blood and have made great wars; you shall not build a house for My name, because you have shed much blood on the earth in My sight. Behold, a son shall be born to you, who shall be a man of rest; and I will give him rest from all his enemies all around. His name shall be Solomon, for I will give peace and quietness to Israel in his days. He shall build a house for My name, and he shall be My son, and I will be his Father; and I will establish the throne of his kingdom over Israel forever.'"* (NKJV)

Because David had spent most of his life fighting—for his life and for God's people—his hands bore many bloodstains. It wasn't appropriate for the purity of the temple to be marred by the fingerprints of unclean hands. Except for when he had Uriah murdered, the violence David had been involved in hadn't been against God's will. Nor had his efforts been futile. Far from it! David's fighting had been a God-ordained, necessary step in the pathway toward a peaceful kingdom. But the blood was still there. (See also 1 Kings 5:2–5.)

key point

what others say

Charles H. Spurgeon

David had prepared the way for Solomon's temple. It was by his fighting that the time of peace came, in which the temple could be erected. Though he is called a man of blood, yet it is needful that the foes of Israel should be overthrown. There could be no peace till her adversaries had been crushed; and David did that.[7]

2. God's plans were bigger and better than David's. David wanted to build God a physical—and therefore temporary structure; God wanted to build David a spiritual—and everlasting—dynasty.

2 SAMUEL 7:18 *Then King David went in and sat before the LORD; and he said: "Who am I, O Lord GOD? And what is my house, that You have brought me this far?"* (NKJV)

go to

prepare for the future
temple
1 Chronicles 22,
28–29

For most people—from toddlers and preteens to adolescents and adults—it isn't easy to accept the word "no." But David was an exceptional man who demonstrated an exceptional understanding of God's loving character. Rather than showing disappointment in God's answer, he allowed God's words and promises to unleash a stream of praise and wonder punctuated by humility, trust, and awe. (See also 1 Chronicles 17:16.)

David graciously took God's "no" for an answer. But he also understood that even though he wouldn't be the one to build the temple, he could help plan for it:

1 Chronicles 22:5 *Now David said, "Solomon my son is young and inexperienced, and the house to be built for the Lord must be exceedingly magnificent, famous and glorious throughout all countries. I will now make preparation for it." So David made abundant preparations before his death. (NKJV)*

The king spent the rest of his life using his time, his energy, and his influence to do what he could to <u>prepare for the future temple</u>. He drew the building designs God gave him; he gathered materials and supplies; and he enlisted workers. He even received the detailed plans for the temple from the hand of God Himself: "All this," said David, "the Lord made me understand in writing, by His hand upon me, all the works of these plans" (1 Chronicles 28:19 NKJV).

Just as God gave David detailed plans for building the temple, so He gives us the detailed plans for building our lives on "the rock" of His foundation—they're in the Bible!

something to ponder

what others say

Randall Price

According to the Bible, the blueprint originated in Heaven, not on earth. . . . Like Moses, King David had been shown by God the "pattern" for the sanctuary's construction and had passed this on to Solomon in the form of divinely inspired "plans."[8]

David could have felt cheated that God hadn't allowed him to build the temple; Solomon could have felt put upon that God dumped his dad's project into his lap. Neither scenario happened because each man simply wanted to do what God had for him to do.

Charles H. Spurgeon

This is the order of God's providence for his Church. It does not happen that he gives a whole piece of work to one man; but he seems to say to him, "You go and do so much; then I will send somebody else to do the rest."[9]

What David Did

1. *Secured the site* by purchasing the property atop Mount Moriah where it would be built (2 Samuel 24:18–25; 1 Chronicles 21:18–27).

2. *Received the plans* from the Lord (1 Chronicles 28:19).

3. *Gathered workers and craftsmen* for all aspects of the construction (1 Chronicles 22:2, 15).

4. *Gathered materials,* which included 100,000 **talents** of gold and 1 million talents of silver; plus large quantities of bronze and iron (2 Samuel 8:6–12; 1 Chronicles 22:14). He set aside the spoils of war for use in the temple as well.

Lambert Dolphin

These materials included 100,000 talents of gold and 1 million talents of silver (1 Chronicles 29). From his own private fortune David also gave 3,000 talents of gold and 7,000 talents of high-grade silver. This is an enormous quantity of gold and silvery by any standard: 100,000 talents of gold = 3750 tons, value today = $45 billion; 1 million talents of silver = 37,500 tons, value today = $10.8 billion. In round numbers the wealth of the first temple was about $56 billion.[10]

Today's believers accumulate treasures of a different sort than did David. We may not win them as spoils of war, or as gifts acknowledging new-formed treaties; but we do amass them in the form of earnings and gifts. It's a good practice to, like David, set aside a portion of our "treasures" to invest in projects that honor God.

apply it

5. *Instructed the workers* to begin preparing the building materials by cutting the stones; hammering the iron for the nails and joints; and bringing in the lumber (1 Chronicles 22:2–4).

go to

instruments
Amos 6:5

6. *Commissioned the Israelite leaders* to help his son (1 Chronicles 22:17–19). Many people of Israel complied with David's request. In fact, archaeologists uncovered an ancient "receipt" for a donation of silver to Solomon's temple.

7. *Prayed for the project* (1 Chronicles 29:16–19) and for all those who would be involved in its construction, especially his son: "And give my son Solomon a loyal heart to keep Your commandments and Your testimonies and Your statutes, to do all these things, and to build the temple for which I have made provision" (1 Chronicles 29:19 NKJV).

8. *Organized the details* involved in temple worship (1 Chronicles 23–26)—from arranging the Levite staff to crafting instruments and writing hymns.

The Heart of the Matter

key point

David threw his time, energy, and enthusiasm into making plans for the construction and furnishings of the temple, but at the heart of all his endeavors was one goal: making it possible for the people of Israel to worship the Lord in His holy temple. As he studied the blueprints, he didn't just see lines and measurements. He envisioned the thousands of priests who would be ministering to the multitude of Israelites filing into the temple courtyard. He smelled the aroma of roasting meat as the priests would lay sacrificial animals across the magnificent altar God had described to him. And he heard the heavenly chorus of the temple musicians who would be using the very <u>instruments</u> he had crafted himself to present musical offerings of praise and thanksgiving.

David not only made the instruments to be used in temple worship; he also wrote many of the songs—the psalms—that would be sung there as well.

Nelson's NKJV Study Bible

Psalms were written for singing. These were songs for public worship in the temple of ancient Israel. They are not merely poems, but lyrics for music from the ancient world.[12]

Alfred Edersheim

The music of the temple owed its origin to David, who was not only a poet and musical composer, but who also invented musical instruments (Amos 6:5; 1 Chronicles 23:5), especially the ten-stringed *Nevel* or lute (Psalm 33:2; 144:9).[13]

An Organizational Giant

Who can possibly know where to start in organizing thousands of people into some semblance of order so they can carry out their holy duties with dignity and purpose? Apparently David did. After counting some 38,000 priests who were of the appropriate age to serve, he assigned:

- 24,000 supervisors, who were in charge of everything having to do with the temple and temple worship, from maintaining the building and ministering to the people to looking after the sacred vessels.

- 6,000 officials and judges, who were stationed throughout the nation in order to serve the people in a religious capacity.

- 4,000 gatekeepers, who guarded the temple night and day against intruders.

- 4,000 musicians.

He then organized these men into twenty-four groups, making each group responsible for serving two weeks each year.

Solomon Steps In

Although David had done lots of preliminary work before he died, much was still left to be done. After he had taken care of other pressing national matters, Solomon knew it was time. Time to blow the dust off the construction plans the Lord had given his father; time to draft skilled workers, secure even more supplies, and get to work.

go to
praying like Jesus
Matthew 6:10

Descriptions of Solomon's temple preparations are featured in both 1 Kings 5 and 2 Chronicles 2:1–18. The two passages include much of the same information, but they aren't exact duplicates. This up-close look at Solomon's preparations for the temple will be based on 1 Kings 5, but will kick off with a look at the first verse of 2 Chronicles because it offers an important detail not mentioned in 1 Kings 5.

First Things First

2 CHRONICLES 2:1 *Then Solomon determined to build a temple for the name of the LORD, and a royal house for himself. (NKJV)*

This verse is important because it highlights the fact that Solomon put his own palace-building plans on the back burner until construction of the temple was complete.

what others say

Roger Hahn

Solomon's desire to build the temple is important. [His military machine] could have enabled Solomon to have embarked on a program of military expansion in several directions. Instead, his first priority was the building of the temple.[14]

It's a simple but powerful principle: Giving God and His plans first priority is always the best idea! We can put God first:

apply it

- *In our plans.* Time is one of the most valuable commodities we can give to the Lord, whether it's time we spend studying His Word, praying, serving others, or worshipping Him with other members of our church family. Try writing time with Him in ink on the lines of your daily planner *before* you schedule all the other appointments and commitments that encroach on your time!

- *In our prayers.* Too many times our prayers are little more than wish lists we attempt to camouflage with lots of nice-sounding religious words. Putting God first in our prayers means <u>praying like Jesus</u>, for His will to be carried out in our lives, allowing it to take precedence over any of our selfish desires or ambitions.

158 ——————— **The Smart Guide to the Bible** ———————

- *In our personal relationships.* We can put God first in every relationship by letting unbelievers know about Christ, and by encouraging believers with our words and actions.

- *In our pocketbooks.* Assigning the first portion of our financial resources to the Lord and His work can be one of the most challenging—yet rewarding—ways to put God first.

Help from Hiram

go to

friend of David
2 Samuel 5:11–12

Tyre
key coastal city in ancient Phoenicia (modern Lebanon) on the Mediterranean

> 1 KINGS 5:1 *Now Hiram king of Tyre sent his servants to Solomon, because he heard that they had anointed him king in place of his father, for Hiram had always loved David.* (NKJV)

King Hiram had been an ally as well as a <u>friend of David</u>; in fact, he had given David supplies and workers to build his palace. When the Phoenician king heard that Solomon had replaced his father following David's death, he sent a delegation of servants to Solomon. This was possibly in keeping with the custom of offering condolences and extending an invitation to renew the treaty since the scepter of Israel had changed hands. However, the 2 Chronicles passage doesn't include the detail that Hiram initiated the communication, but it's important because it highlights the high regard Hiram had for David.

key point

what others say

R. K. Harrison

The Israelites had never shown any desire to attack the powerful fortresses of the Phoenician coast, and the ratification of a treaty of friendship with Hiram had the effect of placing the economic wealth of the maritime kingdom at the disposal of Solomon without the effort and risk of a military campaign.[15]

Even before Solomon became king, a friendship had been forged between his father and Hiram that would be of great benefit to the nation. That's often the way God works in our lives. He begins to make preparations for the plans He has for our lives long before we realize what He is up to. He may bring into our lives certain people; cultivate in our hearts certain attitudes; or bring into our schedules certain activities—seemingly days, months, or even years ahead of time so that, in His perfect timing, His plans can be carried out.

1 KINGS 5:2–6 *Then Solomon sent to Hiram, saying: You know how my father David could not build a house for the name of the LORD his God because of the wars which were fought against him on every side, until the LORD put his foes under the soles of his feet. But now the LORD my God has given me rest on every side; there is neither adversary nor evil occurrence. And behold, I propose to build a house for the name of the LORD my God, as the LORD spoke to my father David, saying, "Your son, whom I will set on your throne in your place, he shall build the house for My name." Now therefore, command that they cut down cedars for me from Lebanon; and my servants will be with your servants, and I will pay you wages for your servants according to whatever you say. For you know there is none among us who has skill to cut timber like the Sidonians." (NKJV)*

As Solomon studied the blueprints for the temple and made an ever-growing list of the materials and workers it would take to get the job done, one thing must have become crystal clear to the wisest man in the world: He would need help, and lots of it, in order to erect the magnificent structure. One can't help but wonder if the message from Hiram had come just when the young king had uttered a prayer for help to the Lord: *"Send someone with the materials and expertise to help me."* That would have been in keeping with Solomon's regular mode of operation; after all, he had seen firsthand the power of prayer when he had asked God for wisdom!

what others say

Woodrow Kroll

Interesting letter! Solomon is writing here and he's building a workforce. Basically what he is doing is, he is developing partnerships. He says to Hiram, the king to the north, he says, "My men will work with your men. I don't have the manpower to get done what I need to do, but you do. Let's work together. Let's form a partnership. We'll develop this partnership and we will get the job done because we are partners." Now, my friends, that is a principle that has worked in ministry since Day One. . . . So this great land developer, Solomon, this God-enthused man, a man enthused about building a temple for the Lord God, first of all builds this temple by developing some partnerships. All the good work of God is done, friends, by developing partnerships.[16]

While no one can know for sure what was going on in Solomon's mind and heart as he proceeded with the temple project, it's not a stretch to believe the greeting from Hiram was music to his ears. Who wouldn't be pleased to hear from an old friend of the family, who not only was kind but who was also known to be generous with the many valuable resources at his disposal? Solomon responded to Hiram's message with familiarity and warmth: *"As a matter of fact, I'm glad you wrote. There is something I need help with and you're just the man who can help me. . . ."*

He presented his needs clearly, asking for:

1. *Timber from Lebanon.* The cedars of Lebanon grew on the western slopes of the Lebanon Mountains east of Tyre. This type of wood was a very old hardwood that wasn't prone to decay or infestation.

what others say

Alfred Edersheim

On the slopes of Lebanon . . . grew those world-famed cedars with which the palaces of Assyria were adorned, and, close by, at Gebal (the ancient Byblos, the modern Jebeil) were the most skilled workmen (Ezekiel 27:9). On the same slopes grew also the cypress, so suitable for flooring, its wood being almost indestructible, and impervious to rot and worms.[17]

2. *Skilled woodcutters.* Solomon wanted to pay Hiram to have his highly skilled woodcutters join his own workers in the endeavor.

what others say

Alfred Edersheim

The extraordinary mechanical skill of the Phoenicians—especially of the Sidonians—was universally famed in the ancient world. Similarly, the best materials were at their command.[18]

Not an Ordinary Temple

At this point, it makes sense to switch back over to the narrative in 2 Chronicles, which records more of Solomon's words to Hiram:

Baal
name for any number of male gods

2 Chronicles 2:4–6 Behold, I am building a temple for the name of the Lord my God, to dedicate it to Him, to burn before Him sweet incense, for the continual showbread, for the burnt offerings morning and evening, on the Sabbaths, on the New Moons, and on the set feasts of the Lord our God. This is an ordinance forever to Israel. And the temple which I build will be great, for our God is greater than all gods. But who is able to build Him a temple, since heaven and the heaven of heavens cannot contain Him? Who am I then, that I should build Him a temple, except to burn sacrifice before Him? (NKJV)

Hiram may have been a friend of David's and Solomon's, but he wasn't of the same faith as the Israeli kings. In fact, Tyre was a center of **Baal** worship. So Solomon worded his request in a way that would let the king, who would have been accustomed to temples that housed many idols of many gods, know exactly what he was doing—and exactly who he was doing it for.

what others say

Eugene H. Merrill

Solomon's reference to other gods does not imply that he believed in their existence. It was a way of setting forth to Hiram, a polytheistic pagan king, the uniqueness and incomparability of the Lord God of Israel (cf. Isaiah 40:18–26; 46:3–7).[19]

It Wasn't Just His Father's Religion

apply it

Solomon referred to "the Lord *my* God" (emphasis added), signaling that he had indeed embraced the faith of his father as his own. No one can get into heaven on the coattails of his or her parents! Whether to follow the Lord or reject His invitation to a relationship with Him is a decision each individual must make . . . well, individually!

Don't miss the fact that Solomon partnered with a foreigner in the temple project. One commentator notes the spiritual significance of that partnership:

Leslie M. Grant

This friendliness between Solomon and Hiram pictures the peace established between Israel and the Gentile nations in the millennium. Gentiles will come to Israel's light and the wealth of the Gentiles will come to Israel (Isaiah 60:3–5). God knew how to dispose Hiram favorably toward Solomon, and He knows how to change the hearts of other Gentiles from enmity to friendliness toward Israel, as He will in the latter days.[20]

Even More Men and Materials

2 Chronicles 2:7–10

The Chronicles passage includes requests Solomon made that aren't listed in the 1 Kings 5 passage. For a construction project of this magnitude and complexity, Solomon needed a man with skills of the highest possible level. However, the majority of Israelites were accustomed to tasks such as farming and shepherding; they weren't very well trained in jobs like engineering. He asked Hiram for an especially skilled worker to supervise the build. He also asked for cypress and algum, another type of lumber, in addition to the cedar. In exchange for the work, he promised generous payment.

Matthew Henry

He did not feed his workmen with bread and water, but with plenty, and every thing of the best.[21]

Hiram's Generous Response

Now, back to the 1 Kings narrative . . .

1 KINGS 5:7–12 *So it was, when Hiram heard the words of Solomon, that he rejoiced greatly and said, Blessed be the LORD this day, for He has given David a wise son over this great people! Then Hiram sent to Solomon, saying: I have considered the message which you sent me, and I will do all you desire concerning the cedar and cypress logs. . . . And you shall fulfill my*

desire by giving food for my household. Then Hiram gave Solomon cedar and cypress logs according to all his desire. And Solomon gave Hiram twenty thousand kors of wheat as food for his household, and twenty kors of pressed oil. Thus Solomon gave to Hiram year by year. So the LORD gave Solomon wisdom, as He had promised him; and there was peace between Hiram and Solomon, and the two of them made a treaty together. (NKJV)

Hiram answered Solomon's letter with one of his own, acknowledging Solomon's position with his people and with his God, and promising to fulfill Solomon's requests.

The trade agreement was a win-win proposition: Hiram would provide the wood, even going so far as to take care of shipping the supplies. In return, Solomon would provide Hiram provisions of wheat and olive oil. Then the subject of Solomon's wisdom is once again highlighted—this time pointing to the king's managerial savvy:

A Massive Labor Force

1 KINGS 5:13–18 *Then King Solomon raised up a labor force out of all Israel; and the labor force was thirty thousand men. And he sent them to Lebanon, ten thousand a month in shifts: they were one month in Lebanon and two months at home; Adoniram was in charge of the labor force. Solomon had seventy thousand who carried burdens, and eighty thousand who quarried stone in the mountains, besides three thousand three hundred from the chiefs of Solomon's deputies, who supervised the people who labored in the work. And the king commanded them to quarry large stones, costly stones, and hewn stones, to lay the foundation of the temple. So Solomon's builders, Hiram's builders, and the Gebalites quarried them; and they prepared timber and stones to build the temple. (NKJV)*

Managing the personnel it would take to gather materials and build a project of this scope was no small part of Solomon's responsibilities. He called into service 30,000 Israelite laborers, who worked in shifts of 10,000, to help Hiram's men cut and transport the timbers from Lebanon. Each shift worked for a month at a time—meaning each man put in four months per year. Beyond that labor force, Solomon pressed into service a permanent group of slave laborers to tackle the more backbreaking work of hauling materials and quarrying the stones. Further, 3,300 men—comprising mostly Canaanites and Israelites—served as supervisors.

As will be seen in later chapters of this book, the workload Solomon placed on those he drafted into service would later cause dissatisfaction among the people.

Chapter Wrap-Up

- The idea for the temple project had originated with Solomon's father, David, who wanted to build a permanent house more suitable for the Lord than the temporary, portable, tentlike tabernacle.

- God had told David that he would not be the one to build Him a temple, because David, a lifelong warrior, had blood-stained hands. God wanted David's son, Solomon, to build the temple because he was a man of peace.

- Although God turned down David's temple-building plans, David prepared the way for his son to build it. Among other things, David received detailed plans from the Lord; he recruited workers and craftsmen; he gathered materials; he donated generous gifts from his own storehouses; and he commissioned the Israelite leaders to help his son.

- When Solomon took over he immediately realized that he needed help and renewed his father's treaty with Hiram, king of Tyre, who gave Solomon the men and materials he needed to get started. Solomon promised to send Hiram wheat and olive oil in return.

- Solomon set up a large-scale labor force to work in the quarries, and at the job site.

Study Questions

1. What had given David the idea to build a temple for the Lord?

2. Why did God veto David's plans?

3. How did David respond to God's refusal to allow him to be the one to build the temple?

4. Who designed the detailed construction plans for the temple?

5. What was one of Solomon's first steps in commencing work on the building project?

Chapter Highlights:
- **Built on Prime Property**
- **Construction Begins**
- **Rubik's Cubit?**
- **Silence Is Golden**
- **Interior Design**

1 Kings 6; 7:13–50; 2 Chronicles 3; 4: The Specs for a Spectacular Building

Let's Get Started

Throughout the ages, people have built all kinds of structures to facilitate the worship of their gods. From the ancient pillars of Stonehenge and the ornate spires of medieval Gothic cathedrals to ultramodern glass-and-metal auditoriums of American mega-churches, artists, architects, and engineers have designed extraordinary buildings in which to meet their deities.

But one structure stands out among the rest as the temple of all temples: the house of the Lord that Solomon built. A glimpse into the most magnificent buildings of worship standing today can offer only a hint of the splendor, significance, and symbolism of Solomon's temple. Premium materials that would cost millions and millions of dollars in today's currency went into every aspect of its construction. Rich imagery graced its design and furnishings. Masterful construction established its structural integrity. Striking carvings and stunning decor adorned every surface of every room—even in spots that most people would never see.

But what set Solomon's temple apart from all others wasn't its intricate craftsmanship or its 24-carat gleam. What set the structure apart was its Designer. Truly, God was in every detail that He provided regarding the layout and construction of the house that He would call "home" among His chosen people, Israel.

key point

Clearly, Solomon carefully followed his father's instructions for building the temple; he was a faithful steward of the monumental project that had been placed into his willing hands.

what others say

Irving L. Jensen

The temple which Solomon built was the first large single structure undertaken by any Israelite ruler.[1]

go to

destroyed
Jeremiah 32:28–44

Nebuchadnezzar
Jeremiah 21–52;
Daniel 1:1–5:18

rebuilt
Ezra 3:8–5:18

Antiochus Epiphanes
Daniel 9:27; 11:31

leveled by the Romans
Matthew 24:15

Nebuchadnezzar
king of the Neo-
Babylonian Empire
who captured
Jerusalem,
destroyed the tem-
ple, and took cap-
tive the people of
Judah

Zerubbabel
head of Judah dur-
ing return from
Babylonian captivity;
builder of second
temple

desecrated
abused something
sacred

Solomon's temple is no longer standing. It was <u>destroyed</u> by **Nebuchadnezzar** in 586 BC. Then it was <u>rebuilt</u> in 536 BC by **Zerubbabel** but later **desecrated** by <u>Antiochus Epiphanes</u>. Herod the Great restored the temple only to have it <u>leveled by the Romans</u> in AD 70.

Despite all that, however, passages in 1 Kings and 2 Chronicles read like an in-depth article in an *Architectural Digest*, offering descriptions of the temple so detailed that scholars have been able to put together very accurate models. Those details are the focus of this chapter. Once again, the two books—1 Kings and 2 Chronicles—describe many of the same details, but at times each offers unique information in differing sequences. So, the discussion in this chapter won't necessarily follow the order in which it is presented in one or both of those books of the Bible. Instead, details about the temple will be presented in a way designed to give you, the reader, a clear sense of what the temple looked like and what its features meant.

what others say

Roger Hahn

These chapters contain the most detailed description of a temple found in ancient literature anywhere. When combined with the descriptions of 2 Chronicles 3:1–5:1, Ezekiel 40–42, and the archaeological remains of ancient temples in the Near East, we have a clearer picture of the temple than of any other ancient structure.[2]

Temples in the Bible

Sancturary	Scripture	Approximate Dates
The tabernacle	Exodus 26:1; 36:8–38; 1 Samuel 4:10–11	Built about 1446 BC Probably destroyed (date unknown)
Solomon's temple	1 Kings 5–8; Jeremiah 32:28–44; Daniel 1:1–2	Built about 960 BC Destroyed 586 BC
Zerubbabel's temple	Ezra 3:1–8; 4:1–14; 6:13–15	Built 516 BC Desecrated 169 BC
Herod's temple: remodeled, enlarged; name changed	John 2:20; Daniel 9:26	Started about 19 BC Destroyed AD 70

Nan Missler

Solomon's temple was special and very unique for three important reasons:

1. It was the only temple in which all the detailed plans—not only of the construction of the temple, but also of all the furniture—were given . . . by the Spirit of God. . . . No other temple could boast of this *supernatural design*.

2. It was the only temple in which the ark of the covenant rested.

3. Finally, it was the only temple in which the Shekinah Glory (God's Spirit) dwelt for 400 years, until the temple was actually destroyed.[3]

plague
2 Samuel 24;
1 Chronicles 21

offered Isaac
Genesis 22:2

Abraham
patriarch of Israel
who modeled great
faith in God

Built on Prime Property

2 CHRONICLES 3:1 *Now Solomon began to build the house of the LORD at Jerusalem on Mount Moriah, where the LORD had appeared to his father David, at the place that David had prepared on the threshing floor of Ornan the Jebusite. (NKJV)*

The first order of business on the construction schedule—securing a building site—had been arranged many years earlier, when David had purchased land atop Mount Moriah.

That property was special for a couple of reasons:

1. Most recently, it had been where God had graciously withdrawn a <u>plague</u> that had decimated Israel as the result of David's sins of pride and self-reliance.

2. It was where God had mercifully provided a substitute sacrifice when **Abraham**, in a breathtaking display of trust in God, had <u>offered his son Isaac</u> upon the altar.

Baker Encyclopedia of the Bible

Fittingly . . . the temple stood where God's grace and mercy had been revealed. The cost of the actual threshing floor, a relatively small area, was 50 silver shekels, but the chronicler probably links in the subsequent purchase for 600 gold shekels of the far larger area needed for the whole temple complex (1 Chronicles 21:25).[4]

go to

living stones
1 Peter 2:5

Dome of the Rock
an Islamic place of
worship in
Jerusalem

Temple Mount
Mount Moriah in
Jerusalem

what others say

Tim LaHaye

This place, purchased by David (2 Samuel 24:18–25) as the site for the temple, became the focus for the construction of the first truly holy building in the history of the world.[5]

Still Sacred

Standing today on the site of Solomon's temple, the Temple Mount, is the gilded-roofed **Dome of the Rock**. Dispute over ownership of this sacred site is at the heart of the ongoing strife in the Middle East.

what others say

William T. James

The **Temple Mount** in Jerusalem has been occupied for the past thirteen centuries by the Dome of the Rock and the Al Aqsa Mosque of the idolatrous Islamic religion.[6]

Construction Begins

1 KINGS 6:1 *And it came to pass in the four hundred and eightieth year after the children of Israel had come out of the land of Egypt, in the fourth year of Solomon's reign over Israel, in the month of Ziv, which is the second month, that he began to build the house of the LORD. (NKJV)*

prophecy

This marks the first level of fulfillment of the prophecy God gave when He said David's son would build Him a temple. The second level of fulfillment will be completed when Jesus finishes building His spiritual temple with the "living stones" of believers and establishes His eternal kingdom. It should never be *surprising*, but it is always *awe-inspiring* when God's prophecies are fulfilled!

what others say

Daymond Duck

In the sense that this prophecy refers to Solomon and the earthly temple, it has been fulfilled. Solomon succeeded David on the throne and he built the first temple. But in the greater and more significant sense that it refers to Jesus, the spiritual temple he is building for God, and the eternal kingdom God is building, this prophecy is yet to be fulfilled.[7]

The Exodus and the Temple

Exodus
Israelites' departure
from captivity in
Egypt

The mention of the **Exodus** in this passage is important for at least a couple of reasons:

1. It provides Bible scholars with a way to establish an accurate chronology of biblical history.

what others say

NKJV Study Bible

Many scholars take this date as the key date for establishing the time of the Exodus. The division of the kingdom at the death of Solomon can be dated at 930 BC (11:41–43). Allowing forty years for Solomon's rule (11:42), the fourth year of his reign would be 966 BC. If the Exodus took place 480 years before 966 BC, its date was 1446 BC. Some consider this date too early for what occurs in the Book of Exodus and date the Exodus in the thirteenth century BC. They suggest that the 480 years may be a round figure representing twelve generations, or that it may have been arrived at by adding the length of various concurrent or overlapping periods as though they were placed in one lineal string of eras.[8]

2. It calls to mind Israel's appointed place in God's far-reaching plan for His people.

what others say

Thomas L. Constable

With the building of the temple Israel would have an opportunity as never before in her history to realize the purpose for which God had formed and freed the nation. That purpose was to draw all people to Himself.[9]

He Didn't Put the Cart Before the Horse

Notice that Solomon began building the temple in the fourth year of his reign—not on the first day, the first month, or even in the first year. The king, it seems, was being careful not to rush into a project of such great importance. He took as long as was necessary to get the nation's political affairs in order, add to the supplies his father had gathered, and line up a top-notch construction crew—all before the first stone was set into place.

Home improvement television programs can be deceiving! Viewers have become accustomed to seeing dramatic transformations take place in the structure and decor of a home inside a thirty-minute time frame, making it easy to forget that the adage "Good things take time" really is true. What the TV cameras don't broadcast, however, are the hours and hours of time it takes to prepare a home for a renovation: the days spent studying blueprints, collecting paint chips; comparing fabric swatches; lining up carpenters; shopping for supplies; priming surfaces. In this era of "instant gratification" and "quick fixes," it can be difficult to regard the slow and steady work of simply *getting ready* to do something as worthy of time and energy. But careful preparation is necessary for anyone who wants to produce good results.

For the Christian, two "P's"—prayer and planning—should be at the top of the to-do list in preparing for any personal, ministry, or professional project.

what others say

Matthew Henry

We are truly serving God when we are preparing for his service and furnishing ourselves for it.[10]

Rubik's Cubit?

1 KINGS 6:2 *Now the house which King Solomon built for the LORD, its length was sixty cubits, its width twenty, and its height thirty cubits.* (NKJV)

The word *cubit* sounds more like the addicting brainteaser of the 1980s than it does a measurement! But a cubit was the common measure of length used in the Bible. Since the term is used dozens of times in the passages describing Solomon's temple, it helps to keep in mind that a cubit is about eighteen inches, or roughly the distance from one's elbow to fingertips. Using that equivalent, the temple measured about 90 feet long, 30 feet wide, and 45 feet high.

A Little on the Small Side

Because of its reputation as such a magnificent structure, it may be surprising to find the dimensions of the temple a little on the small side. Even though it was about twice the size of the tabernacle, it might be comparable in size to a small church today.

Randall Price

In appearance the first temple was a modest building. It was about the size of a small church or synagogue . . . and situated on a platform approximately 10 feet high.[11]

J. Vernon McGee

Even though the temple was small, it was like a jewel. Now a diamond is not as big as a straw stack, but it is much more valuable. That was true of the temple Solomon built.[12]

Rose Book of Bible Charts, Maps and Timelines

Solomon relied on the architects of King Hiram of Tyre. Therefore, his temple was an expression of the Syrian "long room plan" of that region and period of history.[13]

The Temple at a Glance

1 KINGS 6:3–6 *The vestibule in front of the sanctuary of the house was twenty cubits long across the width of the house, and the width of the vestibule extended ten cubits from the front of the house. And he made for the house windows with beveled frames. Against the wall of the temple he built chambers all around, against the walls of the temple, all around the sanctuary and the inner sanctuary. Thus he made side chambers all around it. The lowest chamber was five cubits wide, the middle was six cubits wide, and the third was seven cubits wide; for he made narrow ledges around the outside of the temple, so that the support beams would not be fastened into the walls of the temple.* (NKJV)

Significant physical characteristics of the temple's appearance were its:

- *Front porch*—as high as the temple and extending across the width of the temple.
- *Windows*—for ventilation and light; narrow and possibly covered with lattice so that, some scholars say, one could see out from the inside but not inside from the outside.

- *Chambers*—rooms three stories high—which weren't part of the structure of the temple itself—were built along the outside of the temple. Each floor was progressively wider. The chambers provided the temple priests quiet spots for private time with God as well as a secluded place to prepare for service and to store the various vessels and instruments used in temple worship.

Solomon's Temple
This drawing shows the basic layout of the temple Solomon built in Jerusalem.

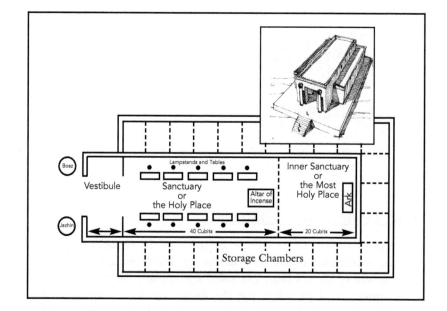

Silence Is Golden

1 KINGS 6:7 *And the temple, when it was being built, was built with stone finished at the quarry, so that no hammer or chisel or any iron tool was heard in the temple while it was being built.* (NKJV)

The noises of a major construction site today can be deafening. Jackhammers, nail guns, and power saws make such a racket that many workers wear earplugs to protect their hearing. But at the ancient temple construction site, things were strangely silent—and not just because these were the days long before power tools. The silence came from the fact that the loudest work—cutting the stones—was carried out at the quarry far away from Mount Moriah. This attests to the outstanding skill of the workers Solomon had recruited, and, more important, it points to the reverence with which the king approached the building of God's dwelling place.

Dorothy Russell

Deep below the old city of Jerusalem, a great cavern extends into the rock. This is where Solomon obtained the stone for building the temple. The marks of the picks used to quarry the rock can still be seen today.[14]

Charles H. Spurgeon

Many of the stones of Solomon's masonry are so enormous that scarcely could any modern machinery move them; and without the slightest cement they are put together so exactly that the blade of a knife could not be inserted between them.[15]

What Are "Living Stones"?

It was a mind-boggling feat of engineering and artistry: From irregular boulders and chunks of rock dug out of the quarries, stoneworkers chiseled out, in assembly-line fashion, row after row of building blocks uniform in shape and size. As the Middle Eastern sun baked the landscape, diligent workers figured and measured, cut and sanded until each stone would fit flush and tight beside the next one. One might say that each stone, individually cut, shaped, and smoothed with extraordinary expertise, was a masterpiece. The crafting and assembly of the stones into the temple offers a great illustration of the way believers—called "living stones" in 1 Peter 2:5 (NKJV)—are being fitted into the spiritual house of God.

David Guzik

God is building a spiritual temple (a spiritual house) using living stones (Christians), those who have come to the ultimate Living Stone (Jesus). This spiritual house shows that as much as Israel had a temple, Christians also have one. But the Christian's temple is spiritual, and they themselves are the temple.[16]

what others say

Henry Morris

This unusual construction practice could be regarded as a type of the manner in which the Holy Spirit quietly is adding "living stones" to the spiritual house of God today, "built upon the foundation of the apostles and prophets, Jesus Christ himself being the chief corner stone; In whom all the building fitly framed together growth unto an holy temple in the Lord" (Ephesians 2:20–21; note also 1 Peter 2:4–5).[17]

Ouch! That Hurt!

Have you ever gone through periods of difficulty, sorrow, or frustration only to emerge on the other side of the dark valley to find that you have learned important lessons, developed more mature character traits, or grown closer to God? That's the process God, sometimes called the Master Designer, often uses to chisel, sand, and shape us into the people He wants us to become. He's preparing each believer—through sometimes painful processes—for placement into his or her designated spot in the "holy temple of the Lord."

what others say

Adam Clarke Commentary

The temple was a type of the kingdom of God; and the souls of men are to be prepared *here* for *that* place of blessedness. *There*, there is no preaching, exhortations, repentance, ears, cries, nor prayers; the stones must be all squared and fitted here for their place in the New Jerusalem, and, being *living stones*, must be built up a holy temple for a habitation of God through the Spirit.[18]

J. C. Ryle

Great is the wisdom with which the Lord Jesus Christ builds His Church. All is done at the right time, and in the right way. Each stone in its turn is put in the right place. Sometimes He chooses great stones, and sometimes He chooses small stones....He often chooses the most unlikely and roughest stones, and fits them into a most excellent work. He despises no one, and rejects none, on account of former sins and past transgressions. He delights to show mercy. He often takes the most thoughtless and ungodly, and transforms them into polished corners of His spiritual temple.[19]

A Heavenly Tap on the Shoulder

1 KINGS 6:11–13 *Then the word of the LORD came to Solomon, saying: "Concerning this temple which you are building, if you walk in My statutes, execute My judgments, keep all My commandments, and walk in them, then I will perform My word with you, which I spoke to your father David. And I will dwell among the children of Israel, and will not forsake My people Israel." (NKJV)*

In an abrupt interruption of the detailed description of the construction of the temple, God spoke to Solomon. Whether He spoke directly to the king in an audible voice or through a prophet isn't made clear, but the message was unmistakable. God:

- Reminded Solomon to remain obedient to Him; and
- Reaffirmed His promises.

How God Makes Promises

The Bible includes hundreds of promises from God to man. Some of those promises are unconditional; their fulfillment requires no action on the part of the people to whom they are made. Nothing a person can do—or fail to do—will cause him or her to lose God's promise. For example, in Genesis 9:11, God said that there would never again be a worldwide flood like the one described in Genesis chapters 7 and 8, no matter how evil people in the world become. That was an unconditional promise. And in the New Testament, Jesus said that He would one day return to the earth. No strings are attached to that promise; He will do what He said He will do.

key point

Others of God's promises are conditional. They are fulfilled when the recipient does what God asks. For example, in Matthew 6, Jesus promised that if a person focuses on the things of eternal value, God will take care of his or her physical needs. The condition for that promise's coming to pass is pursuing spiritual, not physical, riches. And the writer of James 4:7 states that if a person submits to God and resists the devil, the devil will flee. The conditions for that promise coming to pass are surrendering to God's will and deliberately turning away from evil.

go to

promise of land
Genesis 15

**announced the
Messiah**
Luke 1:32–33

something to ponder

God's original promise to David—the promise called the Davidic covenant—was unconditional. That promise:

- Reaffirmed God's <u>promise of land</u>.

- Guaranteed that David's offspring would succeed him as king of Israel.

- Stated that David's heir, not David, would be the one to build a house for God.

- Assured an everlasting kingdom: God promised that David's dynasty would never end.

- <u>Announced the Messiah</u>'s entry into the history of humankind through the lineage of David and the tribe of Judah.

While God's promises to David, and subsequently to Solomon, were unconditional, His words to Solomon did remind the king that a conditional promise was included within the unconditional ones. God would not fail to keep His word concerning each point of the covenant, but Solomon and the kings who followed him would be *at risk of missing out on God's blessings* if they failed to be obedient.

what others say

Tim LaHaye

The tragic history of Israel and the Jewish people is a constant reminder that God keeps His word and blesses those who obey Him, but curses those who disobey Him. Only eternity will reveal what Israel could have accomplished had they obeyed God.[20]

Adam Clarke Commentary

It was a word to encourage him while building; to warn him against apostasy, and to assure him of God's continued protection of him and his family, if they continued faithful to the grace which God had given.[21]

<u>Keeping the Main Thing the Main Thing</u>

Overseeing the construction of the temple must have been an all-consuming project for Solomon. His days were full—managing the immense workforce, fielding questions from supervisors, and supervising the flow of funds and materials. All the while he had to continue carrying out the duties of a king—administering justice, overseeing his staff, strengthening alliances, strategizing ways to keep the nation's economy strong and growing.

Such a weighty workload might have made it easy for Solomon to skip his daily prayers and meditations. Or to forget about keeping the Law and take shortcuts in matters of integrity involving the business end of building. Further, such a glamorous project might have tempted the king to accept the praise of other people, to bask in the limelight of the attention the splendid building was attracting. He was a prime target for suddenly finding himself doing the right thing for all the wrong reasons. But God didn't want any of that to happen. That's why He sent Solomon this urgent memorandum to help the king keep the main thing the main thing.

It happens all the time: We commit to projects at church or in the community, and then become so bogged down with the details and responsibilities that we lose sight of the reason that compelled us to raise our hand to begin with! Listening to God—through prayer, meditation, and Bible study—is essential for keeping on track, spiritually speaking, while undertaking any project.

apply it

Interior Design

the big picture

1 Kings 6:14–36

Once the temple was enclosed, Solomon turned his attention to the interior. The space, like the tabernacle, was divided into two sections: the holy place, or sanctuary; and the most holy place, or inner sanctuary. Finishing touches on the surfaces of the walls, floors, and ceilings involved paneling the walls with cedar, covering the floor with cypress planks, and installing artistic carvings throughout.

Points of Interest in the Temple's Interior Design

Feature of Interest	Description
Ornate Wood Carvings	Wood carvings throughout the temple featured flowers and palm trees—a floral motif that some scholars believe was intended to bring to mind the original dwelling place of God, the Garden of Eden.
Gold Everywhere	Gold was the key word: Solomon overlaid every surface, from the ceilings to the walls and the carvings, with the precious material.
The Most Holy Place	Great attention was paid—and no expense spared—in the completion of the inner sanctuary of the temple where the ark of the covenant would be placed. This room was in the shape of a 30-foot cube and bathed in 600 talents, or about 23 tons, of pure gold. A beautiful, heavy veil separated the holy place from the most holy place. The blue, purple, and red linen drapery featured cherubim woven into its design.
Cherubim	Cherubim carvings adorned the walls; Solomon also positioned two large sculptures of cherubim in the most holy place. Crafted from wood and plated with gold, they stood so that their outstretched, 7-1/2-foot wings overshadowed the ark and spanned the width of the room.
Pillars	In front of the temple were two freestanding bronze pillars. Because of discrepancies in the text and a possible misinterpretation by the scribes, there is some confusion about the height of the pillars. Estimates indicate that they stood anywhere from 27 to 60 feet tall. At any height, they were striking features of the temple. Atop each pillar were intricate carved garlands featuring hundreds of engraved pomegranates. Interestingly, Solomon named the pillars. He called the one on the right Jachin, which means "He Establishes," and the one on the left Boaz, or "In Him Is Strength."

It's a Wrap

1 KINGS 6:37–38 *In the fourth year the foundation of the house of the LORD was laid, in the month of Ziv. And in the eleventh year, in the month of Bul, which is the eighth month, the house was finished in all its details and according to all its plans. So he was seven years in building it. (NKJV)*

The temple was completed several months—eleven to be exact—before the dedication ceremony. This gave Solomon time to make sure that all the furnishings were completed and installed before that great event (to be discussed in the next chapter).

Temple Furnishings*

Furnishing	Location in Temple	Description
Bronze Altar	Inside the courtyard	Altar for burnt offerings
The Sea	Inside the entrance to the courtyard	A massive vessel that held 27,000 gallons of water for ceremonial washing of priests
Ten Lavers	Arranged in two rows of five on the north and south sides of the Sea	Smaller basins—each held 230 gallons—for cleansing of sacrificial animals
Carts	courtyard	Mobile stands to hold the lavers
Ten Lampstands	Interior of the temple—with five on the north side of the holy place and five on the south	Symbolized God's light
Ten Tables	Interior of the temple	To hold the showbread
100 Bowls	Interior of the temple	Golden bowls holding the liquids that were sprinkled
Altar of Gold	In the holy place	Used for offering incense

*2 Chronicles 4 describes in great detail the furnishings that went into the temple.

what others say

J. C. Ryle

Like the altar in Solomon's temple, Christ crucified will be the grand object in heaven. That altar struck the eye of every one who entered the temple gates. It was a great brazen altar, twenty cubits broad—as broad as the front of the temple itself. So in like manner will Jesus fill the eyes of all who enter glory. In the midst of the throne, and surrounded by adoring angels and saints, there will be "the Lamb that was slain." And "the Lamb shall be the light" of the place.[22]

A Massive Building Program

the big picture

1 Kings 7:13–50

Once the temple was completed, Solomon turned his attention to other impressive building projects, both public and private. Solomon's other building projects included:

• **The House of the Forest of Lebanon,** featuring abundant supplies of cedar from that region. The building was possibly used as an armory. The writer of 1 Kings describes elaborate decorative shields that were housed in this structure: "And King Solomon made two hundred large shields of hammered gold; six hundred shekels of gold went into each shield. He also made three hundred shields of hammered gold; three minas of gold went into each shield" (1 Kings 10:16–17 NKJV; see also 2 Chronicles 9:15–16). Further, "all the vessels" used in this facility "were pure gold. Not one was silver, for this was accounted as nothing in the days of Solomon" (1 Kings 10:21 NKJV).

- **The Hall of Pillars,** serving as an entry hall to the Hall of Judgment.
- **The Hall of Judgment,** a throne room from which the king administered justice. (Interestingly, this corresponds to the most holy place, the throne room of God.) The throne wasn't an ordinary chair by any stretch of the imagination; the Bible says that no other throne in the world was like it. Made of wood inlaid with ivory and overlaid with finest gold, it "had six steps, and the top of the throne was round at the back; there were armrests on either side of the place of the seat, and two lions stood beside the armrests. Twelve lions [possibly representing the 12 tribes of Israel] stood there, one on each side of the six steps; nothing like this had been made for any other kingdom" (1 Kings 10:19–20 NKJV; see also 2 Chronicles 9:17–19).
- **Solomon's palace.**
- **A house for Pharaoh's daughter,** Solomon's second wife.
- **An outer court** that encircled the temple, the palace, and all the other buildings, uniting them into an immense and grand royal compound.

The King's Digs

The Bible states that it took Solomon thirteen years to build his palace—much longer than the seven years it took to build the temple. Some scholars suggest that it took longer because all of these buildings—his palace, the house for Pharaoh's daughter, and the halls—were all considered part of the same building project. The arrangement would have been similar to other large palaces of the time. Many of the temple's features were repeated in the palace; similar architecture and the same types of materials characterized both structures.

something to ponder

what others say

Joseph P. Free and Howard F. Vos

The record in 1 Kings 7 tells us that the courts of Solomon's palaces were constructed of "three courses of dressed stone and one course of trimmed cedar beams" (1 Kings 7:12).

Archaeological light on this type of construction was found in the University of Chicago excavation at Megiddo. There the remains of a large building consisted of well-cut stone foundations, the upper surfaces of which were burned black. Fragments of mud brick and ashes from the superstructure lay scattered about. From these ashes was taken a piece of charred wood, which was shown by chemical analysis to be cedar, indicating that the superstructure was built with a "half timber" type of construction similar to the courts of Solomon, which were made with rows of hewn stone and cedar beams.[23]

It's important to remember that while Solomon was not a priest, he was considered a human representative of God. It was, therefore, fitting for him to live in the temple complex.

what others say

Peter Leithart

Solomon's residence in the temple complex stands as a scriptural figure indicating that all earthly rule, not only Israel's, is overshadowed by heaven and a reminder that the gospel we preach is good news about a king of all kings.[24]

Alfred Edersheim

The dwelling of God in His temple and that of Solomon in his house were events between which there was deep internal connection . . . the king was not to be a monarch in the usual Oriental, or even in the ancient Western sense. He was to be regarded, not as the Viceregent or Representative of God, but as His servant, to do His behest and to guard His covenant. And this might well be marked, even by the conjunction of these two buildings in the Scripture narrative.[25]

Chapter Wrap-Up

- What set the temple apart from the temples of other deities was its designer and inhabitant: God. He was in every detail that He had provided regarding the layout and construction of the house that He would call "home" among His chosen people, Isreal.

- The temple was built on Mount Moriah, property with great significance because it was where God had graciously withdrawn a plague that had decimated Israel as the result of David's sin; and it was where God had mercifully provided a substitute sacrifice when Abraham had, in obedience to God's instructions, laid his son upon the altar.

- Surprisingly, the templ   e wasn't much bigger than a small church today.

- The noisy work of finishing and fitting stones together was done at the quarry in order to maintain a holy hush at the building site of the temple.

- Just as master stoneworkers polished and shaped stones for insertion in the temple walls, God polishes and shapes believers, called "living stones," to be fitted into the spiritual temple of God.

- The temple was similar to the tabernacle in design and construction, with many of the same features and furnishings.

- When Solomon had finished building the temple, he turned his attention to building other structures in the temple complex, including his own palace and a home for his second wife, the pharaoh's daughter.

Study Questions

1. What is the condition of Solomon's temple today?

2. What was significant about the property on which the temple was built?

3. Why didn't Solomon begin construction on the temple on his first day as king?

4. What would have been strange about a visit to the construction site?

5. What is the relationship between today's believers and the ancient temple?

6. What did Solomon do when the temple was complete?

1 Kings 8; 2 Chronicles 5:1–7:11: The Dedication of the Temple

Chapter Highlights:
- **The Nation's Biggest Celebration**
- **So Many Sacrifices!**
- **Putting the Throne in the Throne Room**
- **A House of Prayer**

Let's Get Started

Like a new skyscraper going up to reconfigure the silhouette of a city, the structure being erected atop Mount Moriah near Jerusalem had drawn fascinated and reverent attention for the past seven years. During the first months of construction, the people observed a steady stream of workers and caravans of supplies winding up and down the roadways leading to the building site. Each milestone brought new reason to rejoice: *"The foundation is laid!" "The walls are up!" "The roof has been placed!" "Have you seen those magnificent pillars?"*

Once the exterior of the building had been completed, onlookers had seen cart after cart packed with carefully wrapped candlesticks and tables, mounds of jewel-colored fabric, and other treasures hauled up the mountainside. This activity, which had taken place during the last year of construction, signaled that the finishing touches were under way.

And finally, on one special day, Israelites from far and wide began receiving invitations from the king himself. He asked them to attend a one-of-a-kind celebration: the dedication of the nation's first temple.

Even though the discovery of electricity was still many centuries in the future, the streets of the capital city were electric with anticipation anyway as the people made their way toward the sacred mountain, where rays of sunlight piercing the autumn air seemed to cast heaven's spotlights on the holy temple. This promised to be an extraordinary event; after all, it was—in a sense—moving-in day for the presence of the Lord Himself.

Nothing Can Contain God

It's important to make clear before looking further into the temple dedication that God is **omnipresent**—that is, He is everywhere,

omnipresent
everywhere, all the time

go to

**Feast of Tabernacles,
or Feast of Ingathering**
Exodus 23:16; 34:22;
Leviticus 23:33–36,
39–43;
Numbers 29:12–38;
Deuteronomy
16:13–15

**Feast of Tabernacles,
or Feast of
Ingathering**
one of Israel's holiest
celebrations,
commemorating the
nation's wandering
in the wilderness

all the time. Therefore, the temple made of limestone and cedar couldn't contain Him any more than a plastic grocery bag or an indoor sports arena could! The inner sanctuary of the temple would be—merely for God and gloriously for His people—a dwelling place for His presence. It couldn't possibly house the entirety of His being.

what others say

Nelson's Student Bible Dictionary

God is not like the manufactured idols of ancient cultures that were limited to one altar or temple area. God reveals Himself in the Bible as the Lord who is everywhere. God was present as Lord in all creation (Psalm 139:7–12), and there is no escaping Him. He is present in our innermost thoughts. Even as we are formed in the womb, He knows all the days of our future.[1]

Randall Price

We might say that God is like a circle who is at every point the center. Because His presence fills all that He has made He cannot be limited, reduced, or compromised by time or space. However, God can choose to *manifest* His presence temporally, spacially, and locally as He did at the Tabernacle and in the first temple.[2]

The Nation's Biggest Celebration

1 KINGS 8:1–2 Now Solomon assembled the elders of Israel and all the heads of the tribes, the chief fathers of the children of Israel, to King Solomon in Jerusalem, that they might bring up the ark of the covenant of the LORD from the City of David, which is Zion. Therefore all the men of Israel assembled with King Solomon at the feast in the month of Ethanim, which is the seventh month. (NKJV)

A large-scale occasion such as the installation of the ark of the covenant and the dedication of the temple called for a lengthy guest list. Solomon invited all the heads of tribes and families in Israel to attend. It was an invitation no one would have dreamed of turning down. The event was scheduled during the **Feast of Tabernacles**, which commemorated Israel's wandering in the wilderness when the ark had been on the move. (Usually an eight-day celebration that lasted from the fifteenth to the twenty-second day of the seventh month, Tishri, it would ultimately be lengthened to two weeks in honor of this momentous occasion.) The timing—delaying the celebration for eleven months after the temple was completed—was significant for several reasons:

1. **Time to plan.** As anyone who has ever planned a birthday party or the company barbecue can attest, it takes time and lots of preparations to put together a party of any size, let alone one of this magnitude. The span between the temple's completion and the dedication gave Solomon and his "event planners" ample time to get ready for throngs of people.

2. **Practical for the people.** Because of the time of the year when the temple was completed, it would have been extremely difficult for people from all corners of the nation to take time off to come and celebrate.

3. **An automatic draw.** Among all of the feasts celebrated by the Israelites, the Feast of Tabernacles was the greatest. It was one of the three major feasts (in addition to the Feast of Unleavened Bread and Feast of Weeks, or Shavuot), which meant that all males of Israel were required to attend. So it always drew large numbers of people.

Jamieson, Fausset, Brown

As the tabernacle was to be superseded by the temple, there was admirable propriety in choosing the feast of tabernacles as the period for dedicating the new place of worship, and praying that the same distinguished privileges might be continued to it in the manifestation of the divine presence and glory.[3]

The Feast of Tabernacles is considered among the greatest of many feasts and celebrations of Ancient Israel. Others included:

- **The Feast of Unleavened Bread** (Exodus 12:15–20; 13:3–10; Leviticus 23:6–8; Numbers 28:17–25; Deuteronomy 16:3–4, 6), which marked the beginning of the barley harvest.

- **The Feast of Firstfruits** (Leviticus 23:9–14; Numbers 28:26), which accompanied the offering of the first harvested barley to God.

Zechariah
prophet and author
of the book of
Zechariah

tribulation
seven-year period of
God's judgment at
history's end

- *The Feast of Weeks* (Shavuot, or "Pentecost" in English) (Exodus 23:16; 34:22; Leviticus 23:15–21; Numbers 28:26–31; Deuteronomy 16:9–12), which took place fifty days after the barley harvest and involved new grain offerings to the Lord.

- *The Feast of Trumpets* (Rosh Hashanah) (Leviticus 23:23–25; Numbers 29:1–6), which involved a Sabbath rest, the blowing of trumpets, and a holy convocation.

- *The Day of Atonement* (Yom Kippur) (Leviticus 16; 23:26–32; Numbers 29:7–11), which was a day of fasting for the purpose of atoning for the sins of the past year.

The prophet **Zechariah**, in describing things that will happen during the end times, stated that those who survive the **tribulation** will observe the Feast of the Tabernacles.

what others say

Zola Levitt

The Feast of Tabernacles celebrates the fact that God wanted to provide shelter for the Israelites in the wilderness (see Leviticus 23:39–43). Each year devout Jews build little shelters outside their house and worship in them. The Lord's great tabernacle will exist in Jerusalem during the Millennial Kingdom. The entire world will come every year to appear before the King and worship Him.[4]

Tim LaHaye

The survivors of the Tribulation period will go up to Jerusalem annually to worship the King and keep the Feast of Tabernacles because it commemorates the culmination of God's promises to Israel and His plan of the ages.[5]

So Many Sacrifices!

1 KINGS 8:3–5 *So all the elders of Israel came, and the priests took up the ark. Then they brought up the ark of the LORD, the tabernacle of meeting, and all the holy furnishings that were in the tabernacle. The priests and the Levites brought them up. Also King Solomon, and all the congregation of Israel who were assembled with him, were with him before the ark, sacrificing sheep and oxen that could not be counted or numbered for multitude.* (NKJV)

Why were sacrifices on the event's agenda? To answer that question, it's important to remember the reason for, and the role of, sacrifices in the Old Testament system of law:

- God created people (not puppets, but people with free will) for His pleasure, and placed them in an environment of perfect fellowship with Him in the Garden of Eden.

- The people sinned, contaminating their holiness and making it impossible for them to continue to co-exist in close fellowship with their holy Creator.

- Because God loves people, He continued to desire companionship with them and provided a way to cover their sin so that they could reenter His holy presence. He established a system of sacrifices that would allow the blood of an animal to temporarily cover up a person's sin. History's first sacrifices for sin were the animals God killed in order to fashion <u>clothes</u> for Adam and Eve when their sin made them ashamed of their nakedness.

- So, for devout Israelites, making sacrifices was much more than a laborious and time-consuming ritual; it was the doorway through which God welcomed them into fellowship with Himself.

How understandable, then, that on the occasion of God's moving His presence into a permanent dwelling within their midst, the Israelites brought more sheep and oxen than could be counted! (See also 2 Chronicles 5:2–6:2.)

clothes
Genesis 3:21

Calvary
Luke 23:33

dispensation
period of time

Calvary
site where Christ was crucified on the cross

what others say

Beth Moore

Each Israelite's salvation in this **dispensation** prior to <u>**Calvary**</u> was based on faith in God's acceptance of the type, or picture, of atonement He had revealed to them. In other words, just as we are saved by faith as we look back at Christ's atoning work on Calvary, the Israelites were saved by faith as they looked toward it. They placed their faith in the disclosure of Christ given to them through the atoning sacrifices. They were asked to be faithful in accepting the part of Christ that God had made recognizable to them.[6]

Making sacrifices in order to have fellowship with God was no longer necessary when Jesus died on the cross to pay the penalty for everyone's sin.

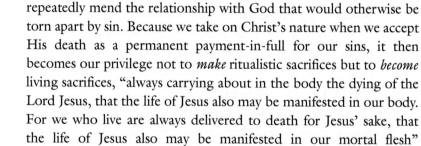

Larry Richards

While the repeated sacrifices of the Old Covenant were annual reminders of the fact that human beings are sinners, the once-and-for-all sacrifice of Jesus is evidence that our sins truly have been forgiven. Because of Jesus there is no longer any sacrifice for sin.[7]

apply it

Because of what Jesus did, sacrifices are no longer required to repeatedly mend the relationship with God that would otherwise be torn apart by sin. Because we take on Christ's nature when we accept His death as a permanent payment-in-full for our sins, it then becomes our privilege not to *make* ritualistic sacrifices but to *become* living sacrifices, "always carrying about in the body the dying of the Lord Jesus, that the life of Jesus also may be manifested in our body. For we who live are always delivered to death for Jesus' sake, that the life of Jesus also may be manifested in our mortal flesh" (2 Corinthians 4:10–11 NKJV). In other words, we respond to Christ's sacrifice by giving up our own lives for His purposes.

what others say

Priscilla Shirer

As Christians we have a responsibility to daily die to the flesh, or let go of those things that distract us from our relationship with the Lord.[8]

According to the Bible, at least two types of sacrifices characterize a Christian's life:

1. *The sacrifice of our bodies.* Romans 12:1 says, "I beseech you therefore, brethren, by the mercies of God, that you present your bodies a living sacrifice, holy, acceptable to God, which is your reasonable service" (NKJV). We can do a million "good" things, such as serve on a church committee, feed the hungry, or read Bible stories to our children. But unless our motives in doing these "good" deeds spring from our willingness to give

our heart, mind, and soul over to obeying and serving God, they're not sacrifices that please Him.

Oswald Chambers

What God wants is the sacrifice through death which enables us to do what Jesus did . . . sacrifice our lives.[9]

2. *The sacrifice of praise.* Hebrews 13:15 says, "Therefore by Him let us continually offer the sacrifice of praise to God, that is, the fruit of our lips, giving thanks to His name" (NKJV). God wants the glory for all that He is and all that He does. We give Him that glory through praise. Praise is the way we vocalize our worship for God; just as important, it's a way we can direct others' attention toward Him.

David Guzik

Because we do have an *altar* (the cross) and we do have a High Priest (Jesus), we should always offer sacrifices. But they are not the bloody sacrifices of the old covenant, but the sacrifice of praise, the fruit of our lips.[10]

Solomon's Temple
This drawing shows none of the opulence of the temple, but does give us the basic shape and proportions of the building itself.

Putting the Throne in the Throne Room

1 KINGS 8:6–8 *Then the priests brought in the ark of the covenant of the LORD to its place, into the inner sanctuary of the temple, to the Most Holy Place, under the wings of the cherubim. For the cherubim spread their two wings over the place of the ark, and the cherubim overshadowed the ark and its poles. The poles extended so that the ends of the poles could be seen from the holy place, in front of the inner sanctuary; but they could not be seen from outside. And they are there to this day. (NKJV)*

The ark of the covenant was the throne of God; the holy of holies was His throne room. Thus the inner sanctuary, splendid though it was, must have seemed strangely empty before the priests—more than 120—reverently carried out the sacred task of placing the ark in the inner sanctuary.

Travels of the Ark

The ark of the covenant had a long history of being on the move:

- The ark was carried around in the wilderness with the Israelites for forty years (Leviticus 16; Numbers 4; 10; 14; Deuteronomy 10).
- Priests carried the ark across the Jordan River into the Promised Land (Joshua 3).
- Priests carried the ark around Jericho (Joshua 6).
- The ark was placed in the tabernacle at Shiloh (Joshua 18:1).
- The ark was taken to Bethel (Judges 20:27).
- The Philistines stole the ark (1 Samuel 4).
- The Philistines returned the ark to Beth Shemesh (1 Samuel 6).
- The ark was taken to the house of Abinadab in Kiriath Jearim for twenty years (1 Samuel 7).
- Saul brought the ark to war camp (1 Samuel 14:18).
- David tried to bring the ark into Jerusalem, but he broke God's Law by allowing it to be moved on a cart, resulting in the death of its mover. David abandoned the mission and left it at the house of Obed-Edom for three months.

- David brought the ark to Jerusalem—the right way this time—and placed it in a tent there.
- David started to bring the ark with him as he fled Jerusalem during Absalom's revolt, but decided to return the ark to the capital city.

The placement of the ark in the temple meant that worship in Israel—which had been divided between two places—would now be centralized. This was according to God's will; He had expressed the desire for the people to worship Him from a central place of worship in Deuteronomy 12:1–14.

temple of the Holy Spirit
1 Corinthians 6:19

key point

what others say

Peter Leithart

Solomon reunites the divided worship of Israel into a single location. . . . The emphasis on the ark and the tablets of the law inside demonstrates the continuity between the order of Solomon and the Mosaic covenant.[11]

The Ark's Only Contents

1 KINGS 8:9 *Nothing was in the ark except the two tablets of stone which Moses put there at Horeb, when the LORD made a covenant with the children of Israel, when they came out of the land of Egypt.* (NKJV)

The ark had previously contained other holy relics, including Aaron's rod and a pot of manna. Now, nothing was in the vessel but the two tablets of stone bearing the Ten Commandments.

what others say

Thomas L. Constable

The sole presence of the Law in the ark reemphasized the importance of the Israelites submitting to the Mosaic Covenant, which these tablets represented. That obedience would be the key to Israel's success (Joshua 1:8).[12]

As mentioned earlier, the temple was a physical illustration of spiritual principles. Not only is each believer a "stone" to be set in the spiritual temple of God; the body of each believer, individually, is the temple of the Holy Spirit. In keeping with that picture, the inner sanctuary of the temple, where the Holy Spirit dwells and where the

something to ponder

Ten Commandments are kept, can be compared to the heart of each believer, where the Holy Spirit lives and where the new law, or new covenant, is kept:

2 Corinthians 3:7–8 *But if the ministry of death, written and engraved on stones, was glorious, so that the children of Israel could not look steadily at the face of Moses because of the glory of his countenance, which glory was passing away, how will the ministry of the Spirit not be more glorious? (NKJV)*

Larry Richards

The Law that God wrote in stone is now being written on the living hearts of believers, each of whom has a personal relationship with the Living God, and each of whom has been forgiven all his or her sins.[13]

Alfred J. Kolatch

The Ten Commandments has become a popular synagogue decorative motif. Sometimes it is made of wood or stone and mounted above the ark or on the outside of the synagogue building. Often times it is embroidered on the ark curtain or Tora mantle.[14]

Paralyzed by God's Glory

1 Kings 8:10–11 *And it came to pass, when the priests came out of the holy place, that the cloud filled the house of the LORD, so that the priests could not continue ministering because of the cloud; for the glory of the LORD filled the house of the LORD. (NKJV)*

A cloud representing God's presence filled the entire temple as God took His place on His throne. The glorious sight stopped the priests in their tracks; they could do nothing but worship God when they found themselves in His overpowering presence. Indeed, without God's presence in His temple, it had been just another building.

God had shown Himself to the Israelites as a cloud in the wilderness (Exodus 14:19–20) and at the dedication of the tabernacle (Exodus 40:34–35). This cloud of God's glory is sometimes called "shekinah" or "shechinah" glory.

what others say

Easton's Bible Dictionary

Shechinah: A Chaldee word meaning resting-place, not found in Scripture, but used by the later Jews to designate the visible symbol of God's presence in the tabernacle, and afterwards in Solomon's temple. When the Lord led Israel out of Egypt, he went before them "in a pillar of a cloud." This was the symbol of his presence with his people.[15]

The Israelites *witnessed* God's glory; today's believers *reveal* it:

what others say

Charles Stanley

When the holy work of God enters the daily preoccupation of our minds and hearts, His glory is revealed like a flower, blooming with each step we take toward Him. His power will not be fulfilled in the church at large, in ministries, in homes, or in businesses until it is fulfilled in each of us as individuals. . . . His glory today is revealed in the lives of ordinary men and women. His glory is revealed now in the transformation that occurs when a broken man brings to the throne shattered fragments of sin and rebellion. When a woman realizes her natural abilities get her nowhere closer to seeing the celebrity of the Lord. When human weariness is exchanged for holy strength, when messy lives are offered to an organized God. The glory of the Lord is unveiled, through His Spirit, to eyes and hearts that expect it in the present as well as in the future.[16]

What Solomon Said

It is difficult to imagine a quieter hush than the one that must have fallen over the entire congregation of Israelites as the radiance of God's glory filled the temple. Out of the reverent silence, however, came a voice anointed with the timbre of God's authority as Solomon spoke, first in a speech to the people, then in a prayer to the Lord.

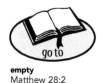

empty
Matthew 28:2

Solomon's Speech

the big picture

1 Kings 8:12–21; 2 Chronicles 6:3–11

Solomon briefly recapped the history of the temple project. By now, it's familiar territory to those who have studied the lives of David and Solomon: The king stated that his father, David, had wanted to build a temple for the Lord, adding that God had said "no" to David but had commissioned himself with the task instead. The king pointed out that God had done exactly as He had promised.

"Just as He Said"

When God kept His word to Solomon and the people of Israel, it wasn't the first time He had done what He said He would—and it wouldn't be the last. Centuries after Solomon died, two women named Mary arrived to find the tomb of Jesus, who had died a criminal's death on a cross between two thieves, empty.

It's an understatement to say they realized that a miracle had occurred. Their minds must have been reeling as they took in the strange sights: the massive boulder blocking the cave's entrance had been pushed aside; there was no form of the body of their beloved lying inside the shadows of the cave; and a beautiful stranger was positioned at the grave's entrance. But their confusion gave way to clarity as the words of the heavenly messenger began to sink in: "He is not here, for He is risen" (Matthew 28:6 NKJV). Then, they heard perhaps the most important words in the angel's message: *as He said* (v. 6 NKJV, italics added). If Jesus had said He would arise from death, and then did it, certainly everything else He had ever promised would come to pass as well!

God's record of keeping His word to people began in the Garden of Eden and won't conclude until every detail of every last promise and every last prophecy He has made is fulfilled. God, who is Truth itself, simply isn't able to fail to keep His word. Seeing the things that God has done in our lives in the light of how they fulfill His promises to us strengthens our faith. When we realize how faithful and sure He has been to follow through on His word before, we are more certain to count on His following through again. Reviewing God's promises fulfilled is a healthy habit for growing believers.

Solomon's Posture of Prayer

Eucharist
rite of Communion

1 KINGS 8:22 *Then Solomon stood before the altar of the LORD in the presence of all the assembly of Israel, and spread out his hands toward heaven.* (NKJV)

The Bible mentions plenty of positions for people to assume when praying:

- Standing (Genesis 24:12–14; Luke 9:28–32)
- Lifting hands (1 Timothy 2:8)
- Sitting (Judges 20:26; look up David's sitting prayer)
- Looking upward (John 17:1)
- Bowing down (Exodus 34:8)
- Kneeling (Mark 1:40; Matthew 18:26; Luke 22:41–44)
- Placing the head between the knees (1 Kings 18:42)
- Pounding on the breast (Luke 18:13)
- Facing the temple (Daniel 6:10)
- Lying down (Matthew 26:38–39)

Notice the posture Solomon took when he prayed to God in this instance: He stood on a bronze platform he had built for the occasion so that everyone could see him, and raised his hands toward heaven (2 Chronicles 6:12–13).

what others say

Kenneth W. Collins

By praying this way, the worshiper acknowledges God as external and transcendant. This posture is for thanksgiving, praises, blessings, benedictions and general prayers. This is still the normal position for prayers in eastern churches and in Jewish synagogues, and it is still used in the western church, particularly when the clergy bless the bread and wine of the **Eucharist**.[17]

Don Walton

Perhaps, the greatest truth we can glean from Solomon's prayer is found in the solid ground he kneeled upon. Solomon based his prayer on God's promises (1 Kings 8:22–30, 56). All who base their prayers on God's promises may be assured of divine attention to their petitions.[18]

pray continually
1 Thessalonians 5:17

model prayer
Matthew 6:8–13

Although the writer of 1 Kings doesn't mention it, 2 Chronicles 6:13 states that the king then dropped to a kneeling position, which is a typical posture for those asking a king for favor.

The "Right" Way to Pray

God instructs us to pray continually, and Jesus gave His followers a model prayer to use as a guideline when praying. But the Bible doesn't suggest a "right" way to pray, physically speaking. The only conditions for praying in the "right" way have to do with the position of one's heart.

what others say

John MacArthur

Rather than external positioning, the Bible emphasizes the posture of the heart. Whether you are standing, sitting, or lying down, the important thing is that your heart is bowed in submission to the lordship of Christ. False religion places a premium on external behavior, while true Christianity is concerned with the heart. And true prayer is characterized by an attitude of humility before God—not the physical posture of the person praying.[19]

When we're talking with others, we can often sense their sincerity or attitude by observing their body language. So it makes sense that our body language during prayer is an indicator of what's inside our hearts.

When you're talking with God, what might your body language of prayer be revealing about your attitude? Are you demonstrating adoration? Humility? Reverence? Helplessness? Gratitude? Or what about indifference? Pride? Impatience? Stubbornness? Since God already knows what's in your heart anyway, the answer to that question is much more helpful to you than to Him. Consider adjusting your prayer posture so it aligns with the position of your heart . . . or, possibly better yet, consider ways that you might adjust the attitudes of your heart so they match up with the posture you assume in prayer.

Solomon's Prayer

With body language that said he was requesting the favor of an all-powerful king, Solomon spoke to the Lord. In his lengthy prayer, Solomon:

- Asked God for *continued fulfillment* of His promises (1 Kings 8:23–26).

- Acknowledged *the inadequacy of the temple* in light of God's greatness (1 Kings 8:27).

- Asked that the temple be identified as *a house of prayer* (1 Kings 8:28–52).

- Requested God's continued attention, acknowledging Israel's unique relationship with the Lord as *a separate nation* (1 Kings 8:53).

Continued Fulfillment

1 KINGS 8:23–26 *And he said: "LORD God of Israel, there is no God in heaven above or on earth below like You, who keep Your covenant and mercy with Your servants who walk before You with all their hearts. You have kept what You promised Your servant David my father; You have both spoken with Your mouth and fulfilled it with Your hand, as it is this day. Therefore, LORD God of Israel, now keep what You promised Your servant David my father, saying, 'You shall not fail to have a man sit before Me on the throne of Israel, only if your sons take heed to their way, that they walk before Me as you have walked before Me.' And now I pray, O God of Israel, let Your word come true, which You have spoken to Your servant David my father." (NKJV)*

The temple hadn't simply materialized on Mount Moriah as had the manna God had sent the Israelites. Like any building project during any century, it was the result of countless hours of preparation and labor. Perhaps no one in Israel knew better than Solomon the full story of its construction: the logistical snags encountered in getting materials shipped in; the engineering challenges that required emergency meetings and tiring brainstorming sessions; the inevitable mistakes that called for troubleshooting and repair; the constant monitoring and supervising of laborers; maintaining the flow of funds; adjusting for schedule setbacks and waiting out weather delays.

key point

"This just isn't going to turn out right," may have popped into the king's thoughts more than once during his eighty-plus months as the project's general contractor.

The Bible doesn't specify what was going on in Solomon's mind and heart during the process, but what Scripture reveals of the king's character and behavior suggests that he stayed focused, worked hard, conducted business with integrity, and kept the prayers flowing. So it's hard not to think of the tremendous personal significance—professionally, emotionally, and most of all spiritually—of his prayer, even though he was presenting it to the Lord on a public platform. His heart was overflowing with praise and gratitude; this was a day of promises kept, of prayers answered, of goals met, of desires fulfilled, and of dreams realized.

The Inadequacy of the Temple

1 KINGS 8:27 *But will God indeed dwell on the earth? Behold, heaven and the heaven of heavens cannot contain You. How much less this temple which I have built!* (NKJV)

The nations surrounding Israel boasted elaborate temples for their gods of wood and stone; now Israel had erected a temple of its own, one that in splendor and beauty rivaled or surpassed that of all others. But Solomon knew that what distinguished the temple of the Lord from all the others wasn't the walls lined with aromatic cedar from Lebanon, the gold-plated surfaces, or the intricate carvings executed by master craftsmen. The difference was in the Deity his nation served. The true God was in all things and above all things. No building could box that in!

what others say

Baker Encyclopedia of the Bible

The temple employed the most sophisticated building techniques of the age, and no expense had been spared in construction, ornamentation, or equipment. Yet Solomon readily confessed its utter inadequacy to house the eternal God.[20]

Randall Price

The theological statement in Solomon's dedication prayer . . . meant that God himself could not be localized on earth. The temple rather stood as the visible station of His invisible, though manifest, presence.[21]

A House of Prayer

1 KINGS 8:28–30 Yet regard the prayer of Your servant and his supplication, O LORD my God, and listen to the cry and the prayer which Your servant is praying before You today: that Your eyes may be open toward this temple night and day, toward the place of which You said, "My name shall be there," that You may hear the prayer which Your servant makes toward this place. And may You hear the supplication of Your servant and of Your people Israel, when they pray toward this place. Hear in heaven Your dwelling place; and when You hear, forgive. (NKJV)

Imagine getting a personal meeting with the president of the United States. Or a Nobel Prize winner. Or a world-famous scientist. As you take a seat in the room with that person, you begin to express your admiration for him or her, and the questions you've longed to ask begin to tumble out. Then you make a terribly disheartening discovery: this person can't hear you or simply refuses to listen. You're in the person's presence, but communication isn't possible.

apply it

That's how the temple would be if God closed His ears to the prayers of the people: They would be in His presence but without the benefit of any communication with Him. Solomon prayed that this would never happen. He asked God to keep His eyes and ears trained on the temple 24/7 so that He would always hear the prayers of the people.

Incidentally, Jesus referred to the temple as a "house of prayer" when He became angry with the people who were buying and selling goods there: "Is it not written, 'My house shall be called a house of prayer for all nations'? But you have made it a 'den of thieves'" (Mark 11:17 NKJV).

something to ponder

key point

After asking God to designate the temple as a house of prayer, Solomon described seven different situations that he expected the people to be praying about. These were primarily based on assorted calamities described in Leviticus 26 and Deuteronomy 28–30, which God had said would befall Israel if the people didn't obey Him. Notice that these verses don't say "*if* Your people sin" but "*when* Your people sin." It's a given that everyone sins, and it's good to have a plan of action in place—prayer and repentance—for when that happens.

Seven Scenarios

Subject	Verses	Context	Request
1. Justice	1 Kings 8:31–32	The temple served as the place where justice was administered.	Solomon asked that, in cases with no human witnesses, God would intervene to administer true justice.
2. Defeat	1 Kings 8:32–34	God repeatedly promises victory to the righteous and defeat to the disobedient (Leviticus 26:17; Deuteronomy 28:25).	Forgiveness for the disobedient person who repented and turned to God in prayer.
3. Drought	1 Kings 8:35–36	Israel, an agricultural nation, relied on rain for its livelihood. At times, droughts were sent by God as a consequence for the Isrealites' disobedience—especially for their tendency to worship Baal, the god of the storm, as their Canaanite neighbors did (Deuteronomy 28:23–24).	Forgiveness of the sin of disobedience and restoration of the rain.
4. Famine, plagues, and enemy invasions	1 Kings 8:37–40	These various calamities were all used by God to censure the Israelites' sins.	Forgiveness of those who repented based on the condition of each person's heart.
5. Foreigners (Gentiles)	1 Kings 8:41–43	Those outside the borders of Israel couldn't be assured that God heard them.	That the Gentiles might be drawn to God as they saw Him working through His people, Israel.
6. Soldiers in battle on foreign soil	1 Kings 8:44–45	They would not have access to God through the temple.	That God would hear and answer their prayers—even when offered from those distant lands.
7. Captivity	1 Kings 8:46–52	God had allowed His disobedient children to be taken into captivity by the enemy.	Restoration for those who asked for forgiveness.

A Separate Nation

1 KINGS 8:53 *For You separated them from among all the peoples of the earth to be Your inheritance, as You spoke by Your servant Moses, when You brought our fathers out of Egypt, O Lord GOD. (NKJV)*

Solomon acknowledged that Israel was set apart by God. Just as Israel has been set apart by God to be different from all other nations and to be used by Him to draw other nations to Him, Christians have been set apart by God to be different from people of all other faiths and to be used by Him to draw others to Him.

something to ponder

what others say

Arnold G. Fruchtenbaum

Israel is truly God's timepiece of history and prophecy. God's overall prophetic program, be it for Israel, the Church, or the Gentile nations, works its way out directly or indirectly through the Jewish people. . . . The true determination as to where we are in history is based upon how world events affect Jewish history and the Jewish people.[22]

Heaven's Fireworks

If anyone present that day might have been wondering whether Solomon's prayer had been heard, God's dramatic response surely put all doubts to rest with a fireworks display that blinded the priests with its light. The writer of Chronicles includes the details the writer of Kings left out about how the Lord ignited the sacrifices the people had brought with His own flame:

2 CHRONICLES 7:1–3 *When Solomon had finished praying, fire came down from heaven and consumed the burnt offering and the sacrifices; and the glory of the LORD filled the temple. And the priests could not enter the house of the LORD, because the glory of the LORD had filled the LORD's house. When all the children of Israel saw how the fire came down, and the glory of the LORD on the temple, they bowed their faces to the ground on the pavement, and worshiped and praised the LORD, saying: "For He is good, for His mercy endures forever." (NKJV)*

John Wesley

The surest evidence of God's acceptance of our prayers is the descent of his holy fire upon us. As a farther token that God accepted *Solomon's* prayer, the glory of the Lord filled the house; the heart that is filled with an holy awe and reverence of the divine glory, to which God manifests his greatness, and (which is no less his glory) his goodness, is thereby owned as a living temple.[23]

Let the Feasting Begin!

I Kings 8:54–66; 2 Chronicles 7:4–11

When Solomon finished praying, he rose to his feet and spoke words of blessing to the people in the gathering. At the conclusion of the benediction, the trumpet sounded, the congregation stood, and the priests sprang into service as the sacrificing and feasting began. The event lasted for days, with Solomon extending the customary feast from seven to fourteen days to allow the people additional time to make thousands of sacrifices and enjoy the food and fellowship. Finally, the people went to their homes, blessed by the king and joyful at what the Lord had done for them.

This was, needless to say, a landmark event in the nation; everyone there knew that fact well. The nation was in the Promised Land and God was on His throne in the midst of His holy temple. The Lord's promises to Israel were truly coming to pass.

Chapter Wrap-Up

- Solomon gathered the Israelites from all over the nation to celebrate the installation of the ark of the covenant in the temple, at a dedication ceremony scheduled during the Feast of Tabernacles.

- When the ark, which now contained only the two tablets of stone on which were engraved the Ten Commandments, was placed in the holy of holies, the glory of God's presence filled the entire temple. Even the priests were paralyzed by His presence.

- After recapping the history of the temple project and pointing out God's faithfulness, Solomon offered a magnificent prayer asking God for continued fulfillment of His promises; acknowledging the inadequacy of the temple; asking that the temple come to be known as a house of prayer for all people; and requesting God's continued favor on Israel as a separate nation.

- God acknowledged the prayer with fire from heaven, which ignited and consumed the sacrifices the people had brought.

- At the conclusion of the feasting and ceremonies, Solomon sent the people to their homes, full of joy because they had been blessed by their king and their God.

Study Questions

1. Would the temple, in the most literal sense, be a place where God lived?

2. With what national celebration did Solomon plan the temple dedication ceremony to coincide with?

3. Why was the temple special not only to Solomon, but to the Israelites as well?

4. What do Christians do today that compares with the sacrifices of the ancient Israelites?

5. What was possibly the most significant petition Solomon made of the Lord concerning the temple?

6. What spiritual truth about human behavior did Solomon clearly understand, according to the nature of his petitions to God?

7. How did Solomon and the people present know that God had heard Solomon's prayer?

Part Four
Peace, Prosperity, and
Public Relations

1 Kings 9:1-9; 2 Chronicles 7:12-22: Hazardous Conditions Ahead

Chapter Highlights:
• God's Good Timing
• God's Answer
• WWDD: What Would David Do?
• The Burden of Being Responsible

Let's Get Started

Much has happened in Solomon's life since the night so many years ago when God had appeared to the king in a dream:

- Solomon had asked God for wisdom and had received it in a big way!

- Solomon had proved that God answered his prayer by demonstrating that wisdom, both in the nation's hall of justice and in its executive offices.

- And, Solomon had prepared for and built the temple, his palace, and all the other buildings in the temple complex.

Then God appeared to Solomon once again. The Lord's message was one of confirmation as well as of caution. God reminded the king of His presence and repeated His promises. But because He could also see the danger ahead for the king and the nation, He spoke words that were like flashing yellow warning lights: God urged Solomon to proceed with care. God said the king's future—and the future of the nation—depended on it.

Like so much of Solomon's story, the account is reported in both 1 Kings and 2 Chronicles. This chapter will explore portions of both passages.

God's Good Timing

God's second appearance to Solomon was clearly a direct answer to Solomon's prayer at the dedication of the temple, as will be discussed in just a bit. There is some debate among Bible scholars, however, as to the timing of His visit. Some insist that God visited the king the very night after he prayed. Others believe the Lord did not visit the king until after the temple, palace, and other building projects were completed. That seems to be the most likely conclusion, especially considering the way the passages in 1 Kings 9:1–2 and 2 Chronicles 7:12 are worded.

think to ask
Ephesians 3:20

1 KINGS 9:1–2 *And it came to pass, when Solomon had finished building the house of the LORD and the king's house, and all Solomon's desire which he wanted to do, that the LORD appeared to Solomon the second time, as He had appeared to him at Gibeon. (NKJV)*

Solomon was a happy camper. He was happy because he had "finished the house of the LORD and the king's house; and Solomon successfully accomplished all that came into his heart to make in the house of the LORD and in his own house" (2 Chronicles 7:11 NKJV).

The king had embraced his father's greatest desire, to build a house for the Lord, as his own magnificent obsession, and had pursued it with passion and persistence to successful completion. In a vivid demonstration that God does more for us than we can even think to ask, Solomon had been given success in other, more personal endeavors as well. In his book of Ecclesiastes, Solomon offered some personal reflections on that period in his life: "I made my works great, I built myself houses, and planted myself vineyards. I made myself gardens and orchards, and I planted all kinds of fruit trees in them. I made myself water pools from which to water the growing trees of the grove" (Ecclesiastes 2:4–6 NKJV).

According to Ecclesiastes 2:10, this work had made him happy: "For my heart rejoiced in all my labor; and this was my reward from all my labor" (NKJV).

what others say

Mark Matlock

Solomon discovered how good it feels to see your hard work lead to success. He discovered the satisfaction that comes from finishing a project you started—and having that project turn out better than you expected.[1]

Ray Bentley

The temple may have been David's legacy, but it was Solomon's crowning achievement. He knew the Lord was pleased, and his heart was at peace.[2]

Aaahhh . . . Sweet Success

Solomon had done everything he had wanted to do. Who could ask for anything more? But the pinnacle he was perched on placed him in a shaky position. His sense of gratitude might grow cold. He could start taking more credit for the attention-grabbing, eye-catching building projects than he deserved. He might start looking for inappropriate activities to help him fill newfound hours of leisure. One misstep off God's good <u>path</u> could cause him to tumble from the pinnacle of success to the pit of failure. Recall that his father, David, had strolled boldly into sin, not when he was out waging war with his men but when he was at home with nothing but time on his hands. Perhaps those risks and others were precisely why God chose to honor Solomon with a personal visit once again.

something to ponder

what others say

Charles H. Spurgeon

I should think that it might have been and probably was so with Solomon that he was in a condition of special need when the temple was finished. He may have been in peril of pride, if not of depression—in either case it was a remarkable season and its need must have been remarkable, also—"and so the Lord appeared unto Solomon the second time, as He had appeared unto him in Gibeon."[3]

Nowhere to Go but . . . Down?

Many people have compared the period following the completion of a major project to postpartum depression: Once the final deadline push is over and the project is completed, they say they experience intense exhaustion, a general sense of letdown, and creative emptiness. Aimlessness can set in after you've accomplished a significant goal, as though you have absolutely nothing left once you've ridden to an emotional, physical, and spiritual crest and achieved all you were aiming for. Plus, when your calendar is no longer full of the demands and details a major project involved, it can seem like the empty squares—the slower pace and the wide-open schedule—open up room for doubt, depression, and lack of direction.

Solomon might have been vulnerable to these very hazards at this particular season of his life. Hour after hour, day after day, week after

go to

path
Psalms 16:11; 25:4;
Hebrews 12:13

go to

no one can see Him and live
Exodus 33:20

Uzzah
2 Samuel 6:1–8

Uzzah
a son of Abinadab who violated the sanctity of the ark and died

theophanies
physical appearances of God

week, month after month, for as long as he could remember, his eyes had been fixed on the construction projects; his mind had been concentrating on the endless details and decisions to be made; and his body had remained in constant motion. Then had come the joy of seeing the fruit of his labor materialize—the highs could hardly have been any higher this side of heaven during those special days of the temple dedication. How very good, then, was God's timing in making this second personal appearance to the king.

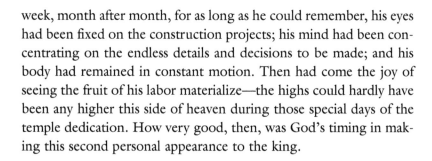

what others say

Dorothy Russell

With the building of a splendid palace and halls for himself and the accumulation of more and more wives, is he forgetting to put God first in his life? With the increase of fame and wealth, is he becoming proud and greedy for more? Is his time so filled with the affairs of this world that even his worship at the temple has become a mere formality? We don't know . . . but God knew. Was this, then, the reason that He appeared to Solomon a second time, standing at the crossroads and pleading with him to take the narrow road that leads to life and true satisfaction?[4]

apply it

Just as He was watching Solomon, ready to step in with guidance at the right moment, God is watching believers today. He's ready to step in with words of comfort and of caution in order to help us stay on track.

God's Appearances

key point

God is so holy and so powerful that <u>no one can see Him and live</u> to tell about it. (Remember when **Uzzah** just touched the ark to try to keep it from falling off the cart? He died from having just a momentary brush with God's holiness, which filled that vessel.) But several times in the Bible, God appeared in a physical form so that He could be seen by people without endangering their lives. These appearances are called **theophanies**. Note that Christ was the ultimate theophany, in that He was the result of God taking on a human form so that He could live among us as Emmanuel, "God with us" (Matthew 1:23 NKJV).

Physical Appearances of God in the Scriptures

preincarnate
appearing in a physical form different from the form He would later take on as Jesus Christ

Reference	Event
Genesis 12:7	The first time God appeared to Abram and promised his descendants the land of Canaan
Genesis 13:14–17	The Lord's second appearance to Abram in the land of Canaan, when He reaffirmed His original promise
Genesis 15	God's third appearance to Abram, when He established His covenant with Abram
Genesis 16:7	The angel of the Lord's visit to Sarah's maidservant, Hagar, announcing the birth of Ishmael
Genesis 17:1	God's fourth appearance to Abram, when He changed Abram's name to Abraham as a sign of the covenant
Genesis 18:1–11	The Lord's fifth visit to Abraham, foretelling Isaac's birth
Genesis 22:11–12	The Lord's sixth appearance to Abraham, to stop him from sacrificing Isaac
Genesis 26:2	The Lord's visit to Isaac, telling him not to go to Egypt
Genesis 32:22–30	The Lord's appearance to Jacob, who wrestled with a "Man"—believed to be the **preincarnate** Jesus Christ or the Angel of God—until he received a blessing
Genesis 35:9	God's visit with Jacob to renew His covenant
Exodus 3:2	God's appearance to Moses in the flames of a burning bush
Exodus 14:19	God's presence with Israel in pillars of cloud and fire
Exodus 33:11	The Lord's intimate conversation with Moses, "as a man speaks to his friend" (NKJV)
Daniel 3:25	The appearance of a figure "like the Son of God" (NKJV) as the fourth man with Shadrach, Meshach, and Abed-Nego in the fiery furnace

God's Answer

1 KINGS 9:3 *And the LORD said to him: "I have heard your prayer and your supplication that you have made before Me; I have consecrated this house which you have built to put My name there forever, and My eyes and My heart will be there perpetually."* (NKJV)

Solomon had prayed an earnest prayer; now God was responding. He said He was "consecrating" the temple, or setting it apart as His own.

apply it

Solomon had built the temple for the Lord, but God would not move in uninvited. The king had asked God to place His presence there, and to set the temple apart as His own. God did just as Solomon asked. Likewise, God will not move uninvited into anyone's heart. But when we ask Him to "move in"—to fill us with His presence—He does just as we ask. He "consecrates" us, or sets us apart, as His own.

Watching and Staying Forever

When God said that His "eyes" and His "heart" would be in the temple "perpetually," meaning forever, He touched on three important topics:

1. *"Eyes"*—Psalm 34:15 tells us that God's eyes "are on the righteous," and His ears are "open to their cry" (NKJV). Like a newborn baby's parent, who keeps an eye and an ear alert to any noise or motion in the cradle, God keeps constant vigil wherever His children are concerned. He wanted Solomon and the people of Israel to know that they could always count on Him, and He wants today's believers to know the same thing. Nothing His followers do escapes His notice. Further, the term "eye" was important to the people of Israel because it alluded to God's judgment.

> **what others say**
>
> **Peter Leithart**
>
> The reference to Yahweh's "eyes" is important. Eyes have to do with judgment (Job 34:21; Psalm 66:7; 94:9; Amos 9:4), and a number of passages of Scripture emphasize the comprehensive vision of the heavenly judge (Proverbs 15:3; 2 Chronicles 16:7–9; Jeremiah 16:16–17; Zechariah 4:10).[5]

2. *"Heart"*—When God stated that His heart would be in the temple, He was assuring the Israelites that, while His eyes were monitoring their actions, His heart would be governing His own. He would deal with them not only out of justice but out of the love and mercy that characterize His heart.

Nelson's NKJV Study Bible

> To the Hebrews, the heart was the seat of the affections, will, and mind. One's emotions and understanding were centered in the heart (Proverbs 15:13, 14).[6]

3. *"Perpetually"*—The gods of the pagan nations surrounding Israel were fickle and temperamental. The idol worshippers and prophets of false gods spent lots of time going through frenzied rituals to try to please and appease their deities. And they never knew from one visit to the next whether their gods would be pleased or angry, or even if their gods would be "present" when they made their appeals. The Lord God, however, could always be counted on to be present. God's constant presence and His availability are among His most striking—and comforting—attributes. "Those who seek me diligently will find me" (Proverbs 8:17 NKJV), He says, "and you will seek Me and find Me, when you search for Me with all your heart" (Jeremiah 29:13 NKJV).

key point

God's Answers to Solomon's Prayers

Solomon Prayed . . .	God Answered . . .
That God would honor His covenant with David by allowing David's descendants to remain on the throne as long as they were obedient to God (1 Kings 8:25–26).	"Yes." God answered that if Solomon would follow in his father David's footsteps of integrity, godliness, and obedience, then He would indeed make sure that one of David's descendants would always remain on the throne of Israel (1 Kings 9:4–5).
That God would keep watch over the temple around the clock, and would hear the prayers the people would present there (1 Kings 8:29).	"Yes." God answered that he had heard Solomon's prayer and assured him that He would be constantly present and constantly watching over the temple and the activity there (1 Kings 9:3).
That God would forgive His people when they cried out to Him and repented after falling into distress because of their sins (1 Kings 8:33–53).	"Yes." God said He would offer forgiveness and restoration if His people were truly repentant (2 Chronicles 7:13).

WWDD: What Would David Do?

1 KINGS 9:4–5 *Now if you walk before Me as your father David walked, in integrity of heart and in uprightness, to do according to all that I have commanded you, and if you keep My statutes and My judgments, then I will establish the throne of your kingdom over Israel forever, as I promised David your father, saying, "You shall not fail to have a man on the throne of Israel." (NKJV)*

God made it no secret that David was the gold standard among kings. For all David's flaws, he was a man whose traits—such as obedience, humility, a teachable heart, adoration of God, and a willingness to repent—exemplified what it meant to be an ideal ruler. David was the yardstick by which all subsequent kings of Israel would be measured, and Solomon was the first in that line. (See also 2 Chronicles 7:17–18.)

apply it

The only descendant of David who would ever surpass his excellence was to come many generations later. That was the One whom God had promised would set up an eternal reign as the King of kings and Lord of lords. In announcing the upcoming birth of this perfect ruler long after Solomon's death, the angel Gabriel told Mary, "He will be great, and will be called the Son of the Highest; and the Lord God will give Him the throne of His father David. And He will reign over the house of Jacob forever, and of His kingdom there will be no end" (Luke 1:32–33 NKJV).

Several years ago, bracelets stamped with the letters "WWJD" became wildly popular, especially among Christian teenagers. The acronym stood for the phrase "What would Jesus do?" and served as a reminder to look to Jesus and His example, rather than to other, more worldly sources for guidance and direction. It was a positive trend in an age when scores of people in society, especially youth, seemed at high risk for misguidance.

The bracelets did help keep many pairs of eyes gazing in the right direction: toward Jesus. But a much more powerful statement about Jesus' influence might be summed up with a slightly different sequence of letters: "WDJD: What Did Jesus Do?" Being a godly person isn't as much about working and striving to copy Jesus' behavior as it is about understanding—and accepting—what He did on the cross. When He died in our place He set us free from the constant pressure of having to do the right thing or act the right way in order to be holy enough to be in God's presence. He set us free from being eternally condemned for our disobedience (even though we still must endure the consequences of our decisions to disobey). When we accept Jesus' payment of His life in exchange for ours, God begins to see us in a completely different way. He sees us through Christ-colored lenses that filter out the splotches of sin in our hearts and present us to the Lord as pure.

God used David the king as an example for all subsequent kings to follow. He also used David as an example for his son Solomon to emulate. When God said "walk as David walked" Solomon certainly heard "walk as the king walked," but he also heard "walk as your *father* walked." David was not a perfect parent and had major problems with some of his sons, but in spite of his personal flaws, he was completely committed to God. He repented when he needed to, and he honored God at every major point in his life.

Still Getting What They Asked For

> 1 KINGS 9:6–9 *But if you or your sons at all turn from following Me, and do not keep My commandments and My statutes which I have set before you, but go and serve other gods and worship them, then I will cut off Israel from the land which I have given them; and this house which I have consecrated for My name I will cast out of My sight. Israel will be a proverb and a byword among all peoples. And as for this house, which is exalted, everyone who passes by it will be astonished and will hiss, and say, "Why has the LORD done thus to this land and to this house?" Then they will answer, "Because they forsook the LORD their God, who brought their fathers out of the land of Egypt, and have embraced other gods, and worshiped them and served them; therefore the LORD has brought all this calamity on them."* (NKJV)

The people of Israel were still receiving what they had asked for years earlier, when they had petitioned God to <u>give them a king</u> like what the other nations had. When God granted the people their request, He made sure they knew what they were getting into. Through His prophet Samuel He said, "If you fear the LORD and serve Him and obey His voice, and do not rebel against the commandment of the LORD, then both you and the king who reigns over you will continue following the LORD your God. However, if you do

give them a king
1 Samuel 8:4–6

not obey the voice of the LORD, but rebel against the commandment of the LORD, then the hand of the LORD will be against you, as it was against your fathers" (1 Samuel 12:14–15 NKJV).

The Burden of Being Responsible

God outlined for Solomon His expectations—and consequences—concerning the behavior of the king and of the nation Israel. (See also 2 Chronicles 7:19–22.) It almost seems like too much responsibility for one man: Why should Solomon have to account for the actions of his people? The answer to that question brings up an essential characteristic of the monarchy: The king acts as God's representative and, as that representative, it's up to him to lead the people down a path of obedience to the Lord.

> **what others say**
>
> **Bob Deffinbaugh**
>
> Both Israel and her king must abide by the commandments God had set down in His law. If they obeyed God's commandments, God would continue to bless them. If not, God would judge His people, as the rest of the world looked on and learned. Israel's king would not set aside the law; the law must be observed, both by the king and by the people.[7]
>
> **Irving L. Jenson**
>
> Great as was Solomon's task in overseeing the construction of the temple, his greater responsibility was his spiritual leadership of the people. God said that His dwelling among the children of Israel depended on Solomon's faithfulness. But Solomon, great and wise as he was, failed in his faithfulness to God and the idolatry which he later introduced (1 Kings 1:1–13) caused the whole nation to be unfaithful to God.[8]

apply it

Ancient Hebrew kings aren't the only people with responsibility for the spiritual behavior of others. God's Word urges believers today to encourage one another, comfort one another, hold one another accountable, teach one another, and keep from causing others to stumble.

What God Expected from Solomon

1. "Walk before Me . . . in integrity of heart and in uprightness" (1 Kings 9:4 NKJV). As the divinely appointed leader of God's

chosen people, Solomon was to conduct his personal and public affairs with "integrity of heart" and "uprightness." His levels of both of these qualities or characteristics, however, would largely depend on how obedient he was to God's commands, decrees, and laws.

2. If Solomon remained obedient, he could look forward to a perpetual reign, through his offspring.

3. If he didn't—that is, if he fell into disobedience or participated in idolatry—the consequences would be severe:

- Israel would be "cut off" and its temple rejected by God (1 Kings 9:7 NKJV).
- Israel would become "a proverb and a byword among all peoples" (1 Kings 9:7 NKJV).
- Israel would experience spiritual and physical "calamity" brought on by the Lord Himself (1 Kings 9:9 NKJV).

Just as God spelled out for Solomon what he—and the people of Israel—must do to receive His blessing and what behavior would result in cursing, He does the same for us.

Solomon's Temple Destroyed

God warned Solomon about the future destruction of the temple if his people disobeyed. They eventually did, and just as God had promised, the temple was destroyed.

"If My People . . ."

The narratives in 1 Kings and 2 Chronicles are quite similar. However, the 2 Chronicles passage includes a verse that has been the subject of many a sermon:

> 2 CHRONICLES 7:14 *If My people who are called by My name will humble themselves, and pray and seek My face, and turn from their wicked ways, then I will hear from heaven, and will forgive their sin and heal their land. (NKJV)*

These words present three possible actions of the people, and three predictable responses from God:

Actions of the people:

- Humble themselves
- Pray
- Repent

Responses of God:

- Hear
- Forgive
- Heal (restore)

Although this passage is directed at the Israelites living during the reign of Solomon, it offers rich application for today. To avoid the consequences of disobedience to God, as God instructed us through His words to King Solomon, we must humble ourselves, pray, and repent. When we do, God promises to hear our prayers and offer us healing and restoration.

Chapter Wrap-Up

- In direct response to Solomon's prayer during the temple dedication, God appeared to the king a second time. His timing was perfect; Solomon was still riding the emotional and spiritual "high" that came from completing the temple and installing the ark, and he was probably at risk for a spiritual stumble.

- God told Solomon that He had not only heard Solomon's prayer but was answering it by setting it apart as His own. He said that His "eyes" and "heart" would be there "perpetually," assuring the king of His continual presence.

- The Lord urged Solomon to follow the example of His father, David, who walked with spiritual integrity, in order to receive His blessings. However, the Lord promised severe consequences if the king (or his sons) failed to follow David's example and turned away from God.

- He also told Solomon that He would hear the prayers of the people and forgive them when they cried out to Him in repentance after falling into distress because of their sins.

Study Questions

1. What was the general state of Solomon's mind and emotions at the opening of this chapter?

2. Why was the timing of God's second appearance to Solomon so good?

3. Why has God, at certain times throughout biblical history, appeared to people in physical form?

4. What did God promise Solomon regarding the temple?

5. What example did God urge Solomon to follow?

6. What consequences did God say would occur if Solomon turned from God?

Chapter Highlights:
• A Sour Deal
• Urban Development
• Solomon's Slaves
• A Visit from a Queen
• Greater Than Solomon

1 Kings 9:10-28; 10; 2 Chronicles 8:3-16; 9:1-28: Dealings with a King and a Queen

Let's Get Started

Solomon stood on the massive front porch of his palace and surveyed the land he governed, land that stretched far beyond what his eye could see. He had many reasons to breathe a quiet prayer of gratitude: the people living in this land were at peace with their neighbors; the national storehouses were overflowing with food and supplies; gifts and revenues were pouring into the nation's coffers; and most important of all, God's presence was residing in the holy temple right in the midst of the City of David.

God had paved the way for the temple to be built via a thousand kindnesses, from providing the plans to sending him much-needed help, especially from the Phoenician king named Hiram. Solomon knew it was time to do something to attempt to repay the debt he owed this friend, without whose assistance the building of the temple would have been so much more difficult.

key point

Meanwhile, as Solomon carried on the business of the nation, word of his wisdom and riches spread throughout the land like the wildfires that sometimes raced through the mountain forests. He never knew from one day to the next who would come knocking at the door of the Hall of Justice to seek an audience with him. Sometimes the visitors were diplomats from other lands bringing him tribute; other times they were sages from the eastern nations who came with a gleam in their eyes, trying to stump him with riddles and challenges. And at least once, it was a stunning, dark-skinned queen who came, it seems, simply to satisfy her own curiosity about the Israelite king she had been hearing so much about.

A Sour Deal

1 KINGS 9:10–14 *Now it happened at the end of twenty years, when Solomon had built the two houses, the house of the LORD and the king's house (Hiram the king of Tyre had supplied Solomon with cedar and cypress and gold, as much as he* *desired), that King Solomon then gave Hiram twenty cities in the land of Galilee. Then Hiram went from Tyre to see the cities which Solomon had given him, but they did not please him. So he said, "What kind of cities are these which you have given me, my brother?" And he called them the land of Cabul, as they are to this day. Then Hiram sent the king one hundred and twenty talents of gold. (NKJV)*

key point

Hiram, the king of Tyre, had befriended David, then Solomon, showing tremendous kindness and generosity by supplying materials and skilled workers for the construction of the temple. In return, Solomon had given Hiram grain and oil. However, that hadn't really been an adequate exchange for the Phoenician king's abundant provision. So, in an effort to balance the books, about halfway through Solomon's reign he gave Hiram twenty cities in Galilee, in the western part of the territory of Asher.

Location, Location, Location

Hiram was certainly no fool who would have been flattered with just the idea of receiving all those cities. He was a wealthy and influential king with far-reaching power and extensive real estate holdings of his own. When he took a tour of his new acquisitions, he found the properties less than desirable. They were not prime property, it seems, for the three reasons that today's real estate agents understand so very well: location, location, and location. It was unproductive land near even more unproductive land. When he made this discovery, Hiram didn't mince words; he called the cities "the Land of Cabul."

what others say

Easton's Bible Dictionary

Cabul How little! As nothing . . . Hiram gave the cities this name because he was not pleased with the gift, the name signifying "good for nothing."[1]

Hiram's History with Israel

Here's a summary of Hiram's kindnesses toward David and Solomon:

- He sent cedar trees, carpenters, and masons for the construction of David's palace (2 Samuel 5:11; 1 Chronicles 14:1).

- He had loved David and was eager to renew their treaty of peace and trading with David's son after Solomon was anointed king (1 Kings 5:1).

- He granted Solomon's request for help in building the temple by providing an abundance of skilled men and high-quality materials (1 Kings 5:8–11; 9:11).

- He gave Solomon 120 talents, or about 9,000 pounds, of gold (1 Kings 9:14).

- He sent Solomon skilled Phoenician sailors to help strengthen Israel's international commerce and trading enterprises (1 Kings 9:27; 10:11, 22; 2 Chronicles 8:18; 9:10, 21).

go to

dealing fairly
Proverbs 11:1

Selfish or Unscrupulous?

Solomon was wise beyond understanding. He was wealthy beyond measure. But was he stingy, too? This episode in his life might suggest so. Some Bible commentators refer to the cities as a "gift" from Solomon. If that's the case, this wasn't a very tasteful or thoughtful gift. It would be like one successful clothing designer giving another one a box full of knock-off, discount-label clothes as a birthday present. It would be downright insulting.

Other scholars refer to Solomon's land grant to Hiram as a business transaction. In that event, perhaps the nature of the deal is a clue that the king didn't always walk the walk he talked concerning how to conduct business.

In the book of Proverbs, the king outlined some sound advice about conducting business with integrity. He spoke of dealing fairly with one another, and he encouraged generosity over greed: "There is one who scatters, yet increases more; and there is one who withholds more than is right, but it leads to poverty. The generous soul will be made rich, and he who waters will also be watered himself" (Proverbs 11:24–25 NKJV). In other words, Solomon was saying that the more one gives, the more one receives. And the stingier a person is, the more impoverished he or she becomes as a result.

go to

returned the cities
2 Chronicles 8:2

Steven K. Scott

Solomon promises that those who are generous will never lack for anything—every true need will be provided—and that you will prosper, and that your prosperity will always increase. . . . And those who are not generous? Solomon says they will fall into poverty. Not necessarily financial or material poverty, but poverty of the soul. They are never satisfied with whatever they have and constantly need more. They become emotionally bankrupt.[2]

something to ponder

Although Solomon did not become materially impoverished, his words in the book of Ecclesiastes certainly suggest that in his later years he might have experienced some of the "poverty of the soul" referred to above. Consider Solomon's words in Ecclesiastes 2:23: "For all his days are sorrowful, and his work burdensome; even in the night his heart takes no rest" (NKJV). Those do, in fact, sound like words springing from an unsatisfied soul. Could it be that the stinginess the king showed with Hiram—giving away the worst instead of the best—was an early symptom of the spiritual maladies he wrote about?

"Thanks, but No Thanks"

Apparently the king of Tyre didn't want the useless land draining his resources and dragging down the value of his investment portfolio, so he returned the cities to Solomon, who later rebuilt them for the Israelites to live in. Oddly enough, at the same time Hiram didn't seem to let the questionable gift damage his friendship with Solomon. According to 1 Kings 9:14, Hiram later even sent Solomon 120 talents of gold—the equivalent of about seventy pounds, an extraordinary quantity.

All nations surrounding Israel had been watching with interest the formation and growth of the nation that called itself "God's people"—and they were studying the king of that nation as well. God had made it no secret that He expected Israel to use that attention to draw people of other nations to Him. Unfortunately, it's not difficult to see how Solomon, as the nation's highest officer, missed his opportunity to do just that. It was the leader of the polytheistic, pagan nation rather than the king of Israel who took the ethical high

key point

road in this transaction. What a pity that Solomon missed this chance to return Hiram's over-the-top generosity with equal liberality! And it's not like he couldn't afford to be generous; the Bible says he was <u>richer</u> than any other king in the world! This would have been an ideal opportunity to give the onlooking nations a reflection of God's goodness in action.

God expects those who follow Him today to draw others to Him through their words and actions. One major arena for that is on the job. The people we work with—many of whom may not know about God, or who may not enjoy a thriving relationship with Him—often see us as representing what it means to be a Christian. With that in mind, a few questions are worth asking every day:

- Are the decisions I'm making on the job reflecting God's character?

- Are my words and actions bringing honor—rather than dishonor—to God's name?

- Does my attitude shut out nonbelievers, or does it compel them to find out more about my faith?

richer
1 Kings 10:23

Millo
2 Samuel 5:9;
1 Kings 11:27;
2 Kings 12:21;
2 Chronicles 32:5

Millo
large architectural terraces

Israel's Urban Development

> 1 KINGS 9:15–16 *And this is the reason for the labor force which King Solomon raised: to build the house of the LORD, his own house, the Millo, the wall of Jerusalem, Hazor, Megiddo, and Gezer. (Pharaoh king of Egypt had gone up and taken Gezer and burned it with fire, had killed the Canaanites who dwelt in the city, and had given it as a dowry to his daughter, Solomon's wife.) (NKJV)*

These next passages of Scripture outline in great detail Solomon's urban development projects. He:

- Built the **Millo**, large terraces on the eastern slope of Jerusalem, likely to fill in the valley to make room for construction of more buildings and to further fortify the city.

- Extended the wall around Jerusalem farther north so that it more than doubled the size of the city.

- Rebuilt the cities of Hazor, Megiddo, and Gezer, three key strategic defense centers. Hazor guarded the north; Megiddo the Valley of Jezreel in central Israel; and Gezer—

which Solomon had received as a wedding gift from Pharoah—in the west.

1 KINGS 9:17–19 *And Solomon built Gezer, Lower Beth Horon, Baalath, and Tadmor in the wilderness, in the land of Judah, all the storage cities that Solomon had, cities for his chariots and cities for his cavalry, and whatever Solomon desired to build in Jerusalem, in Lebanon, and in all the land of his dominion. (NKJV)*

Solomon further fortified Israel by rebuilding and strengthening:

- *Lower Beth Horon,* which—along with Upper Beth Horon—controlled access to Judea from the coast.
- *Baalath*—also known as Kiriath Jearim, where the ark had been kept for some time after it was retrieved from the Philistines.
- *Tadmor*—probably the city in the Syrian Desert later known as Palmyra.

In addition, Solomon designated cities to be used for storage of weapons and supplies, as well as cities to be used to house stables for his horses and chariots.

Solomon: King or Pharaoh?

Israel was to be a nation unlike any other, set apart to be used by God to draw all other nations to Him. Yet in some ways, the nation under Solomon's leadership was beginning to develop some resemblance to its neighbors, and one in particular: Egypt. Two similarities stand out in this passage:

1. *Storage cities.* Storage cities were simply cities throughout the nation designated to house surplus food, supplies, and weapons. Nothing was inherently wrong with setting these up; in fact, doing so showed that Solomon was a man who planned ahead. But the term "storage cities" is only mentioned in one other place in the Bible, when centuries earlier, Israel had been living under oppression in Egypt. The Egyptian taskmasters had divided the Israelites into slave gangs who "built for Pharaoh supply cities." So when the Israelites saw supply-laden caravans building up the inventory of food and weapons in

these designated areas, it may have reminded them of the subjugation and sorrow their forefathers had endured at the hand of Egypt in generations past.

2. *Stables.* Consider the following guideline for kings God had set forth for the Israelites before they took possession of the land God had promised them: "But [the king] shall not multiply horses for himself, nor cause the people to return to Egypt to multiply horses, for the LORD has said to you, 'You shall not return that way again'" (Deuteronomy 17:16 NKJV). It wasn't that God had something against horses; He simply expected those who would lead His people to refrain from putting too much trust in military muscle and horsepower. He wanted them to fully <u>rely on Him</u>.

rely on Him
Psalm 20:7

key point

Incidentally, 1 Kings 10:28–29 notes that the stables housed horses that Solomon had imported from Egypt and a place now known as Cilicia in modern-day Turkey. Each chariot cost about fifteen pounds of silver and each horse cost a little more than three pounds of silver. He probably turned a profit by selling them to the Hittites and Aramaeans—another example of his wisdom manifesting itself in the field of business.

what others say

Peter Leithart

Solomon returns Israel to an Egyptian-like state, setting up for the "Mosaic" liberation of the northern tribes under Jeroboam I.[3]

Henry Morris

Interestingly, remains of some of these stables have been found at Megiddo, which was one of the "cities for chariots" (1 Kings 10:25–26). The University of Chicago archaeologists who excavated these stables estimated that one of them could have accommodated as many as five hundred horses.[4]

Solomon's Slaves

1 KINGS 9:20–23 *All the people who were left of the Amorites, Hittites, Perizzites, Hivites, and Jebusites, who were not of the children of Israel—that is, their descendants who were left in the land after them, whom the children of Israel had not been able*

to destroy completely—from these Solomon raised forced labor, as it is to this day. But of the children of Israel Solomon made no forced laborers, because they were men of war and his servants: his officers, his captains, commanders of his chariots, and his cavalry. Others were chiefs of the officials who were over Solomon's work: five hundred and fifty, who ruled over the people who did the work. (NKJV)

Solomon got the work done on his extensive building projects by using slave labor. He assigned the hardest labor to the descendants of the Canaanite tribes Israel had conquered when it took possession of the Promised Land; the lighter work of soldiering and supervising he left for the Israelites.

In 1 Samuel 8:12–17, the prophet Samuel had warned the nation about this very event. He had told Israel that if they got what they were asking for—that is, if God were to give them a king—one consequence they would have to endure would be slavery. Even though Solomon went easier on the Israelites than he did on foreigners in the land, this eventually created resentment among the people and would be one reason the ten northern tribes would cite as an explanation for seceding from the kingdom.

Did the Canaanites Deserve It?

The groups mentioned in verse 20—the Amorites, Hittites, Perizzites, Hivites, and Jebusites—along with the Canaanites and Girgashites, are people God told Israel to completely annihilate when they entered the Promised Land:

DEUTERONOMY 7:1–2 *When the LORD your God brings you into the land which you go to possess, and has cast out many nations before you, the Hittites and the Girgashites and the Amorites and the Canaanites and the Perizzites and the Hivites and the Jebusites, seven nations greater and mightier than you, and when the LORD your God delivers them over to you, you shall conquer them and utterly destroy them. (NKJV)*

Why did God tell Israel to deal so harshly with these people?

"For they will turn your sons away from following Me, to serve other gods; so the anger of the LORD will be aroused against you and destroy you suddenly....For you are a holy people to the LORD your God; the LORD your God has chosen you to be a people for Himself, a special treasure above all the peoples on the face of the earth" (Deuteronomy 7:4–6 NKJV).

God predicted that if the Canaanites pursued peaceful relations with the Israelites they would become <u>Israel's slaves</u>. Even though God is characterized by love, He is concerned with protecting His people—and that means letting His wrath fall on the ungodly. He wanted Israel to exterminate the Canaanites so their pagan practices wouldn't rub off on His people (see Deuteronomy 20:18).

Just as the Israelites were instructed to destroy the Canaanites when they took possession of the Promised Land, God instructs His followers to <u>put to death</u> all traces of sin in our lives.

A House for His Wife

> 1 KINGS 9:24 *But Pharaoh's daughter came up from the City of David to her house which Solomon had built for her. Then he built the Millo. (NKJV)*

This passage simply repeats the information brought out in 1 Kings 3:1 that Solomon's wife, the Pharaoh's daughter, had lived in the City of David until all the building projects were completed.

Spiritual Leader

> 1 KINGS 9:25 *Now three times a year Solomon offered burnt offerings and peace offerings on the altar which he had built for the LORD, and he burned incense with them on the altar that was before the LORD. So he finished the temple. (NKJV)*

Interrupting this lengthy and detailed description of the extent of Solomon's wealth and power is this note regarding his spiritual life. When the temple had been completed, he stopped sacrificing at the high places and began leading the people in worshipping three times a year. Some speculate that these occasions would have been on the three major feasts the people observed:

- <u>The Feast of Unleavened Bread</u> (Passover), celebration in the first month of the year recognizing the nation's escape from Egypt under the leadership of Moses

- The <u>Feast of Harvest</u> (also called Weeks and Shavuot, but known to most non-Jews as Pentecost), a thanksgiving cele-

Israel's slaves
Deuteronomy
20:10–11

put to death
Romans 8:13;
Colossians 3:5–10

Feast of Unleavened Bread
Exodus 12:1–20;
23:15

Feast of Harvest
Exodus 23:16;
Leviticus 23:15–21

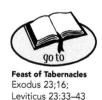

Feet of Tabernacles
Exodus 23;16;
Leviticus 23:33–43

gold
Job 22:24

bration at the end of the grain harvest that occurred seven weeks after Passover.

- The <u>Feast of Tabernacles</u> (or Ingathering), a seven-day celebration in the seventh month—September or October—marking the end of the fruit harvest and recalling the time when the nation had lived in tents in the desert.

Sailor Solomon

1 KINGS 9:26–28 *King Solomon also built a fleet of ships at Ezion Geber, which is near Elath on the shore of the Red Sea, in the land of Edom. Then Hiram sent his servants with the fleet, seamen who knew the sea, to work with the servants of Solomon. And they went to Ophir, and acquired four hundred and twenty talents of gold from there, and brought it to King Solomon.* (NKJV)

The Israelites, by tradition, were landlubbers who made their living off the turf—its fruit, grain, and livestock. Until Solomon, they had never even set up a significant seaport at any point along Israel's Mediterranean coast. But all that changed when Solomon turned his wisdom, wealth, and entrepreneurial spirit seaward. Once again armed with valuable help from Hiram in the form of a team of experienced sailors, Solomon carried out extensive, profitable commerce with Persia, Arabia, and Africa. A jump ahead to 1 Kings 10:22 reveals that the fleet of merchant ships brought in a full load of goods every three years. The exotic cargo aboard these ships included gold, silver, ivory, apes, and monkeys.

The location of Ophir isn't known, but it was considered to be the source of the finest quality <u>gold</u>. The 420 talents would be almost fourteen tons.

Israel's Chief Exports During Solomon's Reign

- Grain
- Olive oil
- Wine
- Cereals
- Fruit
- Honey
- Nuts
- Aromatic gum
- Myrrh
- Wool
- Woven garments

A Visit from a Queen

One of the best-known episodes in the life of King Solomon is his visit from the queen of Sheba. The account adds rich details to the biography of the king in several ways:

go to

wisdom
1 Kings 3:12

wealth and honor
1 Kings 3:13

- It takes readers outside the walls of the City of David to eavesdrop on what people from foreign nations were saying about the king.

- It proves that the reports of his reputation as the wisest and wealthiest man in the world weren't exaggerated. Truly God had given him unsurpassed <u>wisdom</u>, <u>wealth, and honor</u> so that there was not "anyone like [him] among the kings all [his] days" (1 Kings 3:13 NKJV).

- Viewed from a wider angle, what happened between the exotic queen and the son of David illustrates what happens when those who hear about the Lord Jesus Christ—the Son of David—set out to find out more about Him. In that sense, the narrative that centers on the visit of the queen of Sheba doesn't just relate the story of a fact-finding mission of a curious monarch; it reveals a pattern for the lifesaving encounter that can occur between people and God.

something to ponder

Her Inquiring Mind Wanted to Know

> 1 KINGS 10:1–3 *Now when the queen of Sheba heard of the fame of Solomon concerning the name of the LORD, she came to test him with hard questions. She came to Jerusalem with a very great retinue, with camels that bore spices, very much gold, and precious stones; and when she came to Solomon, she spoke with him about all that was in her heart. So Solomon answered all her questions; there was nothing so difficult for the king that he could not explain it to her. (NKJV)*

Solomon's name and reputation had traveled as far and as fast across the globe as his commercial enterprises. People in the lands supplied by every port of trade were hearing the larger-than-life tales of the king of Israel whose wisdom, they said, matched his immense wealth.

J. Vernon McGee

In chapter 10 we have a great illustration of the influence of Solomon in that day.[5]

The stories of Solomon's wit drew many visitors to the king's throne room: "Now all the earth sought the presence of Solomon to hear his wisdom, which God had put in his heart" (1 Kings 10:24 NKJV). Especially intrigued was one person in particular: the queen of Sheba, a bronze-skinned monarch of the land now known as Yemen in southwestern Arabia.

Wealth was not foreign to this woman; her people, the Sabaeans, were known for their trade in fine gold, precious gems, exotic perfumes, and rare spices. Rather, it was the supposed intelligence of this man named Solomon that compelled her to set out on a journey to find out for herself whether the reports from the rumor mill were true. With perhaps nothing more than a quick word to her servants, she set her entourage into action, loading camels and carts with flasks of scented oils, chests of jewels, crates of spices, and extravagant quantities of gold. *She would show this man a thing or two about riches,* she may have been thinking as she watched the valuable gifts being packed for the twelve-hundred-mile journey.

The queen also may have wanted to evaluate the potential economic impact this relatively new player in the global market might have on the existing trading scene. His shipping routes intruded into her territory, and he had the authority to cut off any trading activity she traveled through his land to conduct.

Sue and Larry Richards

Most commentators believe that the queen of Sheba's visit to Solomon was as much intended to establish trade agreements as to satisfy the queen's curiosity about Solomon.[6]

R. K. Harrison

There is every reason to give credence to the historicity of the Biblical narrative concerning the queen of Sheba, for although queens were not prominent in the history of southern Arabia after the sixth century BC, cuneiform inscriptions have been found which indicate that, especially in northern Arabia, tribal confederacies were frequently ruled by queens from the ninth to the seventh centuries BC.[7]

It's too bad that either the court scribes weren't asked to record the conversation between the king and queen, or their transcriptions somehow weren't preserved through the wear and tear of history. That would have been one interesting interview to sit in on!

David Plotz

Sadly, the Bible does not record what Sheba's questions were, only that Solly answered all of them easily. I'm very curious what she asked. Were they savant-type questions like: *What's the cube root of 98,543,306?* Or SAT questions like: *Based on the data supplied, what is the average speed of an ox-cart between Jerusalem and Bethel?* Or Philosophy 101 questions like: *If God is all-knowing, all-powerful, and all-good, why does evil exist?* Or Jeopardy-style questions like: *Category is Patriarchs—He was the king duped by Abraham.* Or trick questions like: *Which is heavier, a pound of feathers or a pound of gold?* What do you think she asked him?[8]

Matthew Henry

Were [the queen's questions] designed to try him? He gave them such turns as abundantly satisfied her of his uncommon knowledge. Were they designed for her own instruction? (as we suppose most of them were), she received abundant instruction from him, and he made things surprisingly easy which she apprehended insuperably difficult.[9]

Whether the queen posed brain-bending riddles, asked weighty philosophical questions, or presented complex mathematical problems, Solomon passed her test with flying colors. All that was left for her to do was to respond.

Thomas
John 20:24–29

"Bring 'Em On"

The queen was likely one of many who set out to find out just how wise Solomon was. Note that nothing in Scripture indicates the king was offended by this testing of his wisdom. Unlike the Wizard of Oz, who hid behind smoke and veils for fear his shortcomings would be exposed, Solomon apparently was happy to throw back the curtains to visitors and welcome their investigation. He probably regarded the opportunity to showcase his great gifts as a chance to introduce others to the God who had indeed bestowed them.

In that sense, Solomon illustrates the attitude of Jesus Christ, who doesn't rebuke those who approach Him with questions or doubts. For example, when His disciple <u>Thomas</u>, like the queen of Sheba, refused to base his beliefs on what he was hearing from others, notice the tenderness in Jesus' response: "Reach your finger here, and look at My hands; and reach your hand here, and put it into My side. Do not be unbelieving, but believing" (John 20:27 NKJV). Jesus wants the chance to prove Himself to us. All we have to do is, like the queen of Sheba, speak with Him "about all that is in [our hearts]" (1 Kings 10:2 NKJV).

Putting God to the Test

Many an account of how a believer came to know God begins not with a powerful sermon or a persuasive friend. It often starts with curiosity, questions, or challenges. Take, for example, Lee Strobel, a journalist who believed that "Jesus was nothing more than the fanciful invention of superstitious people." When his wife became a Christian he noticed dramatic changes—for the better—in her behavior and attitude, and his curiosity got the better of him. Wanting to "get to the bottom of what was prompting these subtle but significant shifts," he "launched an all-out investigation into the facts surrounding the case for Christianity."

His search for answers took him not from Sheba to Jerusalem but from his home in Chicago to the offices of biblical experts across the nation. What he found after a twenty-one-month journey of thorough research and intense probing was conclusive: "All this I now believed," he says in *The Case for Christ*, the book he wrote to report his findings. "The evidence of history and of my own experience was too strong to ignore. . . . So, on November 8, 1981, I talked with God in a heartfelt and unedited prayer, admitting and turning from my wrongdoing, and receiving the gift of forgiveness and eternal life through Jesus."[10]

Notice that the word *came* appears three times in 1 Kings 10:1–2. That happens to be a form of the very word Jesus uses in extending His invitation to all: "Come to Me, all you who labor and are heavy laden, and I will give you rest" (Matthew 11:28 NKJV).

key point

Seeing Is Believing

> 1 KINGS 10:4–7 *And when the queen of Sheba had seen all the wisdom of Solomon, the house that he had built, the food on his table, the seating of his servants, the service of his waiters and their apparel, his cupbearers, and his entryway by which he went up to the house of the LORD, there was no more spirit in her. Then she said to the king: "It was a true report which I heard in my own land about your words and your wisdom. However I did not believe the words until I came and saw with my own eyes; and indeed the half was not told me. Your wisdom and prosperity exceed the fame of which I heard." (NKJV)*

The king's wisdom alone was enough to make the queen of Sheba's bejeweled head spin. But as she listened to the wise words spilling off of Solomon's tongue, it was the "whole package" that really blew her away: The heady fragrance the cedar-lined walls infused into the air throughout each chamber of the palace. The scent of savory meats being roasted by the nation's finest chefs. The quiet and ever-attentive staff of uniformed servants ready to fulfill their master's every need. The ornate carvings above doorways, on table legs, beneath windows. The cool frosting of gold overspreading every surface. And, perhaps most intriguing of all, the devotion and sanctity with which the king entered the magnificent temple to worship his God—the One he referred to as "the one and only God."

Truly, the queen of Sheba had known wise people, wealthy people, and spiritual leaders—but none she had ever met came near to being as wise, as wealthy, or as devoted to his God as this man. Any airs the queen had brought with her on the long desert trip deflated as she saw how lacking was her own wisdom in comparison to his; how diminished was the value of her riches in comparison to his; how empty was the condition of her spiritual life in comparison to his.

H. L. Rossier

All the details of this incomparable reign are of interest to the Queen of Sheba; she rejoices in all, sees all, enumerates all—from the apparel of his servants to the marvelous ramp built by Solomon to connect his palace with the temple.[11]

Greater Than Solomon

Jesus Christ Himself referred to the queen of Sheba in Luke 11:31, drawing a clear comparison between Himself and Solomon: "The queen of the South will rise up in the judgment with the men of this generation and condemn them, for she came from the ends of the earth to hear the wisdom of Solomon; and indeed a greater than Solomon is here" (NKJV).

Charles H. Spurgeon

He tells them that He is greater than Solomon, to convince them of the greatness of their crime in refusing to listen to the messages of love with which His lips were loaded. Foreigners came from afar to Solomon; but I, says He, have come to your door, and brought infinite wisdom into your very gates, and yet you refuse me.[12]

No superlatives are strong enough or vivid enough to adequately describe the scope of God's power, presence, and majesty. Sheba's expression that "indeed the half was not told me" (1 Kings 10:7 NKJV) is the only attempt—albeit a modest one—anyone can make regarding what he or she knows about the Father of all creation, whose riches and wisdom are in fact limitless. In considering the power and majesty of almighty God, Job echoed the queen's sentiment with similar words: "Indeed these are the mere edges of His ways, and how small a whisper we hear of Him! But the thunder of His power who can understand?" (Job 26:14 NKJV).

Jesus Is the Greatest of All

Solomon Was Great	Jesus Is Greater
Solomon was the wisest man who ever lived: His wisdom "surpassed all the kings of the earth" (1 Kings 10:23 NKJV).	Christ is wisdom itself: He is "the wisdom of God" (1 Corinthians 1:24 NKJV) "in whom are hidden all the treasures of wisdom and knowledge" (Colossians 2:3 NKJV; see also Romans 11:33).
Solomon was the wealthiest man around, materially speaking: His riches "surpassed all the kings of the earth" (1 Kings 10:23 NKJV).	Christ is the very source of the "unsearchable riches" (Ephesians 3:8 NKJV) that have eternal value, including: • The riches of goodness, forbearance, and longsuffering (Romans 2:4) • The riches of glory (Romans 9:23; Ephesians 1:18; 3:16; Philippians 4:19) • The riches of grace (Ephesians 1:7; 2:7).
Solomon was a prolific writer: He wrote 3,000 proverbs and 1,005 songs.	Jesus is the Word: "In the beginning was the Word, and the Word was with God, and the Word was God" (John 1:1 NKJV).
Solomon was a good judge for the people of Israel: "And all Israel heard of the judgment which the king had rendered; and they feared the king, for they saw that the wisdom of God was in him to administer justice" (1 Kings 3:28 NKJV).	Jesus Christ is the righteous and holy Judge of all: "My judgment is righteous, because I do not seek My own will but the will of the Father who sent Me" (John 5:30 NKJV). "For we shall all stand before the judgment seat of Christ" (Romans 14:10 NKJV).
Solomon's name meant "peace."	Jesus Christ is the Prince of Peace.
Solomon built a magnificent temple for the presence of God.	Jesus Christ is building the spiritual temple, the house of God.

what others say

H. L. Rossier

We feel our nothingness before this glorious presence; we bow in the dust before such righteousness, wisdom and goodness. But here is what is said to us: "Happy," says the queen, "are these thy servants, who . . . hear thy wisdom." It is not the voice of great waters and loud thunder, but a voice more gentle than the myrrh-scented breeze; a voice that goes through us; the voice of the Beloved, of Jedidiah, the voice of love! All these sentiments come from seeking His face and being admitted to His presence. And as happened with the queen of Sheba, there will be no more spirit in us. There is wonder and worship in the presence of such wisdom, holiness, righteousness, and glory; a very humble love, for it immediately senses that it is not to be compared with this love; the whole heart is ecstatic and longs only to lose itself in the contemplation of its cherished object.[13]

So, confronted with the dazzling truth about Solomon, the queen dropped her guarded language of diplomacy to voice her response to the king. The unadorned, impassioned words issued straight from her heart:

1 KINGS 10:8–9 *Happy are your men and happy are these your servants, who stand continually before you and hear your wisdom! Blessed be the LORD your God, who delighted in you, setting you on the throne of Israel! Because the LORD has loved Israel forever, therefore He made you king, to do justice and righteousness.* (NKJV)

Whether the queen's words indicate that she came to know God through the words and actions of Solomon isn't clear. She may have simply been making polite—albeit passionate—acknowledgment of the God of Israel and His work in the nation through Solomon without claiming Him as her own. But it's also possible that her meeting with Solomon gave her a spiritual wake-up call to follow and serve the one true God. One thing, however, is clear: In recognizing Solomon for who he was, the queen knew exactly where she should direct her adoration: the Lord God.

apply it

Those who enjoy a personal relationship with God today can hope for no less: To be able to direct the attention of others toward God through our actions and words.

Don't miss the impact of the queen's exclamation: "Happy are your men and happy are these your servants, who stand continually before you and hear your wisdom!" (1 Kings 10:8 NKJV). In other words, this woman who slept on the finest linens, wore the finest scents, and ate the finest foods was saying that she would count it an honor to be a servant, if being a servant meant having the opportunity to be in the king's presence.

Going-Away Gifts

the big picture

1 Kings 10:10-13

The queen followed up her words with actions: She gave the king the many gifts she had brought, including an abundance of gold, spices, and jewels. The king, in return, lavished her with gifts before she and her entourage returned to their homeland.

F. B. Hole

If we read 1 Kings 10 we may see how Solomon gave to the Queen of Sheba all she desired, and then capped it by that which he gave her "of his royal bounty." He satisfied her large desires and then went beyond them in the superlative greatness of his kingly munificence. In this he acts as a type. God has acted according to His exceeding riches of grace. The very forgiveness of sins which He has accorded us has been granted in a style and with a fullness worthy of the great and gracious God He is.[14]

Sue and Larry Richards

The Jewish rabbis understood the phrase, "Now King Solomon gave the queen of Sheba all she desired, whatever she asked" (1 Kings 10:13), to indicate that she had a son fathered by Solomon. It is much more likely that the phrase simply reflects that the visit was successful, and the desired treaties were executed.[15]

Solomon's Midas Touch

The queen of Sheba may have visited the king to find out more about the scope of his wisdom, but her journey there inevitably showed her a thing or two about the extent of his riches as well.

1 KINGS 10:14–15, 25, 27 *The weight of gold that came to Solomon yearly was six hundred and sixty-six talents of gold, besides that from the traveling merchants, from the income of traders, from all the kings of Arabia, and from the governors of the country....Each man brought his present: articles of silver and gold, garments, armor, spices, horses, and mules, at a set rate year by year....The king made silver as common in Jerusalem as stones, and he made cedar trees as abundant as the sycamores which are in the lowland.* (NKJV)

In other words, riches were literally pouring into the king's coffers at every turn. Visitors were bringing him expensive gifts; taxes were rolling into the government's accounts at the rate of fifty thousand pounds of gold a year; and traders were bringing in all kinds of exotic goods—including zoo animals!

Chapter Wrap-Up

- Solomon attempted to repay a debt of men, materials, and kindness to Hiram, king of Tyre, with a gift of twenty cities. Upon inspecting the properties, Hiram was disappointed; they were worthless. Whether Solomon's move was borne out of greed or out of bad business sense isn't clear; Hiram, however, didn't seem to let the bad deal disrupt the good relationship between the two parties.

- Solomon continued to expand and fortify Israel, making the nation stronger and wealthier than ever. He also designated cities to store supplies and to house his extensive stables of horses—actions that strongly resembled the behavior of an Egyptian pharaoh.

- Solomon maintained spiritual faithfulness by leading the people in worship three times a year, probably during the three major feasts: the Feast of Unleavened Bread, the Feast of Weeks, and the Feast of Tabernacles.

- With Hiram's help, Solomon expanded his nation's commerce seaward, enabling him to carry out extensive and profitable international trading.

- The queen of Sheba paid Solomon a visit to satisfy her curiosity about whether his wisdom and wealth were exaggerations or fact. When she discovered that Solomon was in fact all that everyone reported—and then some—she was overwhelmed with awe and respect, and gave his God credit for Solomon's amazing gifts.

Study Questions

1. Why did Solomon give Hiram twenty cities?

2. Why did Hiram find the properties unacceptable?

3. What were some of the ways Solomon developed and fortified Israel?

4. How did Solomon venture into new territory, commercially speaking?

5. Why did the queen of Sheba decide to visit King Solomon?

6. What kind of an impression did Solomon make upon the queen?

7. How does the queen of Sheba represent a person who is interested in getting to know more about Jesus Christ?

Part Five
Solomon's Downfall

Chapter Highlights:
• "But"—It's a Big
  Little Word
• 999 Too Many
• From Bad to Worse
• Peace and Politics

1 Kings 11:1–8:
The Godly King Does Ungodly Things

Let's Get Started

Reports of King Solomon's wisdom and wealth were not exaggerated. The queen of Sheba had discovered as much during her visit when she witnessed firsthand the staggering evidence of God's great favor upon the king. But neither the queen nor anyone else could have possibly known what was going on inside the hidden places of Solomon's heart. If she had been able to peer into the king's innermost being, she would have seen traces of disobedience lodging there.

Solomon's failure to obey God's clear commands would soon fester into a full-blown spiritual disease, one requiring the king's biographers, at the beginning of 1 Kings 11, to transform his "brag sheet" into a "scandal sheet" with one tiny introductory word: *But.*

"But"—It's a Big Little Word

1 KINGS 11:1 *But King Solomon loved many foreign women, as well as the daughter of Pharaoh: women of the Moabites, Ammonites, Edomites, Sidonians, and Hittites. (NKJV)*

Solomon had been given many blessings and few restrictions. Wisdom and wealth, power and prestige, a place in history, and a legacy for his descendants . . . these and so much more were all his, God had promised, as long as the king would devote himself to doing things God's way.

And until this time in his life, Solomon—not completely, but for the most part—had done just that. Solomon's outward behavior routinely displayed an inner devotion to the Lord. That's why he scored high marks, at least in the early years of his reign. For example:

- He firmly established, expanded, and fortified the kingdom (1 Kings 2:46; 4:20–21; 1 Kings 9:15–23).

- He followed his father David's example (1 Kings 3:3).

- His prayer and request for wisdom pleased the Lord (1 Kings 3:10; 2 Chronicles 1:7–10).

- His request for wisdom was granted by God (1 Kings 3:11–13; 2 Chronicles 1:11–12).

- He was faithful in worshipping God (1 Kings 3:4, 15; 2 Chronicles 1:3–5; 8:12–13).

- He made wise judgments (1 Kings 3:16–28).

- He demonstrated wisdom in organizing his administration (1 Kings 4:1–19).

- His nation was prosperous, expansive, and secure (1 Kings 4:20–25).

- His personal wealth was immense and renowned (1 Kings 4:26; 10:4–7, 10–12, 14–23, 25–28; 2 Chronicles 1:12, 15–17; 9:9–11, 13–22).

- His wisdom was unsurpassed (1 Kings 4:29–34; 10:1–9, 24; 2 Chronicles 1:12; 9:5–7, 23).

- He was faithful and diligent in supervising the construction of the temple and other buildings (1 Kings 5–7; 2 Chronicles 2–3; 8:16).

- His words of prayer and dedication ushered Israel into a new era of its history (1 Kings 8; 2 Chronicles 5; 6; 7).

key point

However, the small word *but* at the beginning of chapter 11 marks a significant change in the direction of Solomon's biography. Like Eve, who had the entire Garden of Eden to enjoy but wouldn't be happy until she had the fruit of the one tree God had posted as off-limits, Solomon decided his way was better than God's way. Somewhere along the way, the king decided to ignore God's directions.

Boadt and West

In chapter 11 a different mood prevails. This chapter shows us another side of Solomon.[2]

Pharaoh's daughter
1 Kings 3:1

The pattern of disobedience had begun almost imperceptibly when the king had taken <u>Pharaoh's daughter</u> as a wife. In a move that most observers would describe, in light of the culture of the day, as a routine political play, Solomon made a very unwise move by marrying a woman from a nation that worshipped foreign gods. That first small step Solomon took across the line between "what to do" and "what not to do" had become a reckless stride into forbidden territory. Now, he was married not only to "one" such woman; he was married to "many."

Dave Breese

Satan moves in the lives of people from a lesser degree to the greater. He begins his assault by establishing a small beach-head and moves from this point of moral fault into a program of larger conquest. He ultimately intends to consume us, but this devouring begins with the smallest nibble.[3]

<u>Not News to Solomon</u>

1 KINGS 11:2 *From the nations of whom the LORD had said to the children of Israel, "You shall not intermarry with them, nor they with you. Surely they will turn away your hearts after their gods." Solomon clung to these in love.* (NKJV)

There was no way Solomon could have pleaded ignorance on this point of law. The instruction that Israelites were not to marry women who worshipped foreign gods had been issued loudly and clearly:

DEUTERONOMY 7:3 *Nor shall you make marriages with them. You shall not give your daughter to their son, nor take their daughter for your son.* (NKJV)

God's ways
Isaiah 55:8–9

worship no other god
Exodus 20:3

A Divided Heart

Perhaps when Solomon had asked the Lord for a discerning heart he should have also asked for a devoted one as well! <u>God's ways</u> aren't always easy to understand. Sometimes His guidelines and actions cause people to ask why He does certain things, or wonder what He could possibly be up to. The truth is, because He's God—the Creator—He doesn't owe anyone any explanations. He isn't obligated to give reasons for His behavior or account for His decisions.

But in some cases, God does in fact make His motives known. This was one of those occasions. He had good reason to forbid His people from marrying foreigners, and He had shared that reason: "For they will turn your sons away from following Me, to serve other gods" (Deuteronomy 7:4 NKJV). God instructs His followers to <u>worship no other god</u> but Him—it's the first of the Ten Commandments! He knows how difficult it is for His followers to remain faithful to Him if they are eternally and intimately connected to a person of another faith in a marriage relationship.

what others say

Greg Laurie

It's an old, old story, and one I've heard many times about relationships. To keep peace in the home, it is usually the believer who makes compromises to appease the nonbeliever. And this is precisely why God tells us "to not be unequally yoked" (2 Corinthians 6:14).[4]

Henry Morris

Mixed marriages (that is, believers with non-believers) have become all too common even among well-instructed Christians today.[5]

Ron Mehl

Our number-one task as believers is to make sure that nothing—no "god," person, object, task, duty, or pleasure—comes before Him in our priorities, in our plans, and in our affection.[6]

The Baggage They Brought into the Marriage

An earlier chapter of this book discussed the implications of Solomon's marriage to the Egyptian pharaoh's daughter. The baggage she brought into the marriage included a background of idolatry, pride, and superstition. Consider what unsavory issues the king's additional wives—the Moabites; the Ammonites, the Edomites, the Sidonians, and the Hittites—brought along when they moved in with the king. Each woman's ancestors had recorded a history of discord with and even full-blown hostility against Israel. And each group worshipped an assortment of pagan gods. Imagine what a "honey-do" list for Solomon from one of his foreign wives might include! ("Build an altar to pagan gods," for one thing, as revealed later in the chapter.) A relationship with a woman from *any* of those groups would have been inherently fraught with conflict; marrying women from *all* of those groups demonstrates an over-the-top disregard for the dangers God had warned of in telling His people not to marry foreigners.

go to

idolatry
Exodus 12:12;
Numbers 33:4;
Isaiah 19:1

pride
Ezekiel 29:3; 30:6

superstition
Isaiah 19:3

Moabites
Genesis 19:30–37;
1 Samuel 14:47;
2 Samuel 8:2

Ammonites
Deuteronomy 2:19,
1 Samuel 11;
2 Samuel 10;
2 Kings 24:2;
Amos 1:13

Edomites
1 Samuel 14:47;
2 Samuel 8:14;
1 Kings 11:15

Sidonians
Joshua 11:8; 19:28;
Judges 1:31; 10:12

Hittites
Joshua 9:1; 11:3;
1 Samuel 26:6;
2 Samuel 23:39

what others say

Carolyn Nystrom

Solomon's marriages to pagans testified to his lack of whole-hearted commitment to God.[7]

What About Love?

Notice the tiny phrase at the end of verse 2: "Solomon clung to these in love" (NKJV). Can a man really love so many women? It's hard to say for sure, because the Hebrew word for "loved" in this case—*ahab*—can refer to many types of "love." Most scholars agree it's not likely he truly loved these wives—at least not in the sense of the committed, self-sacrificing love that is the glue of godly marriages.

Better words for Solomon's feelings toward his wives might have been *lust* or *pride*. And a better application of the word *love* might be that he "loved" having all those wives. The word *clung* in this phrase comes from the Hebrew word *dabaq*, meaning, among other things, "to catch by pursuit"; "follow close (hard after)"; "overtake"; and "pursue hard." Interestingly, it's the same word used in 2 Samuel 13:1 to describe Amnon's feelings for his half sister Tamar, whom he raped.

Even though Solomon likely did not love *all* of his wives, it's clear he enjoyed a relationship built on God's pattern for love and marriage with at least one person: the unnamed woman of the Song of Solomon. (Much more about that subject in a later chapter.)

Extreme Polygamy

> 1 KINGS 11:3 *And he had seven hundred wives, princesses, and three hundred concubines; and his wives turned away his heart.* (NKJV)

Marrying foreigners rather than multiple wives from Israel was Solomon's behavior that led to condemnation from God. Even so, the king's polygamy—which, given the numbers, might easily be called "extreme polygamy"—can be tough to comprehend, especially in a contemporary context. Almost across the board, modern culture considers marrying more than one wife at a time to be ethically, morally, and culturally taboo.

Three Cheers for Children

Unfortunately, the ancient custom of the Old Testament said that multiple marriages were okay. God seems to have tolerated and even condoned the practice—He even made provisions for it in His law, especially when a first marriage did not produce children or when a woman's husband died and she married her dead husband's brother. And all this for a relatively simple purpose—an ancient Hebrew couple was devastated if they could not have children, for several reasons:

1. First, children went to work at a much younger age than they do today. Even young children provided the family with much-needed help in farming and other chores.

2. Second, male children preserved the family name, which was critical in keeping tribal allotments of property.

3. Third, every Jewish woman harbored the hope that she would be the one to bear the promised Messiah, or to bear the daughter who would. Having no children eliminated that possibility.

Even so, Bible scholars and historians have explored and debated God's view of polygamy for centuries, and they generally agree on these key points:

God's design for marriage
Genesis 2:23–24;
Matthew 19:4–6;
Ephesians 5:21–23

- *Polygamy is not part of God's plan for an ideal marriage.* <u>God's design for marriage</u> clearly involves one man and one woman uniting to become one flesh. Underlining this statement are the instances of polygamy in the Bible that were accompanied by strife and stress.

- *Polygamy was a man-made solution to legitimate problems with the culture and society.* The patriarchal society dictated that women could do little to provide for themselves outside the efforts of a male relative. Thus, even though polygamy didn't follow God's best plan for marriage, it may have seemed like the only way many women could secure the protection and provision of a household. When women lost their fathers, husbands, and brothers in war or to illness, they were vulnerable. Alone in the world and often with children to raise, they could not earn a living, have a home, or buy food and clothing. Often their only options were slavery, prostitution, or utter poverty. Polygamy enabled married men to take such women into their households as additional wives so they could be cared for within the protection of another family.

- *Polygamy added prestige.* It's unlikely that Solomon took in any of his wives because they needed his protection. After all, these wives were princesses—primarily the daughters of kings and of other men of influence. They would have been wealthy, more than adequately protected, and even pampered. These women were Solomon's "trophy wives" in the purest sense. They were the bounty he landed in his wheelings and dealings with kings of neighboring nations.

what others say

William C. Martin

One of [Solomon's] favorite diplomatic devices was the "marriage alliance," in which an agreement of peace was sealed by a marriage between members of the royal families. . . . many [of Solomon's wives] are sure to have been acquired in such an arrangement.[8]

Political, but Not Platonic

It's tempting to presume that since these women were basically political pawns, Solomon had little to do with them once they came into his household. But in all likelihood he took full advantage of the situation, sexually speaking. He admitted as much in Ecclesiastes 2:8, which is usually understood to imply that he had many wives and concubines and is actually rendered that way in several translations of this passage.

Biblical Polygamists

Polygamy wasn't just a practice of the people who lived in the pagan nations neighboring Israel. Many of Solomon's forefathers—some among the godliest men of Israel—had married more than one woman:

- Lamech—Genesis 4:19
- Abraham—Genesis 16
- Esau—Genesis 26:34; 28:9
- Jacob—Genesis 29:30
- Ashhur—1 Chronicles 4:5
- Gideon—Judges 8:30
- Elkanah—1 Samuel 1:2
- David—1 Samuel 25:39–44; 2 Samuel 3:2–5; 1 Chronicles 14:3

999 Too Many

If two wives were one too many by God's ideal standards, then Solomon truly had an excessive number of women—999 too many, to be exact—hanging their underthings to dry in the breezeways of the palace. This was yet another way in which Solomon demonstrated blatant disregard for God's instruction that kings should not have too many wives.

Sue and Larry Richards

> The commandments governing the king were designed to strip him of significant symbols of royalty and keep him humbly subservient to the Lord. There was to be no ostentatious wealth, no great chariot armies, and no multiple wives to produce multiple sons and daughters.[9]

God Told Him So

1 KINGS 11:4–5 *For it was so, when Solomon was old, that his wives turned his heart after other gods; and his heart was not loyal to the LORD his God, as was the heart of his father David. For Solomon went after Ashtoreth the goddess of the Sidonians, and after Milcom the abomination of the Ammonites. (NKJV)*

Just as God had predicted, Solomon's wives led him astray. Be assured, this doesn't mean that Solomon was an innocent victim of circumstances beyond his control. He had deliberately opened the door to evil, despite repeated warnings from God.

Had Solomon taken care in choosing a wife (or even wives) who feared the Lord, imagine how different his life might have been. Rather than turning the king's heart away from the Lord, a godly wife would have worshipped the Lord alongside him, contributing to rather than detracting from his spiritual strength. Further, a godly wife might have seen the red flags being raised by her husband's shifting priorities and warned him of possible danger ahead.

something to ponder

Beth Moore

> Any level of overexposure can open a door in the mind that Satan might one day decide to take for his advantage.[10]

David Plotz

> Solomon's idolatry raises a fundamental question about the difference between wisdom and faith. If Solomon were *truly* wise, presumably he would not build shrines to rival gods because he would know—thanks to his great brain—that the Lord would punish him for it. Such idolatry would be a terribly *unwise* move. The Bible clearly distinguishes Solomon's incomparable intellect from his unreliable faith. He's brilliant in the mind but weak in the soul.[11]

From Bad to Worse

1 KINGS 11:6–8 Solomon did evil in the sight of the LORD, and did not fully follow the LORD, as did his father David. Then Solomon built a high place for Chemosh the abomination of Moab, on the hill that is east of Jerusalem, and for Molech the abomination of the people of Ammon. And he did likewise for all his foreign wives, who burned incense and sacrificed to their gods. (NKJV)

key point

Customarily, people practiced the religion of their king. For example, if a new king conquered a nation, the people living there expected to worship his god or gods. When Solomon took the throne as king of Israel, he placed the worship of the one and only God at front and center of the nation's attention. But after some time, the king stopped insisting that the people living in Israel worship God alone, and he began allowing them to worship pagan gods. Further, Solomon didn't merely put up with the practice; he *participated in it* by helping build the altars to the foreign gods with his own hands. In doing so, he was effectively pulling the plug on the inexhaustible power available to him from the almighty God.

Peace and Politics

There's no question that Solomon allowed the worship of other gods in order to make his wives happy, to keep peace at home. And by making his wives happy, he pleased their respective families and friends in other nations, ensuring peace along the borders. It's also likely that the king tolerated the worship of foreign gods in order to enhance his standing with the conglomeration of peoples now living inside the boundaries of his larger-than-ever realm. Perhaps the king—a savvy politician with matchless wisdom—could see the numbers in his popularity polls spiking with his embrace-all-religions attitude. Maybe he could hear the comments drifting through the city streets: "That King Sol, he's a man of God, all right, but he's not one to beat you over the head with his law. He welcomes people of all faiths inside the borders of his nation."

Incidentally, the worship of other gods wasn't a temptation Solomon, as the nation's religious leader, should have been dangling in front of the Israelites. Their history showed a tendency to abandon God for a multitude of foreign gods.

God's Word is designed to <u>stand alone</u>. It needs no fillers or additives. It is "living and powerful, and sharper than any two-edged sword, piercing even to the division of soul and spirit, and of joints and marrow, and is a discerner of the thoughts and intents of the heart" (Hebrews 4:12 NKJV). When Solomon condoned this influx of assorted pagan religions, he invited the blending of ungodly teachings with God's teachings, corrupting their purity and compromising the spiritual safety of the people who heard it. Today's believers— even so-called "strong" Christians— must always be on guard against <u>false teachings</u> that can creep in unnoticed and destroy the foundations of a person's faith or the effectiveness of one's influence.

apply it

The Worst Kind of Evil

This passage mentions two specific gods. **<u>Chemosh</u>** was the national deity of the Moabites, and **<u>Molech</u>** was the "fire god" deity of the Ammonites. Worship of both gods involved <u>human sacrifices</u>, an abominable practice specifically forbidden by God. The high places Solomon built for Chemosh and Molech remained standing for three hundred years before **<u>Josiah</u>** finally destroyed them.

Everyone Is Susceptible to Sin

If ever a person might be considered immune to sin—particularly of this magnitude—Solomon would have been the one. The son of the person who was closer to God's heart than perhaps anyone else who ever lived, Solomon had come from a godly home. He had established his own history of loving and obeying God. Further, he had a gift of divine wisdom. But no one is ever immune to sin, and nothing—not even godly parents, a high religious ranking, or unsurpassed wisdom—can immunize a person against it. Everyone sins, and in fact many times it's godly people who fall most tragically into sin's snare.

go to

stand alone
Deuteronomy 4:2;
Proverbs 30:6;
Revelation 22:18–19

false teachings
Matthew 7:15;
Mark 13:22;
1 John 4:1;
2 Peter 2:1

Chemosh
Numbers 21:29;
Jeremiah 48:7, 13, 46

Molech
Jeremiah 49:1–3;
Amos 1:15

human sacrifices
Leviticus 18:21;
20:2–5;
Jeremiah 32:35

Josiah
2 Kings 21:23–23:30

Chemosh
pagan god of
Moabites

Molech
pagan god of
Ammonites

Josiah
king of Judah known
for spiritual reform

what others say

Beth Moore

What has terrified me is the growing stack of letters from believers who loved God and walked with Him faithfully for years then found themselves suddenly overtaken by a tidal wave of temptation and unholy assault. Many believers are convinced such things can't happen. . . . They are wrong. . . . Not only *can* the godly suddenly sprawl into a ditch from a solid, upright path, I believe many do.[12]

Oswald Chambers

You no more need a holiday from spiritual concentration than your heart needs a holiday from beating. You cannot have a moral holiday and remain moral, nor can you have a spiritual holiday and remain spiritual. God wants you to be entirely His, and this means that you have to watch to keep yourself fit. It takes a tremendous amount of time.[13]

Dennis Bratcher

Few of us will ever face the problem of idolatry in the same way Solomon did. For us, however, the danger is as real. Our idols are not foreign gods of wood and stone. Our idols are idols of the mind. These are ideas, ideologies, systems of power, cultural influences, even ideas about God, that are completely at odds with faith in the living God of the Bible. Idolatry may be expressed in different ways in different cultures, different cities, or different churches. . . . Religion itself can become idolatrous if it allows a perversion of total devotion to God. Distorted religion can rot the fruit of the Spirit as quickly as outright sin can![14]

Chapter Wrap-Up

- The first part of Solomon's life and reign, for the most part, were characterized by godliness, faithfulness, and obedience to God.

- Solomon compromised his spiritual integrity by marrying women from nations whose people did not worship the true God. God had warned His people not to marry such women because they would present the overpowering temptation to stray from Himself.

- Solomon's polygamy was culturally and socially acceptable, and God even made legal provisions for men with multiple wives. However, the practice strayed far from God's design for an ideal marriage.

- Solomon also disobeyed God's instruction that kings should not marry an excessive number of wives; he had seven hundred wives and three hundred concubines.

- God's warnings about the consequences of marrying women from pagan nations came true; Solomon's wives did in fact turn his heart away from God. He demonstrated this by allowing them to worship their pagan gods, and he even went so far as to help build the altars himself.

- Solomon's willing tolerance of, and participation in the worship of, foreign gods not only affected his own relationship with the Lord; it affected the spiritual health of the entire nation for which he, as its leader, was responsible.

Study Questions

1. How did Solomon's early life and reign differ from his later life and reign?

2. According to God, why was it dangerous to marry women from pagan nations?

3. Why was polygamy commonly practiced—and even condoned by God—during this time?

4. What are some possible explanations for Solomon having such an excessive number of wives?

5. What shocking things did Solomon do as a result of marrying foreign wives?

6. What were some of the possible effects of his actions?

1 Kings 11:9–11; 2 Chronicles 9:29–31: The Wrath of God

Let's Get Started

Solomon's life in the fast lane of wealth, power, and lust had taken him far off the good path of wisdom, obedience, and approval God had graciously paved for Israel's king. The dizzying sensation of breaking the rules and getting away with it must have blinded Solomon to his perilous position far outside the boundaries assuring God's blessing and protection.

Years earlier, the king's father, David, had also strayed off God's good path and into troubling territory. He did it more than a few times, in fact. But, in each situation, David eventually realized what he had done. He saw clearly how far he had fallen, his heart filled with remorse, and he acknowledged—with authentic repentance and utter humility—that his only way out was to cry out to God.

Remorse and repentance, however, weren't on King Solomon's agenda. While he hadn't come right out and denounced God, through disobedience he had pushed the Lord, His Word, and His power to the periphery of his own thinking. He chose instead to operate according to a system that relied on his own abilities, his own resources, and his own guidelines for living. So, sometime near the middle of Solomon's reign, God said, "Enough."

key point

> **1 KINGS 11:9–10** *So the LORD became angry with Solomon, because his heart had turned from the LORD God of Israel, who had appeared to him twice, and had commanded him concerning this thing, that he should not go after other gods; but he did not keep what the LORD had commanded.* (NKJV)

God, who had seen through the grimy film of David's offenses to find a pure heart fully devoted to His own, peered beneath the dark cloak of Solomon's sins and found a divided heart. That made the Lord angry. His anger was compounded by two factors:

1. He had made two personal visits to the king; and,

2. He had given Solomon specific warnings about this very scenario.

go to

pharaoh's daughter
1 Kings 3:1

patience
Exodus 34:6;
Numbers 14:18;
Nehemiah 9:17;
Psalms 86:15; 103:8;
Joel 2:13;
Nahum 1:3

Noah's day
Genesis 6:3;
1 Peter 3:20

longsuffering
Exodus 34:6

wilderness
Psalm 95:10;
Acts 13:18

In spite of God's deliberate efforts to draw Solomon into an intimate and protective relationship with Himself, the king had strayed.

The Luxury of God's Patience

Consider the patience with which God dealt with Solomon:

- He had ample reason to administer justice when the king first dallied in disobedience by marrying the <u>pharaoh's daughter</u>. But He didn't. He had remained patient with the king for whom He had crafted a fantastic future.

- After that, God could have unleashed His judgment on Solomon each time the king married another foreign wife (after another, and another, and another). But He didn't. He remained patient with the king, perhaps watching intently for a sign that Solomon would wake up, realize his wrongdoing, and turn from his defiant ways.

- Even after that, in righteous indignation, God could have struck Solomon dead the first time the king picked up a stone to build an altar to one of the foreign gods his wives worshipped. But He didn't. He extended His mercy to the absolute limits of His patience because of His great love for this man and His people.

The Limits of God's Patience

<u>Patience</u> is one of God's most striking characteristics. He demonstrates patience with His followers more times than it's possible to count! For example:

- He showed patience with the wicked people alive during <u>Noah's day</u>.

- He described himself to Moses as a God who is "<u>longsuffering</u>," or slow to become angry.

- He demonstrated patience with the Israelites' many instances of defiance during their forty years in the <u>wilderness</u> and throughout the following centuries of arrogance and disobedience.

God's patience is of immense <u>personal benefit</u> to everyone on earth. Because of His patience, more people have more of a chance to learn about the eternal life that He has made possible through the work of His Son, Jesus, on the cross:

- "The Lord . . . is longsuffering toward us, not willing that any should perish but that all should come to repentance" (2 Peter 3:9 NKJV).
- "And consider that the longsuffering of our Lord is salvation" (2 Peter 3:15 NKJV).

personal benefit
Romans 2:4;
1 Timothy 1:16

God's patience, however, does have limits. As a God who is holy, He cannot tolerate sin. He loathes it. At some point, as in Solomon's case, the Lord's patience with sinners turns not into impatience but into anger. The anger of God isn't a fit of rage, a flaring temper, or a vindictive spirit. It is God's perfectly controlled, perfectly just response to the wickedness that opposes Him.

Solomon's Sentence

1 KINGS 11:11 *Therefore the LORD said to Solomon, "Because you have done this, and have not kept My covenant and My statutes, which I have commanded you, I will surely tear the kingdom away from you and give it to your servant." (NKJV)*

God, who had spoken directly to Solomon twice before, delivered this news of Solomon's sentence Himself. With the words "because you have done this," He placed responsibility for the judgment right where it belonged: squarely on Solomon's shoulders.

Galatians 6:7 states, "Do not be deceived, God is not mocked; for whatever a man sows, that he will also reap" (NKJV). This principle, written on the pages of each book of the Bible, could hardly be demonstrated more clearly in anyone's life than it was in Solomon's. God had given the king a choice: Obey God's commandments or not. If Solomon chose obedience, God would provide blessing; for disobedience, He would dole out discipline.

PSALM 89:30–32 *If [David's] sons forsake My law and do not walk in My judgments, if they break My statutes and do not keep My commandments, then I will punish their transgression with the rod, and their iniquity with stripes. (NKJV)*

Because Solomon sowed disobedience, angering God after pushing Him to the limits of His patience, he would reap a painful consequence: The kingdom would be taken away from him.

For David's Sake

1 KINGS 11:12–13 *Nevertheless I will not do it in your days, for the sake of your father David; I will tear it out of the hand of your son. However I will not tear away the whole kingdom; I will give one tribe to your son for the sake of My servant David, and for the sake of Jerusalem which I have chosen. (NKJV)*

When God told Solomon He wouldn't impose the sentence during the king's reign and that He wouldn't take the entire kingdom from him, He wasn't acting on a sudden, soft-hearted impulse to cut Solomon some slack. Doubts about the degree of discipline He had decided on weren't creeping into His thoughts. God wasn't waffling. He was simply keeping His word. Remember what God had told David.

2 SAMUEL 7:12–16 *When your days are fulfilled and you rest with your fathers, I will set up your seed after you, who will come from your body, and I will establish his kingdom. He shall build a house for My name, and I will establish the throne of his kingdom forever. I will be his Father, and he shall be My son. If he commits iniquity, I will chasten him with the rod of men and with the blows of the sons of men. But My mercy shall not depart from him, as I took it from Saul, whom I removed from before you. And your house and your kingdom shall be established forever before you. Your throne shall be established forever. (NKJV)*

As discussed earlier, these words, called the Davidic covenant, were God's promise that David's descendants would continue to rule over Israel eternally: "His seed shall endure forever, and his throne as the sun before Me; it shall be established forever like the moon, even like the faithful witness in the sky" (Psalm 89:36–37 NKJV). The first of David's sons to live out that promise was, of course, Solomon.

Although God would discipline Solomon (as well as the kings who followed him when they were unfaithful), He would always make sure a king from David's lineage would rule over Israel. That's why He didn't strip the entire kingdom from Solomon's sons; He would preserve part of it for David's family. Thankfully, God's perfect plans are not altered by the imperfections of His people! And His actions don't waver according to the behavior of His followers; they're always in perfect sync with His character and His Word.

key point

The Perfect Heir

The generations alive during Solomon's time and following, who kept close to the Lord, knew they could count on Him to do what He said He would do. They watched expectantly for a descendant of David to come to the throne who would not fail, as had Solomon and so many kings who came after him. They were watching for a king who was righteous and obedient. The king who would perfectly fit that description was born in a stable in Bethlehem centuries later.

what others say

Charles H. Spurgeon

David's seed lives on in the person of the Lord Jesus, and the seed of Jesus in the persons of believers.[2]

Matthew Henry

David's seed and throne did endure for ever, that, notwithstanding the wickedness of many of his posterity, who were the scandals of his house, yet his family continued, and continued in the imperial dignity, a very long time. . . . the family of David continued a family of distinction till that Son of David came whose throne should endure for ever.[3]

Three Adversaries

1 KINGS 11:14 Now the LORD raised up an adversary against Solomon, Hadad the Edomite; he was a descendant of the king in Edom. (NKJV)

The first phrase of that verse jars the sensibilities. How does God, whose name equals love, grace, and mercy, perform such a seemingly sinister act as stirring up one's enemies? The answer can be given in one word: *discipline*. Discipline is one of the many ways God shows His love.

God's Tools of Discipline

God uses many tools of discipline to teach and shape the hearts of His followers. In this instance, God used Solomon's enemies to discipline the king for his disobedience. Likewise, someone in our lives who apparently "has it in for us" might just be more than a menace. God may be using that person to get our attention, teach us a lesson, or shape our attitudes.

key point

On occasion, God even uses Satan to do His disciplinary work. However, although God may put Satan to work for His purposes, He never gives him completely free rein. The devil has no power except that which God allows him to have.

Adversary #1: The Edomite Egyptian

go to

Edomites
Genesis 32:3;
Numbers 20:18–21

slaughter
2 Samuel 8:13–14;
1 Chronicles 18:12

Edomites
descendants of Esau
who lived south and
southeast of Israel

the big picture

1 Kings 11:15-22

As stated in 1 Kings 11:14, the first of three adversaries the Lord raised up against Solomon was Hadad. The next passage states who that is, explaining that when Hadad was just a boy, David had warred against the **Edomites** and had launched a large-scale <u>slaughter</u>, reducing the population to slaves.

Hadad, a member of Edomite royalty, ran for his life—straight into the lap of luxury in Egypt. The pharaoh took him in, raised him as part of the royal family, and gave him his own sister-in-law as a wife. But while Hadad was walking and talking like the Egyptians, his inner Edomite heart nursed a lingering hostility against Israel. News of David's death was all it took for him to make his move—back to Edom. He didn't have enough power to completely overthrow Solomon's hold on the region, but he did have enough muscle to give the king a real headache. He made it his number one mission to chip away at the peace and stability of the southern part of Solomon's kingdom. (Incidentally, because Solomon was married to Pharaoh's daughter and Hadad was married to Pharaoh's sister-in-law, the Israelite and the Edomite were distant relatives but "by marriage only.")

what others say

Thomas L. Constable

The ancient hostility of the Edomites toward the Israelites must have been aggravated in Hadad's mind by David's slaughter of the Edomites, and Hadad lived for the day he could take revenge.[6]

Adversary #2: The Rebel with a Cause

1 KINGS 11:23–25 *And God raised up another adversary against him, Rezon the son of Eliadah, who had fled from his lord, Hadadezer king of Zobah. So he gathered men to him and became captain over a band of raiders, when David killed those of Zobah. And they went to Damascus and dwelt there, and reigned in Damascus. He was an adversary of Israel all the days of Solomon (besides the trouble that Hadad caused); and he abhorred Israel, and reigned over Syria. (NKJV)*

go to

defeated Syria
2 Samuel 8:3–12

Damascus
capital of Syria

The second adversary God unleashed against Solomon was Rezon. Rezon was a rebel who had moved to **Damascus** with a band of rabble-rousers when David and his troops <u>defeated Syria</u> under the leadership of Rezon's master, King Hadadezer. Rezon whittled away at Solomon's control over the northern part of the kingdom while Hadad continued to work against Solomon's strength in the South.

Adversary #3: The Insider

With Hadad harassing Solomon in the South and Rezon stirring up trouble in the North, circumstances were indeed kicking the sturdy underpinnings from beneath the kingdom. The last thing Solomon's administration needed was trouble from within the ranks, yet that's exactly what God had in mind when He administered His third and most decisive measure of discipline.

> 1 KINGS 11:26–28 *Then Solomon's servant, Jeroboam the son of Nebat, an Ephraimite from Zereda, whose mother's name was Zeruah, a widow, also rebelled against the king. And this is what caused him to rebel against the king: Solomon had built the Millo and repaired the damages to the City of David his father. The man Jeroboam was a mighty man of valor; and Solomon, seeing that the young man was industrious, made him the officer over all the labor force of the house of Joseph.* (NKJV)

Jeroboam's Job

When God had prophesied that He would remove the kingdom from Solomon and give it to "his servant," the person He had in mind was Jeroboam, one of the king's most highly qualified officials. (In fact, that might have been the most painful part of Solomon's punishment—knowing that the kingdom would be taken from the king and given to one of his servants.) Some scholars believe Jeroboam was quite well-to-do, and he certainly shouldered a lot of responsibility. He was in charge of the men Solomon forced into working on his large-scale construction projects. The specific group of workers he supervised were from the "house of Joseph," or the tribes of Ephraim and Manasseh. Those two groups formed the main strength of northern Israel, the faction that would later rebel against Solomon's son, Rehoboam.

Jeroboam's name, which meant "may the people be great," carried great political significance against the backdrop of Solomon's administration that at every turn seemed to glorify, enrich, and exalt the king—all at the people's expense.

Plenty of Reasons to Rebel

These verses state that Jeroboam rebelled against Solomon but they don't say why, other than to hint that there might have been some sort of trouble with the building projects. There were probably as many reasons for a tenth-century BC upper-level manager to rebel against his administration as there are for an employee to revolt against his or hers today.

Consider the possibilities: A boss who expects too much. Long hours. Poor benefits. Uncooperative underlings. Low pay. A dead-end career path. Disagreeable working conditions. Disagreement with company policy. Poor treatment. Discrimination. Favoritism. Unethical or unscrupulous supervisors. An intense craving for the boss's job. Jeroboam may have been enduring one or several of these conditions on the job site, and maybe he had already started daydreaming about his options.

Jeroboam likely wasn't the only man in Solomon's administration who ever rebelled. He may have simply been the next dissenter in line once God decided to raise His holy hand of discipline.

Ephraim: The Tribe with an Attitude

Before the prophet Samuel had ushered Israel into the period of the united kingdom, it had consisted of twelve loosely organized tribes. Each tribe was named after—and traced its ancestry to—one of the twelve sons of **Jacob**.

what others say

Nelson's Student Bible Dictionary

Israel was an association of twelve tribes, designated by the names of the ancestors from whom they were descended (Deuteronomy 27:12–13; Ezekiel 48:1–35). The historial origins of the tribal units may be traced to the book of Genesis.[7]

go to

Jacob blessed them
Genesis 48:5

Manasseh
Joseph's firstborn
son

Joseph
the eleventh son of
Jacob who was sold
into slavery and rose
to prominence in
the Egyptian
government

Each family possessed a unique history. Ephraim, the tribe from which Jeroboam came, had an especially distinctive origin. Its patriarch, the man named Ephraim, wasn't actually Jacob's natural son; he and his older brother **Manasseh** were sons of **Joseph** who were adopted by their grandfather, Jacob. Jacob blessed them.

what others say

International Standard Bible Encyclopedia

Despite their father's protest, Jacob had preferred the younger [son, Ephraim], foreshadowing the future eminence of his descendants (Gensis 41:50 ff; 48:20ff).[8]

In addition to this favored beginning, Ephraim had other claims to spiritual greatness as well. For example, spiritual giants Joshua and Samuel were Ephraimites. Also, the centerpiece of worship, the ark of the covenant, had been located in the territory of Ephraim at Shiloh and Kirjath-jearim. Because of all this, Ephraim became a greenhouse of sorts where a sense of entitlement and righteous indignation flourished. As one observer notes, this attitude escalated into tribal jealousy and resentment when Solomon established Jerusalem as the spiritual headquarters of the nation, drafted tribe members into forced labor on his pet projects, and imposed heavy taxes to bankroll it all.

what others say

Alfred Edersheim

And now, with the reign of King Solomon, all hope of tribal preeminence seemed to have passed from Ephraim. There was a new capital for the whole country, and that in the possession of Judah. The glory of the ancient Sanctuary had also been taken away. Jerusalem was the ecclesiastical as well as the political capital, and Ephraim had to contribute its wealth and even its forced labour to promote the schemes, to support the luxury, and to advance the glory of a new monarchy.[9]

Green with Envy

As a king who was "greater than all the kings of earth in riches and wisdom," Solomon was perfectly positioned to be the object of envy of many of his contemporary heads of state. And according to James, the product of envy is <u>conflict and war</u>. The Bible doesn't list how many of Solomon's foes God held at bay during the years Solomon was living in the light of His favor and blessing, but God probably prevented quite a few from acting against the king.

go to

conflict and war
James 4:1–2

Just What Jeroboam Wanted to Hear

> 1 KINGS 11:29–30 *Now it happened at that time, when Jeroboam went out of Jerusalem, that the prophet Ahijah the Shilonite met him on the way; and he had clothed himself with a new garment, and the two were alone in the field. Then Ahijah took hold of the new garment that was on him, and tore it into twelve pieces.* (NKJV)

One day, as Jeroboam was leaving Jerusalem—possibly after clocking out at the end of a long, hard day on the building sites—he met a prophet named Ahijah. The prophet, whose name means "my brother is the Lord," employed a creative way of presenting Jeroboam with a message from the Lord. The prophet removed the new garment he was wearing and began to tear it into pieces. Twelve pieces, to be exact: one representing each of Israel's tribes.

> 1 KINGS 11:31–33 *And he said to Jeroboam, "Take for yourself ten pieces, for thus says the LORD, the God of Israel: 'Behold, I will tear the kingdom out of the hand of Solomon and will give ten tribes to you (but he shall have one tribe for the sake of My servant David, and for the sake of Jerusalem, the city which I have chosen out of all the tribes of Israel), because they have forsaken Me, and worshiped Ashtoreth the goddess of the Sidonians, Chemosh the god of the Moabites, and Milcom the god of the people of Ammon, and have not walked in My ways to do what is right in My eyes and keep My statutes and My judgments, as did his father David.'"* (NKJV)

Ahijah instructed Jeroboam to take ten pieces of the fabric, explaining that God had plans for him to take his place as king over that number of tribes. Jeroboam's mind must have reeled as the meaning of the prophet's words began to sink in: *A green light from God to revolt against Solomon! Could it be true? God was going to help him accomplish the thing he had been dreaming of and scheming about!*

The prophet also recapped for Jeroboam the Lord's words to Solomon, restating the consequences God had lined out and the rea-

key point

sons He had imposed them. Notice that Ahijah pointed out that Solomon had "forsaken" the Lord, a striking contrast to <u>God's promise</u> that He would never leave or give up on Israel.

Let it be clear: No matter why Jeroboam rebelled against Solomon, and no matter what schemes he might have been working on to accomplish his goals, he would never make any headway that God Himself did not allow.

A Mathematical Mind Bender

The prophet's message to Jeroboam was straightforward enough: Jeroboam was to be placed over ten of the twelve tribes symbolized by the fabric scraps. So when Jeroboam took his share of the pieces of frayed pieces, two remained in Ahijah's hands. But God had promised Solomon one tribe "for David's sake." What about the remaining piece? It doesn't add up!

what others say

Roger Hahn

The mathematics of this passage is puzzling. The garment is torn into twelve pieces representing the twelve tribes. Ten pieces of the garment representing ten tribes will be given to Jeroboam. One tribe will remain for Solomon's son. How does 10 + 1 = 12? The easiest way to understand the problem is to assume that Judah, David and Solomon's tribe, would automatically remain loyal to the Davidic line. To Judah is then added one tribe, the tribe of Benjamin, which also is loyal to Solomon's son. The other ten tribes will secede and be ruled by Jeroboam.[10]

The Twelve Tribes

The ten tribes given to Jeroboam came to be called the *Northern Kingdom*, or *Israel*; and the two that remained with Solomon were the *Southern Kingdom*, or *Judah*.

The Northern Kingdom, or Israel

go to

God's promise
1 Kings 6:13; 8:57

- Ephraim
- Manasseh
- Naphtali
- Dan

- Issachar
- Zebulun
- Asher

- Simeon
- Gad
- Reuben

The Southern Kingdom, or Judah

- Judah
- Benjamin

light
1 John 1:5

apple of God's eye
Zechariah 2:8

Leaving the Light On

1 KINGS 11:36 And to his son I will give one tribe, that My servant David may always have a lamp before Me in Jerusalem, the city which I have chosen for Myself, to put My name there. (NKJV)

"We'll leave the light on." The foregoing was the tagline in a well-known motel chain's 1980s TV and radio commercial that aimed to tug at potential travelers' heartstrings. It worked; the words landed awards and made Motel 6 a household word. The power behind that plainspoken assurance lies in the way it stirs up a powerful sense of belonging, and of being cared for.

In a sense, "I'll leave the light on" is what God was saying when He declared that He would preserve the tribe for David's offspring so that His "lamp" would "always" remain in Jerusalem. It hadn't been too many years since the brightness of God's glory had nearly blinded the priests, as on the day God moved His presence into the holy of holies in the temple atop Mount Moriah. For a wonderful stretch of time the entire nation had basked in the bright light of God's blessing and affirmation under the leadership of its wise and godly king. But step-by-step, Solomon's misdeeds had blocked out the radiance of God's favor. Now, it seemed the division of the kingdom would cast a final, dark shadow of hopelessness over the land.

But darkness isn't what God wants for His people. Ever since He issued the powerful words "Let there be light" (Genesis 1:3 NKJV), God—who is in fact <u>light</u> itself—has been in the business of offering light and hope to a world living in the darkness of wickedness and despair. Jerusalem, called the "<u>apple of God's eye</u>," is God's way of "leaving the light on" in a dark world: He used Jerusalem as a light pointing the pagan nations toward Him.

Millennium
Isaiah 60:1–14;
Ezekiel 37:24;
Zephaniah 3:14–17

Millennium
the thousand-year
reign of Jesus on
earth

International Standard Bible Encyclopedia

The Gentiles were to come to her light (Isaiah 60:3). Her mission as the enlightener of the world was symbolized in the ornamentations of her priesthood. The Urim of the high priest's breastplate signified light, and the name itself is but the plural form of the Hebrew 'or. It stood for revelation, and thummim for truth.[11]

He used Jerusalem to bring His Son, Jesus Christ, the "brightness of [God's] glory" (Hebrews 1:3 NKJV), into the world. Christ's birth fulfilled the prophecy of "the true Light which gives light to every man coming into the world" (John 1:9 NKJV). The One who was to be "a light to the Gentiles" (Isaiah 42:6; 49:6) called Himself "the light of the world" (John 8:12; 9:5 NKJV; see also John 12:46).

Ann Spangler

According to Jewish tradition, one of the names for the Messiah is "Light." How fitting, then, that Jesus is called the "Light of the world." John's Gospel portrays Jesus as the light that vanquishes the darkness brought on by sin—a darkness that ends in death. Christ has opened the eyes of a sin-darkened world to the truth of the gospel. We who believe in him have moved from darkness to light, from death to life. When we pray to Jesus as the Light of the world, let us remember that we are calling on the One who was so determined to draw us into his light that he spent nine months in the darkness of his mother's womb in order to become one of us.[12]

He will use Jerusalem as His seat of government during the **Millennium**.

Mark Hitchcock

[Jesus Christ] will rule the world from Jerusalem. All nations and peoples will flood there to pay homage to the King and His chosen people, the Jews.[13]

Believers are instructed to "put on" the characteristics of Christ, so it follows that, like Jesus, we, too, have the important mission of being the light of the world. We are the lamps He lights to show others the way to Him.

put on
Romans 13:14;
Galatians 3:27

light of the world
Matthew 5:14;
Luke 16:8;
John 12:36;
Ephesians 5:8;
Philippians 2:15

The Same Offer God Gave Solomon

> 1 KINGS 11:37–39 *So I will take you, and you shall reign over all your heart desires, and you shall be king over Israel. Then it shall be, if you heed all that I command you, walk in My ways, and do what is right in My sight, to keep My statutes and My commandments, as My servant David did, then I will be with you and build for you an enduring house, as I built for David, and will give Israel to you. And I will afflict the descendants of David because of this, but not forever. (NKJV)*

Notice that even though Jeroboam didn't have David's royal blood running through his veins, and even though he was rebellious, God presented him with the same proposition He had presented to Solomon: "Obey, and you will be blessed." It would be up to Jeroboam to choose whether to follow the Lord's commands and receive His blessings or to disregard them and lose His favor. It's the same offer God gives believers today: Our standing is not based on the strength of our spiritual ancestry or track record, but on whether we choose to obey God's Word. Unfortunately, Jeroboam would later prove to be a very ungodly leader.

Shishak
first named pharaoh
in the Bible; he
reigned from about
945 to 914 BC

Jeroboam Fled

> 1 KINGS 11:40 *Solomon therefore sought to kill Jeroboam. But Jeroboam arose and fled to Egypt, to Shishak king of Egypt, and was in Egypt until the death of Solomon. (NKJV)*

Somehow Solomon must have discovered the truth. Whether he caught Jeroboam instigating treachery or he heard about God's message through the grapevine, the king determined to have his servant killed for treason. Jeroboam sought safety in Egypt, where Pharaoh **Shishak** offered him asylum.

Solomon's Death

1 KINGS 11:41–43 Now the rest of the acts of Solomon, all that he did, and his wisdom, are they not written in the book of the acts of Solomon? And the period that Solomon reigned in Jerusalem over all Israel was forty years. Then Solomon rested with his fathers, and was buried in the City of David his father. And Rehoboam his son reigned in his place. (NKJV)

key point

In a familiar pattern used by the ancient historians who recorded the epitaphs of biblical kings, the author of 1 Kings noted other sources of information about the king's life, the length of his reign, the place he was buried, and the name of his successor. Solomon died in 930 BC, leaving the kingdom he had unified in shambles when his son, Rehoboam, succeeded him as king. Judah remained loyal to Rehoboam, but the ten northern tribes set up a rival kingdom—which kept the name Israel—under the leadership of Jeroboam. (See also 2 Chronicles 9:29–31.)

what others say

Larry Richards

When Solomon died, the people appealed to his son Rehoboam for tax relief. The foolish young king refused. The ten northern tribes rebelled and crowned Jeroboam as their king.[14]

As mentioned earlier, neither kingdom was left in very good hands. The rivalry between Israel and Judah continued for more than two hundred years, when, in about 722 BC, Israel was finally taken into Assyrian (i.e., Babylonian) captivity.

what others say

William C. Martin

[Judah] outlived her northern sister by several generations, hanging on stubbornly until 587 B.C., at which time Jerusalem was finally destroyed by the armies of Nebuchadnezzar and thousands of the inhabitants of Judah were taken captive to Babylonia.[15]

The period of Israel's history that occurred during Solomon's reign would be looked upon by later generations as a golden age, or what today's language might refer to as "the good old days." With Solomon on the throne, success had coated every facet of the Israelites' lives, much like gold had adorned every surface of the temple and the king's palace:

1. *Politically*—The Israelites had enjoyed unprecedented peace because of the alliances Solomon had forged with neighboring nations.

2. *Militarily*—The Israelites lived without fear; Solomon had guaranteed their security with massive, well-organized, and well-armed military forces.

3. *Economically*—The Israelites reveled in the economic security that came from the extensive trade agreements and commercial ventures Solomon had put into place.

4. *Culturally*—The Israelites living under Solomon's rule no doubt enjoyed the cultural benefits brought about by their famous king: His scientific research, wise sayings, music, and architecture educated their minds and enriched their lives.

5. *Religiously*—The Israelites lived—for a period, at least—under the leadership of a man who governed the nation with divine wisdom and authority, and put the worship of God at the center of attention, both physically and figuratively speaking.

These were the days the prophet Jeremiah must have had in mind in his plaintive cry to the Lord on behalf of his sinful people in the book of Lamentations. Begging the Lord to restore his people after Jerusalem's fall to the Babylonians, he lamented over the destruction of the temple, noting "how the gold has become dim! . . . The stones of the sanctuary are scattered at the head of every street" (Lamentations 4:1 NKJV). He observed that the people (who, during Solomon's reign had been the picture of contentment and happiness) would now be better off dead than starving and "stricken for lack of the fruits of the field" (Lamentations 4:9 NKJV). Describing how far from God's best his people had fallen, Jeremiah begged the Lord to restore the "good old days": "Renew our days as of old" (Lamentations 5:21 NKJV).

Solomon's Destiny

Such a small obituary for such a grand life as Solomon's! But his life, in truth, didn't end there. Like every human on the planet, his spirit would continue to live eternally after his body experienced physical death. Even though he spent his latter years suffering the political and physical consequences of his disobedience to God and enduring the bitter taste of doubts and regrets (more about that in the last chapter of this book), there is no reason to believe he didn't eventually repent and turn back to God with confidence that he would, like his father, David, live in the house of the Lord forever (Psalm 27:4).

what others say

Henry Morris

It is worth considering the possibility, at least, that Solomon may, in his last years, have turned back to the Lord in true repentance and faith.[16]

Chapter Wrap-Up

- God became angry with Solomon because, in spite of God's personal appearance to the king and specific warnings, the king had allowed his pagan wives (whom he shouldn't have married in the first place) to lead him astray into worshipping foreign gods.

- God had shown great patience with the king before unleashing His wrath, just as He demonstrates patience with everyone.

- God punished Solomon by promising to remove the kingdom from his hands.

- Showing mercy, however, God said that He would not carry out this sentence during Solomon's lifetime; He would do it after the king's death.

- Further honoring His promise of an everlasting reign to David, God said that He would not strip away the entire kingdom; He would preserve a portion of it for David's family.

- God—who had been blessing Solomon with peace—removed His restraining hand from the king's enemies—Hadad, Rezon, and Jeroboam—allowing them to stir up dissention and discord in the kingdom as a means of divine discipline.

- Through a prophet, God told Jeroboam that he would be the one to take control over ten of Israel's twelve tribes, and that He would give Solomon's son one tribe (comprising Judah and Benjamin) to preserve David's dynasty.

- Jeroboam then fled to Egypt, where he remained until after Solomon died.

Study Questions

1. Why was God angry with Solomon?

2. What did God do to punish Solomon?

3. How did God demonstrate mercy to Solomon?

4. How did God honor the Davidic covenant in spite of His need to discipline Solomon for His sins?

5. Who were Hadad, Rezon, and Jeroboam?

6. What news did Jeroboam receive through the prophet Ahijah?

7. Did Jeroboam overthrow Solomon right away?

Part Six
A Legacy of Wisdom

A Legacy of Wisdom

What made the wisest, richest, and arguably the most powerful man in the world tick? What were the secrets of his success, the motivations that fueled his ambitions? The passions of his heart and the principles that undergirded his practices? Did he ever have questions, or doubts—and if so, what were they?

The historical report of Solomon's life, as recorded in 1 Kings and 2 Chronicles, leaves many questions unanswered for those who would like to know more about the man who had it all—or, at least, who seemed to have had it all. Few of the king's spoken words were recorded, and many of his thoughts and motives went unexplained by the writers who put together those important books of Bible history.

But, amazingly, Solomon answered many questions himself in three of his books that are included in the Bible. Proverbs, Ecclesiastes, and the Song of Solomon add rich color, texture, and dimension to the drawing of the king that is outlined in his basic biography.

Although Solomon's books appear in the Bible in the sequence listed in the preceding sentence, most scholars believe he wrote them in a different order:

1. *Song of Solomon*—Solomon probably wrote this eloquent, extended love poem when he was a young man as a passionate—and quite detailed—celebration of married love.

2. *Proverbs*—Solomon probably wrote many of these brief statements of practical wisdom that apply to believers and nonbelievers alike when he was in his middle years, at the crest of his success and maturity.

3. *Ecclesiastes*—Solomon probably wrote this book near the end of his life to record his questions concerning the meaning of human life apart from a personal relationship with God.

The next three chapters will offer an overview of each of these books—in the order in which they are presumed to have been written—to help shed even more light on Solomon's intriguing life.

Solomon's Song: It's All About Love

Let's Get Started

Rewind the video of Solomon's life to a time many years before his death. After a nerve-racking struggle over the succession to his father's throne, he has just been crowned as Israel's third king. For now, at least, he rules over the nation as a co-regent with his father. But David is declining in health, and with each passing day he becomes less and less involved in governing the nation.

This means that each passing day, for Solomon, brings tremendous, ever-increasing responsibilities and pressures. Men are ordered to live or die by his justice, matters of war and peace are determined by his diplomatic skills, and the day-to-day lives of the Israelite families are profoundly affected by his economic decisions.

Solomon has the job of a mature man, so it would be easy to forget that he has a very young man's heart and a young man's passions . . . until reading the Song of Solomon. This lengthy poetic drama finds the youthful king retreating from the hustle and bustle of the capital city to enjoy the tranquillity of the surrounding countryside, by disguising himself as a shepherd so he can inspect his vineyards without being recognized. While there he sees a beautiful young maiden who captures his heart. She falls in love with him, too, but has no idea that he is also her king. He leaves her, promising to return. When he does, she is overjoyed to discover his identity. The two are married, and their relationship embodies God's principles for married love.

Before looking more closely at the plot of Solomon's Song, however, it's important to keep in mind some significant facts.

Four Threes

1. *Three Titles.* Solomon's Song is referred to by scholars and in literature by three titles:

Abishag
1 Kings 1:3–8

Naamah
2 Chronicles 12:13

Solomon's successor
1 Kings 11:43

Naamah
one of Solomon's
wives; Rehoboam's
mother

- *"Song of Solomon"*—the title used in most modern translations of the Bible

- *"Song of Songs"*—the title used in the Hebrew Bible

- *"Canticles"*—the title taken from the Latin word for "song," which is *canticum*

In the Hebrew Bible, the Song of Solomon is the first of the "Five Megilloth," or scrolls, followed by the books of Ruth, Lamentations, Ecclesiastes, and Esther. Parts of it were sung on the eighth day of the Passover Feast, the first and greatest of the Jews' annual feasts.

2. *Three Voices.* Three main characters—or groups of characters—speak in the book:

- *The Lover* (Solomon)—This book discloses more personal information about Solomon than readers can possibly glean from his biography detailed in 1 Kings and 2 Chronicles. For example, by reading his Song, readers learn that he had wavy, black hair (5:11), gentle eyes (5:12), and stood tall, with a chiseled physique (5:14–15).

- *The Beloved Bride* (Shulamite)—Not much is known about this woman's hometown of Shulam since it isn't mentioned anywhere else in the Bible or on any maps of that time and region. It was probably just a small village. Some scholars also believe this might have been <u>Abishag</u>, the beautiful young virgin hired to keep the elderly David warm while he slept. Other scholars believe this to be **Naamah**, the mother of Rehoboam—who then would have been Solomon's firstborn son, possibly confirmed by the fact that he was <u>Solomon's successor</u> to the throne. Whatever this woman's identity, she possessed some striking characteristics:

  - She was a "regular" girl. Unlike the princesses Solomon later married, she was not from a royal family, and she knew what it meant to work.

  - Even though she was an ordinary farm girl, she had a refreshing confidence, a boldness not always associated with women in this era. Like most other women throughtout the ages, she might have changed some things about herself if she could have (she thought her skin was too dark, for example), but she was the first of the couple to speak.

- *The Chorus* (Shulamite's friends)—These women, also called "daughters of Jerusalem," may have been friends or companions of the bride. They often interrupt the scene with songs, comments, or warnings.

go to

godly marriage
Matthew 19:3–9;
Hebrews 13:4

God's love for His people.
Isaiah 54:5–6;
Jeremiah 2:2;
Ezekiel 16:8–14;
Hosea 2:16, 18–20

Christ's love for the church
Ephesians 5:22–33;
2 Corinthians 11:2;
Revelation 19:7–9;
21:9

what others say

Robert Davidson

Indeed within the book more verses are attributed to the woman than to the man. Is this a welcome counter-balance to the male chauvinism which often seems to speak in the biblical text?[1]

3. *Three Ways to Read the Book.* Many scholars suggest at least three ways to interpret the book:

- As a literal description of the emotional, physical, and spiritual relationship between Solomon and the Shulamite, and as an ideal for any <u>godly marriage</u>.
- As an illustration of <u>God's love for His people</u>.
- As an illustration of <u>Christ's love for the church</u>.

what others say

Ray Bentley

Wedded life in Israel represented the highest, deepest, and most respective form of affection. The *Song of Solomon* expresses the heart of a satisfied husband and devoted wife.[2]

Irving L. Jensen

If your study of the Song of Solomon will arouse in you a more genuine love for your Lord, as well as a deeper gratitude for His love to you, then it will not surprise you that God chose to include such a love story in His Holy Scriptures.[3]

Ann Spangler

The New Testament presents Christ as the church's Bridegroom. He is the Holy One who did not cling to his divinity but left his Father's house to dwell among us, calling us to become one with him in the most intimate way possible. To all of us, male and female, Christ offers himself as our provider and protector, the one who has forever pledged himself in faithfulness and love.[4]

key point

The richest interpretation of Solomon's Song probably involves reading it primarily for the literal love story that it is, while enjoying the beautiful images it presents of God's love for Israel and Christ's love for the church—always remembering that, whether speaking of love between a man and a woman, God's love for Israel, or Christ's love for His church, it's all about <u>love</u>.

It's "love"-saturated: Hebrew words used for "love" in the Song of Solomon appear about sixty times in the brief book.

4. *Three Questions.* When surveying what Bible scholars have written about the Song of Solomon down through the centuries, certain topics seem to surface again and again as points of special interest, debate, or controversy. Those topics raise three thought-provoking questions:

- *What's It Rated?* It's no secret that the Song of Solomon is the "raciest" book in the Bible. Passages include vivid (and very unusual!) descriptions of the lovers' physical appearances, as well as pointed remarks about their desire for one another. The frankness used in describing this very passionate affair have caused some to argue that the book has no place in the Bible at all. Traditionally, Jews would not allow a young man to read the Song until he reached the age of thirty. Maybe that means it was rated "PG-30." Admittedly, though it takes far more to make today's readers blush than it did twenty-five, fifty or one hundred years ago, such talk about physical attraction and sexual activity isn't something most people expect to read in the pages of the Holy Bible! But the very fact that these words are in the Bible says a whole lot about God's views on the matter of love and sex.

go to

love
John 3:16;
Romans 12:10;
1 Corinthians 13;
Philippians 1:9;
1 John 3:1, 16;
4:9–11

- *Where's God?* Another subject of much discussion about the Song of Solomon is the absence of God's name in the book.

- *How Could a Man with So Many Wives Write a Book About Love?* Was Solomon a hypocrite? He hardly qualifies as an expert on the advantages of monogamous love, considering the number of wives and concubines that shared his home. But most commentators agree that the explanation has to do with the timing—it was written before he acquired all those wives!

The Song of Solomon

Now, for a look at the book itself. The narrative of the Song of Solomon jumps around quite a bit; in places it puzzles even Bible scholars. Sometimes, for example, it's often difficult to figure out who's speaking, and to whom. And the sequence of events isn't easy to pin down. But here are the broad strokes of the story told in the eight chapters that make up the book a very smitten Solomon wrote in his younger days.

Love Struck

"Nothing Can Ruin Our Day!"

SONG OF SOLOMON 2:15 *Catch us the foxes, the little foxes that spoil the vines, for our vines have tender grapes.* (NKJV)

In the second chapter of the book, the Shulamite gives Solomon more glowing reviews, then she turns away from the chorus as she hears her lover approaching. He invites her to come outside with him to enjoy the beautiful spring day. This chapter makes it evident that the couple's connection is growing, that they long to be together, and that they are determined not to let anything spoil their relationship.

The phrase "little foxes" refers to the pesky animals that would creep into vineyards and destroy the roots of the plants. It's a metaphor for the little annoyances that can creep into and damage a relationship.

A wise couple sees the "little foxes"—such as the clichéd dispute over how to squeeze the toothpaste tube and spats caused by bothersome habits or disagreeable in-laws—for what they are. They make a deliberate decision *not* to let those minor issues inflate to cause bigger problems down the road.

What a Nightmare!

SONG OF SOLOMON 3:1–4 *By night on my bed I sought the one I love; I sought him, but I did not find him. "I will rise now," I said, "and go about the city; in the streets and in the squares I will seek the one I love." I sought him, but I did not find him. The watchmen who go about the city found me; I said, "Have you seen the one I love?" Scarcely had I passed by them, when I found the one I love. I held him and would not let him go, until I had brought him to the house of my mother, and into the chamber of her who conceived me. (NKJV)*

In this passage, the bride-to-be relates a nightmare she had the night before her wedding. In the dream, she was searching for her lover, who was missing. After a frantic search through the city, she is relieved to finally find him. She then takes him to her mother's house, as if to make sure he would not slip away from her again.

Here Comes the Groom

SONG OF SOLOMON 3:6–11 *Who is this coming out of the wilderness like pillars of smoke, perfumed with myrrh and frankincense, with all the merchant's fragrant powders? Behold, it is Solomon's couch, with sixty valiant men around it, of the valiant of Israel. They all hold swords, being expert in war. Every man has his sword on his thigh because of fear in the night. Of the wood of Lebanon Solomon the King made himself a palanquin: He made its pillars of silver, its support of gold, its seat of purple, its interior paved with love by the daughters of Jerusalem. Go forth, O daughters of Zion, and see King Solomon with the crown with which his mother crowned him on the day of his wedding, the day of the gladness of his heart. (NKJV)*

After waking from the dream and advising the young "daughters of Jerusalem" to be patient in matters of love, the bride-to-be is thrilled to see her fiancé, whom she now understands is King Solomon, approaching in all his royal majesty to take her to the wedding.

He Can't Stop Talking About Her!

The fourth chapter of the Song of Solomon—with the exception of the very last verse—expresses more of the king's adoration of and desire for his bride. He describes her appeal with vivid imagery from nature, raving about her beautiful hair, her white teeth, and her fine figure, until she invites him to consummate their marriage.

Descriptions of physical beauty that are odd to modern readers appear throughout the entire Song of Solomon, but chapter 4 features an especially concentrated and colorful collection. Here's a sampling of the strange phrases, with explanations that might help readers better understand why the Shulamite woman would have considered them compliments rather than very creative insults.

What He Said and What She Heard

Solomon Describes	He Compares Her Features To	She Hears
Her eyes	Doves	Her eyes are soft and gentle and reflect purity of soul.
Her hair	A flock of goats	Her (black) hair is long and flowing, like the appearance of a flock of goats on a mountainside.
Her teeth	Newly shorn sheep, each with a twin	Her teeth are white and none of them are missing.
Her lips	Red thread, or ribbon	Her lips are appealing and well-formed.
Her "temples"	Pomegranates	Her complexion is beautifully colored and healthy-looking.
Her neck	Tower of David	Her neck is long and beautiful, possibly because it is encircled by many rows of beads in keeping with the Egyptian style of fashion.
Her breasts	Two fawns grazing	She has a nice figure.

SONG OF SOLOMON 5:1 *I have come to my garden, my sister, my spouse; I have gathered my myrrh with my spice; I have eaten my honeycomb with my honey; I have drunk my wine with my milk. (NKJV)*

Solomon doesn't hesistate to accept the invitation his new wife has just extended at the end of chapter 4. He gladly enters "the garden," then afterward describes the rapturous experience the two enjoyed on their wedding night. Someone—possibly the chorus or, as some scholars speculate, even God Himself—blesses the union with the words: "Eat, O friends! Drink, yes, drink deeply, O beloved ones" (5:1 NKJV).

what others say

Jill Savage

I love how the Bible often uses the analogy of nature to describe sexual intimacy. Sometimes we see a garden analogy; another time it is water or a flowing stream; often the analogy is of fruit. All of these metaphors for sexual intimacy describe an environment of refreshment. A garden is a place of sensual, fragrant delights. A flowing stream is fresh, cool, sparkling water. Fruit is a sweet, refreshing taste experience.[12]

Another Bad Dream

the big picture

Song of Solomon 5:2–8

The Shulamite has another dream. This time, she refuses to let her husband into her bedroom, then regrets her decision and changes her mind only to find that he has disappeared. While conducting a feverish search, the watchmen find her and mistake her for a criminal because she is a single woman roaming around at night. Desperately, she turns to the chorus and asks them to remind Solomon that she still loves him very much.

Most commentators agree that the Shulamite's rejection of Solomon's sexual advances describes the indifference that can plague a marriage once the honeymoon is over. The "headaches" that can prevent a couple from nurturing physical closeness can spring from many factors, including:

- Taking a husband or wife for granted
- Having a "me-first" attitude
- Not having time for each other
- Being tired or (really!) having a headache

what others say

Alistair Begg

It is all too easy to neglect to provide genuine expressions of gratitude because we have come to believe that our spouse is just doing what is expected and it is not deserving of special mention.[13]

SONG OF SOLOMON 5:9–16 *What is your beloved more than another beloved, O fairest among women? What is your beloved more than another beloved, that you so charge us? My beloved is white and ruddy, chief among ten thousand. His head is like the finest gold; his locks are wavy, and black as a raven. His eyes are like doves by the rivers of waters, washed with milk, and fitly set. His cheeks are like a bed of spices, banks of scented herbs. His lips are lilies, dripping liquid myrrh. His hands are rods of gold set with beryl. His body is carved ivory inlaid with sapphires. His legs are pillars of marble set on bases of fine gold. His counte-*

nance is like Lebanon, excellent as the cedars. His mouth is most sweet, yes, he is altogether lovely. This is my beloved, and this is my friend, O daughters of Jerusalem! (NKJV)

When the chorus asks the Shulamite what's so special about Solomon, she launches into another starry-eyed description of her husband. She concludes her honey-coated praise of him with what many find to be the sweetest, most intimate words in the song: "Yes, he is altogether lovely. This is my beloved, and this is my friend, O daughters of Jerusalem!"

Just as a deep and growing friendship is a vital part of a thriving marriage, it is also a vital part of a flourishing relationship with Christ. "I have called you friends" (John 15:15 NKJV), He tells His followers.

She Knew Where He Was All Along!

SONG OF SOLOMON 6:2–3 *My beloved has gone to his garden, to the beds of spices, to feed his flock in the gardens, and to gather lilies. I am my beloved's, and my beloved is mine. He feeds his flock among the lilies.* (NKJV)

At the beginning of chapter 6, the young women want to help the Shulamite find her lover. But now, the Shulamite realizes she doesn't need their help because she knows where he is: in his garden. This could mean that he was literally in the garden tending his plants—which makes perfect sense for a man such as Solomon who has many vineyards to care for. Or, the phrase "gone to his garden" (Song of Solomon 6:2 NKJV) could also suggest Solomon's taking care of other pressing responsibilities—after all, he is king of Israel! Surely he has lots of people to see, places to go, and things to do.

But whether he's really up to his elbows in fertilizer or busy with the affairs of the kingdom, these words speak of the Shulamite's confidence that the relationship is secure. In spite of her worries, she knows he hasn't betrayed her; he is just tending to other matters.

apply it

Marriages don't exist in a vacuum! Once the honeymoon is over, other obligations at work, with extended family, at church, and in the community are always vying for a couple's time. A spouse with a mature attitude understands and respects the balance his or her mate must try to achieve in order to keep all the proverbial plates spinning.

> **SONG OF SOLOMON 6:4–13** *O my love, you are as beautiful as Tirzah, lovely as Jerusalem, awesome as an army with banners! Turn your eyes away from me, for they have overcome me. Your hair is like a flock of goats going down from Gilead. Your teeth are like a flock of sheep which have come up from the washing; every one bears twins, and none is barren among them. Like a piece of pomegranate are your temples behind your veil. There are sixty queens and eighty concubines, and virgins without number. My dove, my perfect one, is the only one, the only one of her mother, the favorite of the one who bore her. The daughters saw her and called her blessed, the queens and the concubines, and they praised her. Who is she who looks forth as the morning, fair as the moon, clear as the sun, awesome as an army with banners? I went down to the garden of nuts to see the verdure of the valley, to see whether the vine had budded and the pomegranates had bloomed. Before I was even aware, my soul had made me as the chariots of my noble people. Return, return, O Shulamite; return, return, that we may look upon you!* (NKJV)

Soon, Solomon returns. Apparently absence has made his heart grow even fonder. He expresses more lavish praise—again using some of those compliments that can sound so strange to modern ears. Then he punctuates his song of admiration with a question expressing his awe of this woman: "Who is she who looks forth as the morning, fair as the moon, clear as the sun, awesome as an army with banners?" (6:10 NKJV).

Don't miss the picture! The king of Israel, the son of the mighty warrior, David, is as unnerved by his wife's beauty as he would be if he stood before a formidable army!

key point

"I Am His"

SONG OF SOLOMON 7:10 *I am my beloved's, and his desire is toward me.* (NKJV)

As the marriage matures, so do the boldness and intimacy of the images the couples use to describe each other. This short verse includes a rarely used Hebrew word for "desire" that clearly expresses sexual longing.

what others say

Jack S. Deere

This is a more emphatic way of stating possession. How much more could a husband belong to his wife than for him to desire only her? She had so grown in the security of his love that she could now say that his only desire was for her. She had become so taken by his love for her that here she did not even mention her possession of him.[16]

A Romantic Getaway

SONG OF SOLOMON 7:11–13 *Come, my beloved, let us go forth to the field; let us lodge in the villages. Let us get up early to the vineyards; let us see if the vine has budded, whether the grape blossoms are open, and the pomegranates are in bloom. There I will give you my love. The mandrakes give off a fragrance, and at our gates are pleasant fruits, all manner, new and old, which I have laid up for you, my beloved.* (NKJV)

Sometimes the concerns and stresses of day-to-day life can press in on a couple's relationship to the point that it's critical to do as the Shulamite suggested and get away for the weekend. She longs to enjoy a change of scenery and have some time alone with her husband.

what others say

Larry and Thelnita Fincher

One piece of advice we have consistently given couples over thirty years of family ministry is to plan a night away as husband and wife at least once a year. This time is critical to keeping a focus on the marriage relationship. While this is an investment of a very scarce commodity, our time, it is an investment that pays huge dividends.[17]

Sealed and Secure

The final chapter of Solomon's song, chapter 8, begins with the bride saying she would like to enjoy even greater intimacy with her husband. She wishes she could experience the freedom to show affection in public that society then allowed sisters and brothers, but not husbands and wives. She then asks her husband to "set me as a seal upon your heart" (8:6 NKJV), indicating that she wants the king to understand her complete commitment to him alone.

what others say

Jack S. Deere

In Old Testament times a seal was used to indicate ownership of a person's valued possessions. So the beloved asked to be her lover's most valued possession, a possession that would influence his thoughts and his actions.[18]

Solomon Wrote the Book on Love and Marriage

This overview has just "hit the high spots" of the Song of Solomon, but the book—in its entirety—is a must-read for married couples, engaged couples, or even young people who anticipate being married one day. In a world inundated with skewed ideas about marriage and sex, it offers a fresh glimpse into God's intentions concerning those subjects. Here are just a few of the most important points contemporary readers can glean from this ancient poem:

1. *Just say "No" to premarital sex.* Notice that the rapture of Solomon and his bride's physical union wasn't experienced until *after* they were married. The bride herself even cautioned her attendants—twice—to guard their viriginity until they, too, were married (see 2:7; 3:5). Further, Solomon made it no secret that he admired rather than scorned her premarital purity, which he tactfully described in Song of Solomon 4:12 as "a garden enclosed," "a spring shut up," and "a fountain sealed" (NKJV).

what others say

Alistair Begg

Perhaps nowhere has society's thinking changed more drasti-cally than in regard to sex outside of marriage. Once clearly regarded by the majority as wrong, now only about one-third of the population thinks so. . . . But if we are to uphold the Maker's instructions, we have no other alternative open to us. The ever increasing percentages of failed marriages should indicate that secular society's approach to marriage with its lack of absolutes is not working.[19]

2. *Just say "Yes" to sex within marriage.* The Song of Solomon makes it clear that sex isn't to be limited to the process of pro-creation. God designed it to also provide married partners with mutual pleasure and unmatched intimacy. The book also strongly suggests that withholding sex from a marriage partner isn't a great idea.

what others say

Kathy Collard Miller and D. Larry Miller

Although no couple will have a mutual desire to make love every time one of them suggests it, they both need to be sen-sitive to the other's needs and make every effort to cooperate.[20]

3. *Marriage isn't always a bed of roses.* Solomon and his bride faced trials—from everyday annoyances to insecurity—just like any married couple today faces challenges. Growth and deep-ening intimacy often spring from overcoming those trials together.

4. *The foundation of a sturdy marriage is <u>commitment</u>.*

what others say

Dennis Rainey

Marriage is not some kind of social contract—something you just "do" for as long as you both shall "love." Marriage is a sacred covenant between one man and one woman and their God for a lifetime. It is a public vow of how you will relate to your spouse as you form a new family unit.[21]

The Ultimate Romance

The Song of Solomon offers a captivating, yet realistic, look at the story of a long-ago romance. As mentioned near the beginning of this chapter, it's also a fitting portrayal of the ultimate love story: the one between God and His people.

what others say

Ray Bentley

From Genesis to Revelation, we can hear the story, resounding through the ages, of the Shepherd who came down from the mountain heights of glory into the lives of those who yearn for love. There He fell in love with His beloved, His own creation, and sought to win her love, this bride who so often has thought herself unworthy. Falling in love with the Shepherd, we discover Him to be the King of kings and Lord of lords, who gave His life for us, desiring to fill us with love and joy, and prepared to carry us into eternity. This is the ultimate romance![22]

Chapter Wrap-Up

- Solomon probably wrote the Song of Solomon as a young man, before he took multiple wives, to describe the unfolding of the love story between him and an unnamed Shulamite woman.

- The love story can be interpreted literally as a description of physical, emotional, and spiritual principles of relationships and marriage; as an illustration of God's love for His people; and as a picture of the relationship between Christ and the church.

- The book includes frank descriptions of the couple's passion, revealing God's plan for the physical aspect of married love to be pleasurable for both spouses.

- The drama features an honest look not only at the romantic aspect of a love affair, but also at the everyday challenges married couples meet—from insecurities about time spent apart to petty annoyances that can sour a relationship.

- A highlight of the love story is the Shulamite's exclamation that her husband was her friend, capturing the closeness that marriage partners can enjoy and mirroring the closeness a believer can enjoy with Jesus Christ.

Study Questions

1. Who are the three main characters in the love story?

2. What are three ways to interpret the Song of Solomon?

3. How was the Shulamite different from the other women Solomon would eventually marry?

4. What features of the book have stirred up controversy through the years?

5. What are some practical tips the book offers for today's marriages?

6. What principles regarding marriage does the book support?

Proverbs:
A Word from the Wise

Chapter Highlights:
- Handbook for Life
- Wisdom
- Words
- Wealth
- Work

Let's Get Started

Shifting away now from the tranquil countryside where Solomon found his first love, it's time to return to the commotion of Israel's capital. There in Jerusalem, Solomon's thoughts have surely plummeted from the lofty, romantic places in the heart he described in his Song to land—possibly with a painful thud!—on more concrete matters. The kingdom is growing exponentially; tributes are pouring in from neighboring heads of state; tax monies are flowing into the nation's treasury; building projects are reconfiguring the landscape.

It's all basically good, but it's also all Solomon can do to stay on top of everything. Even though he's had plenty of sound advice from his father, plus the help of the nation's most skilled leaders and unlimited resources, he still realizes one important thing. He can't do it on his own. He needs help.

Maybe that's why Solomon takes off for a worship retreat to offer an extravagant number of <u>sacrifices</u> as a way of crying out to the Lord. And maybe that's why, when God approaches him with the open-ended invitation for Solomon to tell Him what he wants in 1 Kings 3:5, the king asks for the one thing he knows will help him the most. "Wisdom," he answers. The book of Proverbs puts into words the result of God's "yes" to that appeal.

sacrifices
1 Kings 3:4

Handbook for Life

Proverbs is a collection of concise sayings written by Solomon and others to offer practical advice about an array of life experiences.

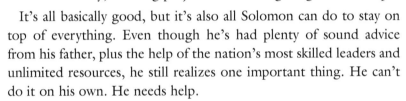

what others say

Halley's Bible Handbook

Solomon's fame was a sounding board that carried his voice to the ends of the earth, and made him an example to all the world of the wisdom of God's ideas.[1]

key point

The Proverbs were written during a period when many people from across the ancient Near East had become keenly interested in the topic of wisdom. What set the book of Proverbs apart from the wisdom writings produced by Egyptian sages and others was its spiritual dimension. Solomon and the other writers of Proverbs stressed the fundamental truth that "the fear of the LORD is the beginning of knowledge" (Proverbs 1:7 NKJV).

Because of its practical approach, Proverbs has remained popular reading for believers and nonbelievers alike throughout the centuries. Its pages present a gold mine of timeless teachings. Its principles can guide people to success in areas from relationships and work ethics to money management and communication skills.

apply it

Despite its universal appeal, it's important not to approach the book of Proverbs as if it were a "Tips and Tricks for Wisdom and Success" article in the latest issue of a popular magazine. To ignore the book's spiritual element is to miss its main point: True wisdom cannot be achieved apart from a thriving relationship with the Lord.

Wisdom Literature in the Bible

In the Christian Bible (as opposed to the Jewish Bible), the books of the Old Testament are divided into five different sections. The book of Proverbs belongs in the poetry section.

Sections of the Bible

Type of Literature	Books Included	Theme
Pentateuch (the Law)	Genesis Exodus Leviticus Numbers Deuteronomy	Foundation of the Hebrew faith
History	Joshua Judges Ruth 1 & 2 Samuel 1 & 2 Kings 1 & 2 Chronicles Ezra Nehemiah Esther	Israel's spiritual growth and decline
Poetry	Job Psalms Proverbs Ecclesiastes Song of Solomon	The worship of the Lord and individual faith
Major & Minor Prophets	Isaiah Jeremiah Lamentations Ezekiel Daniel Hosea Joel Amos Obadiah Jonah Micah Nahum Habakkuk Zephaniah Haggai Zechariah Malachi	God's revelation of His blessings, judgments, and promises through the prophets

The Basics

These are the fundamental things you need to know about the book of Proverbs:

Agur and Lemuel
contributors, along
with Solomon, to
the book of
Proverbs

- *Who Wrote It*—Credit for writing most of the Proverbs goes to Solomon, but two other little-known people—men named **Agur and Lemuel**—also contributed sections to the book.

- *When It Was Written*—Solomon probably penned his portion some time between 970 and 930 BC. As mentioned earlier, this was probably when he was still a young man, but after he had married the Shulamite and the Egyptian princess. Other proverbs continued to be added to the collection many years after Solomon died.

- *What It Means*—The word *proverbs* is translated from the Hebrew word *masal*, which has several meanings:

  - To be like or to be compared with

  - An object lesson

  - A prophecy

  - A parable

  - An allegory

  Certainly each saying in the book of Proverbs embodies one or more of those definitions.

- *How It's Organized*—To be a book about wisdom, Proverbs sure doesn't seem to employ a very "wise" system of organization! The sayings aren't in any way arranged according to topic. For example, the thirty-plus maxims about working hard don't appear in the same chapter; they are scattered throughout nineteen of the book's thirty-one chapters.

what others say

Gleason L. Archer

They are not grouped according to a comprehensive plan, except for certain sections which contain a series linked together by common characters or analogies.[5]

key point

Because of the way it's organized (rather, because of the way it's *not*), anyone looking for information about a specific topic—such as parenting or money—in the book of Proverbs should have a good concordance on hand!

Even though the subject matter isn't orderly, the book does follow a straightforward outline, as shown in the table below.

How the Book of Proverbs Is Organized

Example	Function
Proverbs 1:1–7	Statement of purpose
Proverbs 1:8–9:18	Solomon's fifteen lessons on wisdom
Proverbs 10:1–22:16	Solomon's 375 wise sayings
Proverbs 22:17–24:34	Sayings of the wise men
Proverbs 25–29	Proverbs of Solomon collected by Hezekiah's men
Proverbs 30:1–31:9	Wisdom of Agur and Lemuel
Proverbs 31:10–31	Acrostic poem describing an excellent wife

- *How It's Written*—In Hebrew poetry, words don't always rhyme but ideas do. This pairing of ideas is called parallelism. Four kinds of parallelism appear in the book of Proverbs. The words may seem complicated, but their meanings are really quite simple.

Four Kinds of Parallelism in the Book of Proverbs

Type	Description	Example
Synonymous	The words or thoughts in line 1 *parallel* the words or thoughts in line 2.	"A foolish son is a grief to his father; and bitterness to her who bore him" (Proverbs 17:25 NKJV).
Antithetical	The words or thoughts in line 1 *contrast* the words or thoughts in line 2.	"A wise son makes a glad father, but a foolish son is the grief of his mother" (Proverbs 10:1 NKJV).
Emblematic	The words or thoughts in line 1 *amplify* the words or thoughts in line 2 with a simile or metaphor.	"Like an earring of gold and an ornament of fine gold is a wise rebuke to an obedient ear" (Proverbs 25:12 NKJV).
Synthetic	The words or thoughts of line 1 are *continued or developed* in line 2. Many of these are signaled by the words "Better than."	"Better is a dry morsel with quietness, than a house full of feasting with strife" (Proverbs 17:1 NKJV).

Not only is the poetry of Proverbs mechanically tight, but its language and imagery are descriptive and vibrant.

Reading Proverbs

Because it has thirty-one chapters, an excellent way to study the book of Proverbs is by reading a chapter a day (and two on one day of the months with fewer days). Some people even make it a practice to go through the book of Proverbs several times a year. Many say this simple habit dramatically affects every aspect of their lives. That shouldn't come as a surprise, considering that Proverbs, like the rest of God's Word, is "living and powerful" (Hebrews 4:12 NKJV).

There's not enough space here to explore Proverbs verse by verse and chapter by chapter. So it might be most helpful to take a brief look at what Solomon and the other writers had to say about a short list of topics covered in the book of Proverbs.

What Solomon (and Others) Had to Say About...Wisdom

The most prominent subject in the book of Proverbs is wisdom. Solomon and the other writers described wisdom in great detail. They noted what it looks like, what it's based on, how to get it, how to use it, and what happens to those who put it into practice.

1. *What does it look like?* Picture wisdom as a person. That's what Solomon did in Proverbs 1:20–33 and in chapters 8 and 9. He described wisdom as a woman calling out to people and inviting them to follow her. She gives her gift of wisdom to those who accept the offer, but she laughs at the disastrous results that fall on those who refuse her.

No one is "wise" or "foolish" according to the whims of God or a circumstance of genetics. This woman named "Wisdom" makes it clear that she is available to *every* individual, but that it's up to each person to decide whether or not to follow her.

2. *What is it based on?* As mentioned earlier in this chapter, the foundation of wisdom is the fear of God. There is no wisdom apart from God, and He alone is its source: "For the LORD gives wisdom; from His mouth come knowledge and understanding" (Proverbs 2:6 NKJV).

3. *How do I get it?* Reading textbooks and attending lectures might make a person *educated*, but those activities won't make a person *wise*. The only way to obtain true wisdom is to say "yes" to God's invitation to take it.

wisdom
Luke 2:52;
Colossians 2:3;
Revelation 5:12

ask
James 1:5–6

Holy Spirit
1 Corinthians
2:11–12; 6:19;
John 14:26

what others say

Billy Graham

I believe we ought to get all the education we can, but we dare not make it our god. John Dewey once defined education as the systematic, purposeful reconstruction of experience; but so much of modern education leaves out God. . . . We need education, but not just for the mind and the body; we also need education for the spirit.[6]

We accept Wisdom's invitation in a number of ways, beginning with a vital prerequisite: a personal relationship with Jesus Christ. The Bible states that Jesus not ony has wisdom; He is <u>wisdom</u> itself. Unless we have a relationship with Him, the door to His wisdom remains locked. But having a relationship with Christ unlocks that door.

Once that happens we can freely step inside and, like Solomon, we can <u>ask</u> for it with the confidence of knowing that we will receive our request. A relationship with Christ also brings the <u>Holy Spirit</u> into our lives. The Holy Spirit gives us a supernatural ability to understand the spiritual dimension of the issues we face. And the Holy Spirit also lends us the insight we need to interpret and understand God's "encyclopedia of wisdom"—the Holy Bible.

what others say

John MacArthur

The holy scriptures, of course, if you really look at it from cover to cover, contain everything a person needs to know to live life according to the will of God. Now it may not tell you how to build a cabinet, it may not tell you all the little ins and outs and techniques of child rearing and so forth. But what it does do is produce principles and generates proper attitudes out of which all kinds of wisdom and application can flow. . . . I think the first thing to do in pursuing wisdom is study the Bible.[7]

Acquiring wisdom and applying it can be two very different things. It takes a tremendous amount of self-discipline to put wisdom into practice. Solomon's life is a perfect example of that. The fact that he fell into a destructive pattern of disobedience doesn't raise a question about whether he really had wisdom to begin with; we know he did because the Bible says it, and we see evidence of his wisdom throughout his biography. His disobedience simply suggests that he didn't always apply his wisdom as he should.

Those who obtain and apply wisdom receive many blessings—even beyond the obvious benefits of having the wisdom itself. Just a small sampling of those "extra-added" blessings includes a better relationship with God (Proverbs 2:5), protection (Proverbs 2:7–8; 3:23–26), favor with God and man (Proverbs 3:4), guidance (Proverbs 3:6), provision (Proverbs 3:9–10), contentment (Proverbs 3:13–15; 8:11), ever-increasing wisdom (Proverbs 9:9), and long life (Proverbs 9:11).

what others say

Woodrow Kroll

Don't lose that tandem—wisdom and discipline. I think what happened in Solomon's life was that he attained the wisdom; he just did not exercise the discipline.[8]

What Solomon (and Others) Had to Say About...Words

Today, words fly through cyberspace, soar along the airwaves, and pulse through cables by the billions. They're spoken and retracted, typed out and edited, printed out and thrown away. But in the tenth century BC, the spoken and written word carried much more weight and permanence. With no means of recording words apart from the trained, careful hand of the scribes, ancient Isrealites couldn't afford to treat words carelessly or casually. They treasured words—especially God's words—as if they were money. For example, when the prophet Samuel was just a boy listening to the Lord, the Bible states that he "let none of [God's] words fall to the ground"

(1 Samuel 3:19 NKJV). It's as if God's words were "pennies from heaven" that Samuel could treasure!

Because words were so important, and because they still are—even though they may seem more disposable than ever—the Lord saw fit to use Solomon and the other writers to return to the topic of the power of words again and again throughout the book of Proverbs. By one count, at least ninety proverbs address words, speaking, and speech. Many of these proverbs support at least two key points:

1. *Words prove a person's wisdom (or foolishness).* People demonstrate the wisdom they receive from God in many ways. For example, their wisdom shows in the decisions they make and in the way they treat people. One of the best indicators of a person's wisdom—or lack of it—is his or her use of words. In Proverbs 23:16, a father tells his son that he can gauge his son's wisdom by listening to his son talk: "Yes, my inmost being will rejoice when your lips speak right things" (NKJV). A wise person can be recognized by using words with restraint (Proverbs 10:19; 21:23; 29:20), gentleness (Proverbs 15:10), and kindness (Proverbs 15:26; 16:21, 23–24; 22:11). And a foolish person can be spotted from a mile away: He or she talks too much (Proverbs 10:19 and 13:3), answers too quickly (Proverbs 18:13), spreads gossip (Proverbs 17:9), breaks confidences (Proverbs 11:13), and is quarrelsome (Proverbs 20:3; 26:17).

2. *Words are the power tools of communication.* The book of Proverbs uses strong language to describe the power of words. For example, the tongue has power over life and death (Proverbs 18:21) and the potential to either build a person up or tear a person down. A person who doesn't use words carefully can experience—and cause—harm (Proverbs 12:18; 13:3).

Just as a person using heavy-duty power tools can ensure safety and success by following the directions for safe operation, we can protect the safety of those we're talking to and enjoy successful communication when we follow the "speech manual" God provides us in the book of Proverbs.

Steven K. Scott

Why was the wisest and richest man who ever lived so insistent that we guard our mouth and be "slow to speak"? I believe it's because as king he sat in the company of many who pretended to be wise, but whose words exposed them as fools. I'm sure he witnessed many who were quick to speak, and spoke foolishly.[9]

Billy Graham

The problems of the world could be solved overnight if men could get victory over their tongues. Suppose there was no anger, no profanity, no lying, no grumbling, or complaining; suppose there were no dirty stories told, no unjust criticism—what a different wold this would be! . . . If we would always think before we speak, there would be much less evil speaking, and there would soon be a spiritual awakening that would sweep the church in America.[10]

What Solomon (and Others) Had to Say About...Wealth

As discussed throughout this book, Solomon was no stranger to affluence. If the wise king were alive today, he would probably make the Fortune 500 Club on a routine basis!

Wilfred J. Hahn

In 1 Kings 10:14–15 we read, "The weight of the gold that Solomon received yearly was 666 talents, not including the revenues from merchants and traders and from all the Arabian kings and the governors of the land." This surely was a large income. Based upon recent gold prices, this would amount to an annual income of about one-half billion in US dollar terms. Based upon the average income of that time, King Solomon would have earned an income equivalent to about 200,000 laborers. In those terms, his annual income would be closer to an equivalent of $8 to $10 billion per year. As the Bible confirms, no other king was as rich as he was during that time.[11]

Because he was able to see his wealth through the lens of his great wisdom, Solomon was well aware of the pitfalls opened up by riches:

disappear
Luke 12:15;
Colossians 3:2

1. **Wealth is fleeting.** Proverbs 23:4–5 says that people shouldn't wear themselves out trying to get rich because riches are temporary and can only provide benefits this side of eternity: "For riches are not forever, nor does a crown endure to all generations" (Proverbs 27:24 NKJV). Chasing after wealth should not become a person's number one priority. If it is, as many can attest, the consequences can ripple out to affect one's home life and family: "He who is greedy for gain troubles his own house" (Proverbs 15:27 NKJV). Further, putting "money grabbing" at the top of one's to-do list usually backfires, bringing poverty rather than prosperity: "A man with an evil eye hastens after riches, and does not consider that poverty will come upon him" (Proverbs 28:22 NKJV).

2. **Wealth can give way to greed.** The Lord makes it clear that His people should show generosity to those in need. Solomon warns that chasing after riches easily gives way to greed, which is the opposite of generosity. Greed can spiritually and even physically drain the life out of a person (Proverbs 1:19).

what others say

Steven K. Scott

Solomon used two Hebrew words to describe greed. One means "to deeply yearn or long for something"; the other implies wanting something so badly that you are willing to violate the rights of others to get it. Combining these two words gives us a fuller picture of what Solomon means. Greed is a deep longing for something that creates a willingness to do whatever it takes to acquire it. In other words, greed is not defined by *what* you want, but rather by *how badly* you want it.[12]

True wealth, Solomon said—possibly even as he was running his finger across the glimmering gold surface that overlaid the walls of his palace—isn't money, or gold, or silver. It's righteousness. Even valuables that are socked away in state-of-the-art vaults, and assets deposited in the safest investment accounts, can <u>disappear</u> in a heartbeat. But righteousness carries eternal value: "Riches do not profit in the day of wrath, but righteousness delivers from death" (Proverbs 11:4 NKJV).

There's no guarantee of happiness or prosperity to those who are righteous, but Proverbs points out that those who apply wisdom to their financial situation will likely enjoy certain blessings, whether material or otherwise:

something to ponder

- "The hand of the diligent makes rich" (Proverbs 10:4 NKJV).
- "The righteous will flourish like foliage" (Proverbs 11:28 NKJV).
- "In all labor there is profit" (Proverbs 14:23 NKJV).
- "By humility and the fear of the LORD are riches and honor and life" (Proverbs 22:4 NKJV).
- "A faithful man will abound with blessings" (Proverbs 28:20 NKJV).

What Solomon (and Others) Had to Say About...Work

Solomon was a king in the most magnificent sense of the word. But even given his luxurious lifestyle afforded by his wealth and position, he didn't laze around his throne and eat grapes all day. Among the many titles that could be stamped on his business card, if such things had existed during Solomon's day, were "diplomat," "architect," "judge," "scientist," "musician," "author," and "businessman." His daily grind involved recruiting supervisors; making decisions about his staff's pay and benefits; managing building projects; budgeting and tracking expenses; overseeing logistics; and administering the nation's finances. So when Solomon wrote about work it's safe to assume that he spoke from experience. Proverbs concerning work emphasize:

1. The value of work. Diligence—working hard and working consistently—ensures that a person will be able to enjoy the necessities of life such as food and shelter. The vocabulary included in verses addressing this topic include words such as "plenty" (Proverbs 28:19 NKJV) and "satisfied" (Proverbs 12:11, 14 NKJV), indicating that those who work hard will

always have more than enough. On the other hand, those who are lazy place their own well-being—and that of their families—at risk. Poverty is a certain outcome of laziness:

2. "How long will you slumber, O sluggard? When will you rise from your sleep? A little sleep, a little slumber, a little folding of the hands to sleep—so shall your poverty come on you like a prowler, and your need like an armed man" (Proverbs 6:9–11 NKJV).

3. "The soul of a lazy man desires, and has nothing" (Proverbs 13:4 NKJV).

4. "The lazy man will not plow because of winter; he will beg during harvest and have nothing" (Proverbs 20:4 NKJV).

5. The importance of planning ahead. Had Solomon not been a man of foresight, how different his biography might have turned out! Planning ahead was essential to every facet of his accomplishments—from his political maneuverings to his scientific research and construction projects. Planning ahead for any endeavor is a step that's often the easiest to skip; but failing to do so can only ensure failure. "He who gathers in summer is a wise son; he who sleeps in harvest is a son who causes shame" (Proverbs 10:5 NKJV).

key point

It's Just the Beginning

Having a relationship with Christ and fearing Him, or recognizing Him for who He is, allows access to His wisdom. But having access doesn't mean obtaining a lifetime supply all at once; in fact, it's just the "beginning," according to Proverbs 1:7. Once we step through the "door" the woman named "Wisdom" beckons us through, we can spend the rest of our lives soaking up her infinite supply. Even if memorizing the entire book of Proverbs could never reveal all of God's wisdom!

Chapter Wrap-Up

- The book of Proverbs proves Solomon's divine gift of tremendous wisdom—and records it for the benefit of others, offering practical advice about an array of life experiences through concise sayings.

- Distinguishing Proverbs from other wisdom literature of the day is its fundamental truth that the fear of God is the starting point for obtaining wisdom.

- The Proverbs state that wisdom is available to everyone but that no one can receive it apart from fearing the Lord. Further, one can receive wisdom without applying it. Having the self-discipline to put wisdom into practice is a believer's most rewarding challenge.

- The power of words is stressed throughout the Proverbs; words reveal a person's wisdom and serve as power tools of communication. Used carefully they can build up and bring healing; used carelessly or maliciously they can destroy.

- Because he was able to see his wealth through the lens of his great wisdom, Solomon was able to see the pitfalls of riches. It is temporary, it can give way to greed, and it offers nothing of eternal value.

- Many Proverbs stress the value of work and the importance of planning ahead.

- Wisdom is a perpetually renewable resource: No matter how much a person obtains, he or she can always obtain more.

Study Questions

1. What set the book of Proverbs apart from other wisdom literature?

2. According to Solomon and the other writers of Proverbs, what is the key to obtaining wisdom?

3. What characteristic of the Proverbs have made it a time-tested, often-used "guidebook for living" by Christians and non-Christians alike?

4. What's one of the biggest challenges in handling the gift of wisdom?

5. What is one way to tell whether a person has wisdom?

6. Why isn't obtaining riches a wise or worthy goal?

7. What are some principles the Proverbs communicate regarding work?

Ecclesiastes: The Search for Satisfaction

Let's Get Started

Hindsight is 20–20—especially when you're the wisest man in the world. During the last days of his life, Solomon had the chance to look back over the years and try to make some kind of sense of it all by processing it through his great wisdom. The result was the book of Ecclesiastes, his final work of literature that's included in the Bible. It contains twelve chapters of the philosopher's musings on the meaning of life, and features some of the most well-known phrases and passages in Scripture.

Ten of the Best-Known Expressions from Ecclesiastes

1. "Vanity of vanities, all is vanity" (1:2 NKJV).

2. "There is nothing new under the sun" (1:9 NKJV).

3. "All the rivers run into the sea, yet the sea is not full" (1:7 NKJV).

4. "To everything there is a season, a time for every purpose under heaven" (3:1 NKJV).

5. "Two are better than one" (4:9 NKJV).

6. "A man has nothing better under the sun than to eat, drink, and be merry" (8:15 NKJV).

7. "Whatever your hand finds to do, do it with your might" (9:10 NKJV).

8. "Cast your bread upon the waters" (11:1 NKJV).

9. "Remember now your Creator in the days of your youth" (12:1 NKJV).

10. "Fear God and keep His commandments, for this is man's all" (12:13 NKJV).

Who's the Writer?

ECCLESIASTES 1:1 *The words of the Preacher, the son of David, king in Jerusalem. (NKJV)*

Solomon. Throughout his biography, readers have seen this man fulfill many roles, from king and judge to manager and architect. But … "preacher"? Does that title really refer to the man who is the subject of this *Smart Guide to the Bible*?

As a matter of fact, many Bible scholars have disputed the authorship of the book of Ecclesiastes. They claim that certain cues in the language suggest it might have been written much later than during Solomon's lifetime.

But strong evidence within the book, pointing directly to Solomon, leads many other Bible researchers to conclude that he was in fact a "preacher" among all his other positions. The book lists traits of an author that fit Solomon to a T. The writer:

- Was the son of David (1:1)
- Served as king in Jerusalem (1:12)
- Had unmatched wisdom (1:16)
- Undertook extensive building projects (2:4–6)
- Knew much about the natural world (2:4–7)
- Maintained large numbers of servants (2:7)
- Enjoyed great wealth (2:8)
- Wrote many proverbs (12:9)

something to ponder

The Hebrew word translated "preacher" is *Qohelet*, which also means "one who addresses an assembly" or "teacher." Those definitions might draw a more acccurate picture of Solomon, a man of great wisdom and influence who conducted an end-of-life research project of sorts, and was compelled to share his findings with a group of scholars or students.

Was His Cup Half Empty or Half Full?

Depending on whose comments you're reading, when Solomon wrote the book of Ecclesiastes he was either a cynical, despairing man who had strayed from his faith or a wanderer who had returned to his faith and embraced a realistically optimistic view of life on earth. Or as he puts it, of life "under the sun."

KJV Study Bible for Women

Some describe the contents of the book as pessimistic, cynical, skeptical, hedonistic, or agnostic and picture the author as a man of doubt who has wandered far from God. On the other hand, many interpret the book quite positively: the author is a man of faith, a realist, who sees that man simply cannot put the whole of life together. The latter view is favored since the author believes God is good (2:24; 3:13); believes God has a wise plan (3:11, 14; 7:14; 8:17); believes God is just (3:17; 8:11–13); and always exhorts men to fear God (8:12, 13; 12:13,14).[2]

Revolve: Psalms & Proverbs

The book of Ecclesiastes gets a bad rap as a downer because it ditches the superficial and offers these two essentials for living: Fear God and enjoy every day as a gift from him. Then evaluate each thing in life—like money, power, success, adventure, and knowledge—against what is really important. Anything that doesn't measure up is out. It's not worth building your reason for being on.[3]

The rest of this chapter will hit some of the high spots, if they can be called that, in the book of Ecclesiastes, with a closer look at the first and last chapters as well as a few key passages in between. But it's important to remember that to gain the most benefits from Solomon's "hindsight insight," it's essential to read the entire book while prayerfully considering how his observations translate to life—to your life—today.

apply it

Vanity: It's Not the Bathroom Sink

ECCLESIASTES 1:2 *"Vanity of vanities," says the Preacher; "Vanity of vanities, all is vanity."* (NKJV)

go to

vanity
Isaiah 5:18;
Hosea 12:11

vanity
meaningless, empty

The word *vanity* is used in a few other places in the Old Testament, but it appears a whopping twenty-nine times in the New King James Version of the book of Ecclesiastes alone. That makes it a "key word" in the book, and because Solomon saw fit to use it so many times, it's well worth looking at more closely.

The word is translated from the Hebrew *hebel*, which means "breath," or "vapor." Picture the way the foggy vapor of a person's warm, moist breath vanishes from the air on an icy winter morning. On the other hand, perhaps the most accurate way to describe it today is with terms such as "empty," "useless," "meaningless," or "fleeting."

Remember how the title of the "Song of Songs" was called that as a way of indicating its superiority? The same idea is behind the phrase "vanity of vanities." It's a way of referring to the epitome of emptiness or uselessness; if something is a "vanity of vanities," it's "utterly meaningless."

Round and Round

the big picture

Ecclesiastes 1:3–11

Solomon describes the endless cycles of God's creation, from the birth and death of generations of people to the perpetual rhythms of nature. This emphasizes his point that "there is nothing new under the sun" (1:9 NKJV) and pounds a drumbeat of monotony and futility.

key point

The first verse of this passage—Ecclesiastes 1:3—includes the first instance of another often-used phrase (twenty-seven times, to be exact) in the book of Ecclesiastes—"under the sun." This sets up a contrast Solomon will stick with throughout the rest of the book. This contrast weighs events and motives that take place "under the sun"—or on earth during the physical, material experience of living—against the divine agenda carried out on the other side of the sun, in the heavenly realm.

Researcher Extraordinaire

pleasure
Proverbs 21:17;
2 Thessalonians
2:12;
1 Timothy 5:6;
2 Timothy 3:4;
James 4:1; 5:5

the big picture

Ecclesiastes 1:12–18

In Ecclesiastes 1:12–18 the king:
- Identifies himself—"the Preacher . . . king over Israel in Jerusalem" (1:12 NKJV).
- Describes his mission—"I set my heart to seek and search out by wisdom concerning all that is done under heaven" (1:13 NKJV).
- Cites his credentials—"I have attained greatness, and have gained more wisdom than all who were before me in Jerusalem. My heart has understood great wisdom and knowledge" (1:16 NKJV).

It's as if Solomon wanted to make sure his listeners understood that of all the people on the earth, *he* was best qualified to conduct this research project. If that project had a title, it might be called "So What?" because that seems to be what Solomon set out to discover about all the activities people carry out.

what others say

Lawrence Boadt

The author undertakes the investigation of experience at all levels, and asks questions about creation, justice, the wise versus the fool, just and unjust, and even quotes a large number of proverbs that he actually thinks will work in life.[4]

The Pleasure Principle

the big picture

Ecclesiastes 2:1–11

Ecclesiastes 2:1–11 summarizes Solomon's determination to find the meaning of life by seeking <u>pleasure</u>. He details the kinds of things he did to pursue that end. Even though his hedonism offered some temporary benefits, he concludes that pleasure-seeking wasn't a worthwhile endeavor; it "all was vanity and grasping for the wind" (v. 11 NKJV).

Consider the details this passage reveals about the high life Solomon lived:

death
Psalms 48:14; 56:13;
89:48;
Romans 5:14; 6:23;
1 Corinthians 15:26;
Revelation 1:18

apply it

- He took a headlong dive into laughter and merriment (Ecclesiastes 2:1–2).

- He overindulged in drinking (Ecclesiastes 2:3).

- He engaged in an over-the-top pursuit of the biggest, the best, and the most, whether it was homes, orchards, servants, or sheep (Ecclesiastes 2:4–8).

Truly, Solomon's was the original "lifestyle of the rich and famous," possibly comparing to the way some of the most famous sports and movie celebrities live today. Many of the ways Solomon sought meaning in life—by refusing to withhold from himself any desire or pleasure (Ecclesiastes 2:10) are the ways people seek meaning in life today. Consider the time and money spent today on such pleasures as entertainment, partying, and home improvements. Not too much has changed throughout the centuries since Solomon conducted his experiment! None of these things provided him with true satisfaction any more than they can provide a person with true satisfaction today.

what others say

Ray C. Stedman
Imagine how the palace must have rocked with laughter. Every night they had stand-up comics, and lavish feasts, with wine flowing like water. Harrah's Club was never like this![5]

Wisdom and Foolishness

In Ecclesiastes 2:12–26, Solomon observed that the wise man as well as the fool can expect the same fate: <u>death</u>. He also grieved over the fact that working hard only allows the fruit of one's labor to be enjoyed by someone else; and he expressed frustration that hard work doesn't offer much of a gratifying reward. He concluded that "nothing is better for a man than that he should eat and drink, and that his soul should enjoy good in his labor. . . . For God gives wisdom and knowledge and joy to a man who is good in His sight" (Ecclesiastes 2:24–26 NKJV).

Solomon's conclusion marks a change in the book's tone, and it's one that he ultimately repeats five additional times in the book: Ecclesiastes 3:12–13, 22; 5:18–19; 8:15; 9:7–9. He also revisits that comparison again: On the one hand (this side of the sun) there are

326 ———— **The Smart Guide to the Bible** ————

things to do, like work and obtaining wisdom, that aren't in and of themselves especially rewarding. In fact, they can be quite frustrating.

On the other hand (or the other side of the sun—and this is an important point), *adding God to the equation changes everything.* Carrying out earthly activities transforms from an exercise in frustration to an experience of joy.

Ray C. Stedman

Emptiness and vexation were Solomon's own experience when he tried to live it up without the missing element that it took to meet the hunger of his heart.[6]

A Time for Everything

ECCLESIASTES 3:1–8 *To everything there is a season, a time for every purpose under heaven: a time to be born, and a time to die; a time to plant, and a time to pluck what is planted; a time to kill, and a time to heal; a time to break down, and a time to build up; a time to weep, and a time to laugh; a time to mourn, and a time to dance; a time to cast away stones, and a time to gather stones; a time to embrace, and a time to refrain from embracing; a time to gain, and a time to lose; a time to keep, and a time to throw away; a time to tear, and a time to sew; a time to keep silence, and a time to speak; a time to love, and a time to hate; a time of war, and a time of peace. (NKJV)*

Robert Davidson

There are many people for whom the book of Ecclesiastes really means this passage. . . . Take a few moments to read it aloud. You will find yourself under its spell; the fascinating rhythm of its language, the finely balanced and contrasting experiences to which it points. It has been a passage for all seasons and all moods: from that of a young man trying to come to terms with a quickly broken marriage, to that of the girl bubling with enthusiasm as, for her, success and love walk hand in hand; from that of a woman silently mourning the loss of a life-long companion, to that of a mother joyfully greeting the birth of her first child.[7]

joy
Psalms 27:6; 30:5;
John 15:11;
Romans 14:17;
Galatians 5:22

This familiar passage brings to light two important principles:

1. *God has established a divine order for the activities of His creation.* From a human perspective, life can seem unpredictable, and many times doesn't make sense. But Ecclesiastes 3 reminds us that God is the Divine Designer who remains in control—even though things "this side of the sun" often seem to be leaning more toward chaos than order.

2. *We have a responsibility to operate within the appropriate boundaries set by this "divine design."* Ever known a person who seems to always say the right thing at the right time? Then there are others who inevitably say the *wrong* thing at the wrong time. Whether he or she realizes it or not, the person who says the right thing at the right time is demonstrating an understanding of his or her place at that moment in the grand scheme of God's design.

More Words About Work

ECCLESIASTES 4:4–6 *Again, I saw that for all toil and every skillful work a man is envied by his neighbor. This also is vanity and grasping for the wind. The fool folds his hands and consumes his own flesh. Better a handful with quietness than both hands full, together with toil and grasping for the wind.* (NKJV)

A Little Help from Friends

ECCLESIASTES 4:9–12 *Two are better than one, because they have a good reward for their labor. For if they fall, one will lift up his companion. But woe to him who is alone when he falls, for he has no one to help him up. Again, if two lie down together, they will keep warm; but how can one be warm alone? Though one may be overpowered by another, two can withstand him. And a threefold cord is not quickly broken.* (NKJV)

friendship
1 Samuel 18:1–4;
20:14–17;
Proverbs 17:17,
18:24; 27:10;
Luke 11:5–8

Family, friends, coworkers, neighbors . . . King Solomon offers a clear outline of the benefits of teaming up with others in <u>friendship</u> and cooperation. He notes that:

- ***Two people are twice as good (9)***—In fact, each half of a pair can exert half the effort yet enjoy twice the yield.

None of us, individually, have every gift God gives to those who are His followers (see 1 Corinthians 12). When we learn to partner with others and depend on them to complete our deficiencies, we can accomplish much!

- ***Safety in numbers (10)***—This statement takes on even more punch when considered in the context of when it was written. With today's round-the-clock emergency assistance as close as a 9-1-1 call away, it can be hard to fathom just how dangerous it was to live and travel during the time Solomon was alive. A person who "fell"—who experienced some kind of an emergency—often had to wait days for help unless he or she had a friend along. Today, a friend can offer a welcome hand up—whether it's a physical, spiritual, or emotional tumble.

- ***Warmth in togetherness (11)***—Nights in the Middle East can be very cold. Some solo travelers during Solomon's day even curled up against their donkeys to keep warm overnight! A much sweeter smelling scenario, however, found friends huddled up together to generate some much-needed body heat against the frigid desert air. Today, friendship can offer a warm blanket of love, help, security, and encouragement against the harsh challenges of life.

- ***Strength in numbers (12)***—Traveling in pairs was the best way to ensure safety against the elements, wild animals, and bandits. A traveling companion's extra set of eyes and ears helped detect danger approaching and a way to overpower an enemy in case of attack. Today, friends—especially close, spiritually discerning friends—can serve in a similar capacity. They often have the perspective that enables them to see danger ahead and warn of possible pitfalls and stumbling stones. And if we are "attacked" by trials and tribulations, a friend can often lend us the strength we need to fight back.

Was It Lonely at the Top?

"On the surface, it wouldn't appear so. After all, [Solomon] had a full staff of servants, an entourage of musicians and hundreds of wives to keep him company. He also, no doubt, had numerous business acquaintances and political buddies to pal around with. But . . . being surrounded by people doesn't preclude loneliness. . . . Perhaps Solomon's insight into the benefits of sharing the burdens of life with friends sprang from his longing for something he wished he had. We can almost hear the bitter ring of sarcasm in his words recorded in Proverbs 14:20: 'the rich has many friends' and Proverbs 19:4: 'wealth makes many friends' (NKJV)."[10]

Proper Worship

Solomon had gone from the highest of highs to the lowest of lows as far as his worship life was concerned. High points included his extravagant sacrifice before God visited him with the mind-boggling offer of his heart's desire and his moving prayer at the dedication of the temple. His lowest point found him erecting altars to the pagan gods worshipped by his foreign wives. This gave him an array of experiences from which to draw some significant conclusions about worship, which he details in Ecclesiastes 5:1–7.

Do's and Don'ts of Worship

DO:

- *Be reverent when going to worship.* (Had Solomon cringed as he watched some people who were irreverent as they entered the temple he had poured all his time and energy into building for the presence of the Lord?)

- *Worship for the right reasons* ("Obedience is better than sacrifice," Samuel had told Saul. However, did Solomon realize how profoundly the disobedience he demonstrated in his later years would affect his worship?)

DON'T:

- *Try to "bribe" God with conditional promises or try to win His favor with foolish chatter.* (Once he began to stray from a close relationship with the Lord, had he tried to talk his way out of hot water with God?)

- *Forget who He is.* (Solomon showed he had in fact forgotten who God was when he participated in worship of foreign gods.)

what others say

Robert Davidson

Worship is not like going to a concert and coming away inspired and uplifted by great music. You can do that and remain totally insensitive to what is going on around you: indeed you can be so uplifted that common everyday things and the needs of people around you seem trivial and unimportant. But worship must never be merely spiritual self-indulgence or the satisfying of our emotional needs. It must mean listening, opening ourselves to the obedience that God wants from each one of us. It must flow out into action.[12]

You Can't Take It with You!

In Ecclesiastes 5:8–6:2, Solomon summarizes his take on money matters. Key points he makes include:

- Money can't buy happiness or satisfaction.

- More peace and contentment come from putting in a good day's work than from the riches it provides.

- The value of money expires at death.

Again, the aging king was writing from hard-earned experience. He had more riches and wealth than anyone around, and had seen firsthand that gold coins and treasures offer little in the way of lasting benefits.

Some Somber Thoughts

ECCLESIASTES 7:1–6 *A good name is better than precious ointment, and the day of death than the day of one's birth; better to go to the house of mourning than to go to the house of feasting, for that is the end of all men; and the living will take it to heart. Sorrow is better than laughter, for by a sad countenance the heart is made better. The heart of the wise is in the house of mourning, but the heart of fools is in the house of mirth. It is better to hear the rebuke of the wise than for a man to hear the song of fools. For like the crackling of thorns under a pot, so is the laughter of the fool. This also is vanity.* (NKJV)

Who would choose a funeral over a birthday party? Tears over giggles? A scolding over praise? Passages like this make it easy to see how the book of Ecclesiastes earned its reputation as a "downer." Was Solomon just having a blue day when he wrote these words, or is there credence to his gloomy observations? One scholar helps make sense of the king's dark thoughts by noting that people are more apt to discover the big truths about life when they're not soaring on the wings of emotional highs.

What Solomon Said About His Wife

Actually, the heading for this section probably ought to say, "What Solomon didn't say about his *wives*." Because this man who had seven hundred wives (plus three hundred concubines) only visits the topic once in the book—and it's strikingly singular:

> ECCLESIASTES 9:9 *Live joyfully with the wife whom you love all the days of your vain life which He has given you under the sun, all your days of vanity; for that is your portion in life, and in the labor which you perform under the sun.* (NKJV)

The fact that Solomon ignored mentioning the *quantity* of his wives and focused instead on the *quality* of life with one—"the wife"—practically shouts the Shulamite's name from the pages of Scripture. Many scholars agree that this underlines the authenticity of the love between himself and the Shulamite and highlights the political nature of his marriages to the other women.

key point

what others say

Selwyn Hughes

Husbands, enjoy your wives (v. 9). Enjoy, not put up with. You have a wife? Love her. Live it up and have fun in your marriage. Don't wait until you retire to enjoy life.[15]

One Last Bit of Advice . . .

> ECCLESIASTES 12:1 *Remember now your Creator in the days of your youth, before the difficult days come, and the years draw near when you say, "I have no pleasure in them."* (NKJV)

After further explorations of life and its paradoxes, Solomon offers a last bit of advice before summing up his conclusions. The aging king, again speaking from experience, urges young men to get their lives right with God. He says they should do that while they are still young, while they have great strength, health, and vitality.

what others say

Ray Stedman

Remembering God does not mean merely thinking about Him once in awhile. It means to relate to Him, walk with Him, discover Him, learn to know Him while you are young.[16]

. . . Before His Closing Remarks

ECCLESIASTES 12:13–14 *Let us hear the conclusion of the whole matter: Fear God and keep His commandments, for this is man's all. For God will bring every work into judgment, including every secret thing, whether good or evil. (NKJV)*

The book of Ecclesiastes has detailed Solomon's end-of-life search for satisfying answers to life's inconsistencies, and this passage records his conclusions. It's really a threefold revelation. To find fulfillment in life on earth a person must:

1. *Fear God.* As discussed earlier in this book, fearing God doesn't mean running from Him in fright. It means recognizing Him for who He is: the Creator of the universe who is all-powerful and all-knowing, and who loves His creation dearly.

2. *Keep His commandments.* Because God loves His creation so much, He gives guidelines that can keep wayward people safe and sound. These guidelines can be found in the Bible, and obeying them is a way people demonstrate their love for and commitment to the Lord.

3. *Anticipate judgment.* Work accomplished, relationships formed, wisdom acquired . . . these are all part of life "under the sun" and they may seem futile enough ("vanity") on their own. But Solomon urges people to carry them out with eyes focused forward to a future that reaches beyond the boundaries of the material world. Having God upfront and center brings certain eternal rewards, just as pushing Him away brings certain eternal doom.

> **what others say**
>
> **Life Application Study Bible**
>
> All people will have to stand before God and be judged for what they did in this life. We will not be able to use life's inconsistencies as an excuse for failing to live properly. To live properly, we need to (1) recognize that human effort apart from God is futile, (2) put God first—now, (3) receive everything good as a gift from God, (4) realize that God will judge both evil and good, and (5) know that God will judge the quality of every person's life.[17]

The Bible Almanac

Ecclesiastes argues that life has meaning only when a person serves God. If a person follows other goals, he will fall into utter hopelessness: "vanity of vanities" (Ecclesiastes 1:2). Ecclesiastes says that a person can find happiness only when he pursues godliness, not when he pursues pleasure or comfort. . . . The writer declares that life is "vanity of vanities" only if it is lived apart from God. Though His ways are inscrutable, God gives meaning to life.[18]

Chapter Wrap-Up

- Although there is some dispute among scholars as to who really wrote the book of Ecclesiastes, strong evidence within the book points directly to Solomon, who recorded his end-of-life insights after researching the meaning of the human experience.

- The key word *vanity* means meaningless, or worthless, and is used frequently by Solomon to describe life and activities on earth.

- Throughout the book Solomon weighs events and motives that take place "under the sun"—or on earth during the physical, material experience of living—against the divine agenda carried out on the other side of the sun, in the heavenly realm.

- One way Solomon sought meaning in life was by refusing to withhold from himself any desire or pleasure. That's not unlike the method of many people today who spend time and money on entertainment, partying, and home improvements in an effort to find contentment.

- Solomon discovered that on the one hand (this side of the sun) there are things to do, like work and obtaining wisdom, that aren't in and of themselves especially rewarding. In fact, they can be quite frustrating. On the other hand (or the other side of the sun), adding God to the equation changes everything: Carrying out earthly activities transforms an exercise in frustration to an experience of joy.

- Solomon's ultimate conclusion was threefold: To find fulfillment in life on earth, a person must (1) fear God, (2) keep His commandments, and (3) anticipate a future that reaches beyond the boundaries of the material world.

Study Questions

1. Why was Solomon, of all people, best qualified to look into the matter of life's meaning?

2. What do the terms and phrase "vanity" and "under the sun" mean, and what did he use those words to describe?

3. What were some ways Solomon tried to find fulfillment?

4. What is one of the most famous passages in the book of Ecclesiastes, and what is its message?

5. What is Solomon's advice concerning relationships?

6. What was Solomon's conclusion about the meaning of life?

Appendix A—The Answers

2 Samuel 11, 12; 1 Chronicles 20
Conceived in Sorrow

1. Some factors that put David at risk for sinning with Bathsheba included: refusing to go out to battle with his men, according to custom, and allowing his actions to progress *toward* sin rather than *away* from it. In other words, instead of averting his eyes when he saw Bathsheba, he kept looking. Rather than putting her out of his mind, he summoned her. Instead of controlling his passion for her, he allowed his lust to control him.

2. David first tried to deal with his sin by covering up the evidence: He manipulated situations and even the lives of others to suit his own purposes. But that didn't work. Although he appeared to have things under control on the surface, his psalms indicate that his heart remained in distress.

3. At first, David responded to Nathan's parable with anger at the thief. Then, he was overcome by grief when he realized Nathan's words were illustrating his own actions. Filled with remorse, he repented.

4. God forgave David of his sin but predicted that the son he and Bathsheba had conceived would die.

5. God showed mercy and kindness to David and Bathsheba after the death of their infant son, by allowing them to conceive another son, to be named Solomon (as well as "Jedidiah").

2 Samuel 13–19; 1 Kings 1; 2 Chronicles 1
The Man *After* the Man After God's Own Heart

1. Amnon's rape of Tamar ruined her prospects for ever marrying and having children, and touched off a string of violence in David's household. The crime made Absalom angry; in turn, he had Amnon killed.

2. Absalom's resentment for his father, possibly because of David's apparent lack of concern for Tamar and possibly because of his apparent over-

concern for Amnon, prompted him to attempt to seize the throne from his father.

3. As David was fleeing Jerusalem in the wake of his son's attempted coup, he stopped at the Mount of Olives to worship and to pray.

4. Nathan approached Bathsheba with the news of Adonijah's attempted power play because she was Solomon's mother, and because she apparently had such a good relationship with the king that she could expect to be given an audience with him.

5. When Adonijah discovered his plot against the king had failed and that Solomon had been anointed, he became afraid for his life. He ran to take hold of the horns of the altar, a place of safety. David promised to let Adonijah live as long as he behaved himself.

2 Samuel 23:1–7; 1 Kings 2:1–12
David's Death

1. David's two sets of "last words" were directed to the nation (2 Samuel 23:1–7) and to Solomon (1 Kings 2:1–9), highlighting his tremendous responsibilities both as a king and as a father.

2. In David's formal address to Israel he stressed the importance of being a just king and being a God-fearing king. A lack of either trait would render the king ineffective and powerless.

3. David acknowledged that his kingdom fell far short of ideal, but he looked forward to the fulfillment of God's promise of a perfect, coming kingdom.

4. In David's final words to his son, he stated that Solomon's success would hinge on his willingness to submit to God's authority.

5. David offered his son specific advice concerning how to deal with Joab, Barzillai, and Shimei. He believed it necessary to give Solomon a head start in figuring out how to deal with the people who were likely to be among Solomon's most pressing concerns after David's death.

1 Kings 2:13–46
Politics and Power

1. Adonijah may have taken his request to Bathsheba rather than to Solomon himself because: she might be sympathetic; she apparently enjoyed some influence over her son; and Solomon or one of his men might be quicker to suspect the motives behind his request.

2. Adonijah's remark that "the kingdom was mine" and "the kingdom has been turned over" betrayed his true feelings about Solomon's position as king.

3. Solomon responded to the request Bathsheba brought him on behalf of Adonijah by ordering Adonijah's execution.

4. Solomon had Abiathar banished rather than executed for his act of treason, in deference to the priest's former faithful service to David.

5. Joab was so frightened that he clung to the horns of the altar, hoping for protection, because he saw what had happened to other traitors in the administration and he knew he was equally guilty.

6. Shimei broke the conditions of his house arrest, converting Solomon's rather lenient discipline into an order of execution.

7. Solomon had to carry out these harsh acts of justice because, as God's anointed king, he needed to rid the kingdom of any threats to peace.

1 Kings 3; 2 Chronicles 1:2–13
Foreign Relations and a Famous Request

1. An alliance with Egypt benefited Solomon by helping fortify the western border of the land, expanding Israel's political sphere of influence, and improving the nation's trade potential. Pharaoh would benefit from the alliance by gaining Egypt safe passage through Israel.

2. Some of the "evil" influences Egyptians could have brought into Israel included idolatry, witchcraft, and superstitions as well as attitudes of pride, arrogance, and ambition.

3. The high places were altars erected on mountaintops where people could make sacrifices. They were frequently used by pagans. God directed Israel to destroy the altars at the high places and to refuse to worship Him in such spots. Instead, they should worship Him as He specified: in the tabernacle.

4. Solomon and a large number of his people convened at Gibeon to make sacrifices. Solomon presented a thousand burnt offerings before the Lord—truly an extravagant amount.

5. Solomon received his remarkable gift of wisdom after the Lord approached him, asking the king to tell Him what he wanted. Because Solomon's request for wisdom pleased the Lord, He granted his request.

6. God gave Solomon even more than he asked by giving the king riches and honor in addition to unsurpassed wisdom.

1 Kings 3:16–28; 4
Solomon—Chief Justice and CEO

1. It was surprising that Solomon bothered to give his attention to the two prostitutes, because under the ancient codes they had no legal, economic, or social status.

2. The case was an especially tough one to resolve because there were no witnesses and there was no evidence; the dispute simply pitted one woman's word against the other's.

3. Solomon's judgment earned him the sincere respect and admiration of his people.

4. Solomon organized his administration by appointing chief officers to key leadership positions, and by dividing the nations into twelve sections, with each section under the supervision of a governor.

5. The size and scope of his kingdom marked the partial fulfillment of the Abrahamic covenant and of the covenant God had made with his father, David.

6. Solomon distinguished himself in the fields of literature and science in addition to justice and administration.

1 Kings 5; 2 Chronicles 2
Getting Ready to Build

1. David wanted to build a temple for the Lord because he was dismayed by the incongruity between the lavish surroundings he—a mere mortal—inhabited and the temporary tent that served as the tabernacle of the Lord.

2. The Lord said "no" to David's plans because He wanted a man of peace, not war, to build the temple. David had been a warrior; therefore, his bloodstained hands would mar the sanctity of the temple. On the other hand, Solomon's reign had been largely one of peace. He, God said, would be the one to build the temple.

3. David responded to God's refusal of his plans by throwing his energy into making preparations for his son to build the temple.

4. According to David, he received detailed plans for the temple construction directly from the hand of God.

5. One of the first things Solomon did was renew his father's treaty with the king of Tyre, enabling the Israelite king to capitalize on Hiram's kindness, generosity, materials, and manpower.

1 Kings 6; 7:13–50; 2 Chronicles 3; 4
The Specs for a Spectacular Building

1. Solomon's temple is no longer standing; it was destroyed and rebuilt several times. The biblical description of the structure, however, is so detailed that experts have been able to reconstruct models of it with extraordinary accuracy.

2. The temple was built on property with great significance because it was where God had graciously withdrawn a plague that had decimated Israel as the result of David's sin. And, it was where God had mercifully provided a substitute sacrifice when Abraham had, in obedience to God's instructions, laid his son upon the altar. Today the property—the location of the Dome of the Rock—is the source of much dispute in the Middle East.

3. Solomon did not begin construction on the temple until the fourth year of his reign in order to allow ample time for planning and preparation.

4. The construction site was eerily quiet—the noisy work of finishing and fitting stones was done at the quarry in order to maintain a holy hush at the building site.

5. The temple serves as a visible illustration of numerous spiritual principles; further, today's believers are assured that, as "living stones," they are being shaped for insertion into God's spiritual temple.

6. When the temple structure was complete, Solomon had all the furnishings installed and then turned his attention to building other structures in the temple complex, including his own palace and a home for Pharaoh's daughter.

1 Kings 8; 2 Chronicles 5:1–7:11
The Dedication of the Temple

1. Because God is everywhere, all the time, He could not possibly be confined within the walls of the temple. For the sake of His people, however, He could establish a dwelling place for His presence there.

2. Solomon planned the temple dedication—delayed it, in fact—to coincide with the Feast of Tabernacles, which commemorated Israel's wanderings in the wilderness. As one of the three feasts Israelites were required to attend, the timing was ideal.

3. The temple was very special, not only to Solomon but to the other Israelites as well because this was the place where, through the system of sacrifices, they could enter into fellowship with God. They also understood the significance of the fact that the construction of the temple fulfilled God's plan for them to worship Him in one central location.

4. Because Jesus served as the once-for-all sacrifice for the sins of those who accept Him as Savior, today's Christians do not need to offer sacrifices to atone for their sins. They do, however, enjoy the privilege of offering their bodies as living sacrifices for the Lord's use and honor.

5. Solomon pleaded with the Lord to always be available to listen to the prayers of the people who came to the temple, or who prayed toward the temple from faraway lands.

6. According to the nature of the petitions Solomon made to God, he understood that all humans are sinners. Solomon prayed for the times "when" the people would sin—not for "if" they would sin.

7. Solomon and the people knew God heard the king's prayer because He sent a fire from heaven to ignite and consume the sacrifices they had brought.

1 Kings 9:1–9; 2 Chronicles 7:12–22
Hazardous Conditions Ahead

1. As this chapter opens, Solomon had done everything he had wanted to do for the Lord and for himself. He was probably enjoying the spiritual, emotional, and physical rewards of having completed the temple, celebrating its dedication, and then building his own palace.

2. The timing of God's second appearance to Solomon was especially good because the king may have been at risk of spiritual maladies such as depression, excessive pride, or aimlessness after riding the crest of such spiritual success. He very much needed a reminder of his place in God's plans, and of the possible dangers ahead.

3. Because His glory and holiness make it possible for no one to see Him and live, God has taken on a physical form several times throughout biblical history, in order to be seen by people without endangering their lives.

4. God promised Solomon that He had set apart the temple as His own; He assured him of His continual presence there.

5. God urged the king to follow the example of his father, David, who walked with integrity and uprightness. If he would do that, God said, the

king and his descendants could enjoy a continual reign over Israel.

6. God said if Solomon or his sons turned from God, He would bring "calamity" on them by bringing his reign over Israel to an end. (That would not, however, nullify His promise to David of an "everlasting kingdom.")

1 Kings 9:10–28; 10; 2 Chronicles 8:3–16; 9:1–28
Dealings with a King and a Queen

1. Solomon gave Hiram the twenty cities in an effort to repay the king of Tyre for the kindness and generosity he showed in providing Israel with skilled craftsmen and materials for the construction of the temple.

2. The properties were on or near unproductive land; the king of Tyre, who already had extensive wealth and land, had no need for such undesirable properties.

3. Solomon had large architectural terraces built to fill in the valley surrounding Jerusalem; he extended the wall around the city; he rebuilt key strategic defense cities; he designated cities for storage of supplies and weapons; and he designated cities to house his numerous stables and chariots.

4. Solomon, with Hiram's help, established a fleet of ships to be used for international maritime trading.

5. The queen had heard of Solomon's fame and wanted to come see for herself whether the rumors of his wisdom were true. She also brought gifts, indicating she hoped to establish good diplomatic relations with Israel.

6. After Solomon had answered all of the queen's questions, and she looked around to see the magnitude of his wealth and success, she was literally left breathless with the realization that the truth far exceeded the stories she had heard. She said as much and then acknowledged the God who had so obviously blessed the king and his nation.

7. Sheba represents any believer who brings honest questions—and even doubts—about what he or she has heard about Jesus Christ. Like Sheba, once a person seeking this information is confronted with the dazzling truth, he or she can't even begin to describe His wonders, wealth, or riches—and is inevitably changed.

1 Kings 11:1–8
The Godly King Does Ungodly Things

1. Solomon's early life and reign were characterized by godliness, obedience, and spiritual integrity. During his later years he drifted away from his God-centered worldview. His first, tiny steps of compromise (which started when he married the Egyptian pharaoh's daughter) turned into blatant disobedience over time. His actions demonstrated increasing disregard for God's instructions and for his own responsibility to be a spiritual leader of the people of Israel.

2. God had specifically warned that marrying women from pagan nations put the men at risk for being tempted to turn away from God, to follow the false gods of their wives.

3. Polygamy was commonly practiced—and even condoned by God—during this time because it often seemed to be the only way to provide for a woman's safety and well-being.

4. Solomon accumulated such an excessive number of wives in his diplomatic dealings with other nations. Having a large harem also symbolized a monarch's strength and power, so Solomon—the greatest king alive during his time, as the Bible states—apparently wanted to have more wives than his fellow heads of state.

5. Solomon's foreign wives not only persuaded him to allow them to continue to worship their native gods, but he also allowed the construction of high places where they could do so. Further, he himself helped build altars to these gods, who were particularly abominable because their worship was often associated with human sacrifice.

6. Solomon's disobedient and unfaithful actions took him outside the realm of God's blessing and protection, leaving him personally vulnerable to certain consequences and discipline. His actions also had dire public consequences. They opened the nation's door to false teachings, compromising the spiritual health of his people.

1 Kings 11:9–11; 2 Chronicles 9:29–31
The Wrath of God

1. God was angry with Solomon because the king had not only allowed his pagan wives to worship their gods, but he had also begun to participate in their worship. He did this in spite of God's personal visits and in spite of His warnings against that very event.

2. God punished Solomon by promising to remove the kingdom from his hands.

3. God demonstrated mercy by withholding that event until after Solomon's death.

4. God honored the Davidic covenant by preserving part of Israel.

5. Hadad, Rezon, and Jeroboam were three enemies of Solomon whom the Lord allowed to cause strife and dissension in the kingdom.

6. The prophet Ahijah conveyed God's message to Jeroboam, to the effect that he would be the one to become king over ten of Israel's twelve tribes.

7. Jeroboam did not overthrow Solomon right away; in fact, fearing for his life, he fled to Egypt until after the king died.

Solomon's Song
It's All About Love

1. The three main characters in the love story are Solomon, the Shulamite woman, and the chorus of women.

2. The Song of Solomon may be interpreted (1) as an example of godly principles of relationship and marriage; (2) as an illustration of God's love for His followers; and/or (3) as a picture of Christ's love for His church.

3. The Shulamite was different from the other women Solomon would eventually marry because she was an "ordinary" girl. That is, she wasn't a princess or a political pawn.

4. Controversy surrounding the Song of Solomon has noted its frank discussions of physical attraction and sex, and its omission of the name of God.

5. The Song of Solomon offers a number of practical tips for today's married couples, including the advice not to let everyday frustrations damage a relationship and the value of getting away alone together.

6. The book strongly states that premarital sex is not an option; that sex within marriage is designed to provide pleasure and intimacy; that every marriage will face trials; and that the foundation of a sturdy marriage is commitment.

Proverbs
A Word from the Wise

1. The book of Proverbs incorporates a strong spiritual element into its wisdom, setting it apart from other wisdom literature of the day.

2. According to Solomon and the other writers of Proverbs, the key to obtaining wisdom is the fear of the Lord.

3. The universal appeal of Proverbs hinges on its concise, practical advice on a wide range of issues that continue to affect readers as much today as they did during the tenth century BC.

4. One of the biggest challenges in handling the gift of wisdom is learning how to apply the wisdom to one's words and actions.

5. Words go a long way toward demonstrating whether a person is wise or foolish.

6. Obtaining riches is not a wise or worthy goal, because riches don't last and they have absolutely no eternal value.

7. The Proverbs assert that work is important: Wise people not only work, but they work hard and they plan ahead.

Ecclesiastes
The Search for Satisfaction

1. Solomon, of all people, was best qualified to look into the matter of life's meaning, first and foremost because he was the wisest man in the world. Further, he had the advantage of age and a broad range of experience—an excellent vantage point for someone attempting this kind of research.

2. The word *vanity* means "worthless," "fleeting," or "meaningless"; "under the sun" refers to life and activities on earth, apart from divine realities. Solomon used the word *vanity* to describe life "under the sun."

3. Solomon tried to find fulfillment in pleasure-seeking, wealth, and wisdom, among other things, and found that none of those activities delivered.

4. Ecclesiastes 3:1–10, one of the most famous passages in the book of Ecclesiastes, emphasizes God's beautiful, rhythmic design for the earth and the activities of those who live in it. It stresses the need to act within the appropriate boundaries He has set by the passage.

5. Solomon encourages friendship over solitude, citing benefits that include safety, warmth, and strength.

6. Solomon concluded that the only way to find meaning in the natural world is to maintain a meaningful spiritual relationship with God. That comes by fearing God, following His guidelines, and living in anticipation of eternity.

Appendix B—The Experts

Alter, Robert—professor of Hebrew and comparative literature; widely respected Bible translator.

Archer, Gleason L.—Bible scholar and author of a number of books; instrumental in the preparation of the Old Testament portion of the New American Standard Bible.

Barbieri, Louis A., Jr.—professor of theology at Moody Bible Institute in Chicago.

Beasley, Sabrina—writer and articles editor for FamilyLife, a division of Campus Crusade for Christ that presents conferences on marriage and family. She and her husband live in Little Rock, Arkansas.

Begg, Alistair—minister, Bible scholar, and author of several books, including *Made for His Pleasure: Ten Benchmarks of a Vital Faith*.

Bentley, Ray—pastor/teacher of Maranatha Chapel in San Diego; his teachings are webcast live on the Internet and on the radio.

Boadt, Lawrence—professor and well-known scholar of biblical literature who has written numerous articles and books on Old Testament subjects.

Bodmer, Judy—author of *When Love Dies: How to Save a Hopeless Marriage* and a contributor to the #1 New York Times best seller *Chicken Soup for the Mother's Soul*.

Bratcher, Dennis R.—executive director of The CRI/Voice Institute, a global and ecumenical ministry dedicated to providing biblical and theological resources for growing Christians.

Breese, Dave—pastor and theologian whose work until his death in 2002 was committed to advancing Christianity through evangelistic crusades, the distribution of literature, and the broadcast media.

Buzzell, Sid S.—professor of Bible exposition at Colorado Christian University, Lakewood, Colorado.

Castleman, Robbie—assistant professor of biblical studies at John Brown University; author of numerous study guides.

Chambers, Oswald—prominent early twentieth-century Scottish Protestant Christian minister and teacher, best known as the author of the devotional book *My Utmost for His Highest*.

Clarke, Adam—British Methodist theologian most widely known for writing commentaries on the Bible in the early 1800s.

Coffman, James Burton—Bible scholar, author, preacher, and teacher who was considered one of the most influential figures among Churches of Christ until his death in 2006.

Collins, Kenneth W.—minister and biblical scholar who received his Master of Divinity degree from Wesley Theological Seminary in Washington, D.C.

Constable, Thomas L.—Bible scholar, professor of Bible exposition at Dallas Theological Seminary, pastor, and speaker who has ministered in nearly three dozen countries and has written commentaries on every book of the Bible.

Cowman, L. B.—pioneer missionary to Japan and China whose book, *Streams in the Desert*, has become one of the best-selling devotionals since its first publication in 1925.

Davidson, Robert—professor of biblical studies, University of Glasgow, and author of several books.

Deere, Jack—associate senior pastor of Trinity Fellowship Church in Amarillo, Texas.

Deffinbaugh, Robert L.—graduate of Dallas Theological Seminary; a Bible teacher who has contributed a great many of his Bible study series to the Web site Bible.org.

Dolphin, Lambert—retired Christian physicist and prolific writer whose work focuses on science and theology.

Duck, Daymond—best-selling author who has written numerous books, including several for this Smart Guide to the Bible series. He is a much-sought-after guest for Christian programs, and frequently speaks at prophecy conferences and revivals.

Edersheim, Alfred—Vienna-born biblical scholar who converted from Judaism to Christianity and wrote several widely recognized books about the traditions of the Jewish faith and the life of Christ.

Fincher, Larry and Thelnita—cofounders of HomeBuilders Ministry, presenting practical teachings for the family in the subject areas of marriage, parenting, finances, leadership, and career. On the staff of Rowland Road Baptist Church, Monroe, Louisiana.

Free, Joseph P.—late chairman of the department of archaeology at Wheaton College, and professor of archaeology and history at Bemidji State College in Minnesota.

Fruchtenbaum, Arnold G.—founder and director of Ariel Ministries, which offers intensive biblical and theological training of Jewish believers. He has written several books and often speaks and teaches at conferences and seminars.

Gibson, Joyce L.—A Bible curriculum and devotional writer and editor whose book of Genesis appears in this same Smart Guide to the Bible series.

Graham, Billy—best-selling author and evangelist who has led millions of people to Christ through his crusades on every continent, and through his radio and television messages.

Grant, Leslie M.—Canadian evangelist, writer, speaker, and a frequent contributor to various periodicals, Bible study lessons, and calendar readings.

Guzik, David—director of Calvary Chapel Bible College in Germany; also widely known for his online study materials and Bible commentaries.

Hahn, Roger—noted biblical scholar, teacher, preacher, pastor, and writer.

Hahn, Wilfred J.—formerly a top-ranked global analyst and one-time head of a large global investment company with worldwide operations; his writings focus on the end-time roles of money, economics, and globalization.

Harrison, R. K.—late professor of Old Testament who wrote the classic work *Introduction to the Old Testament*, and was the general editor of the *New International Commentary on the Old Testament*.

Henry, Matthew—English clergyman who lived from 1662 to 1714, most noted for his commentary of the Bible.

Higgs, Liz Curtis—popular author and award-winning speaker who encourages Christian women with her humor and insight.

Hitchcock, Mark—graduate of Dallas Theological Seminary who has served as a pastor and has written several books about prophecy.

Hole, F. B.—late evangelist, teacher, and publisher whose books include *The Great Salvation* and *Foundations of the Faith*.

Hughes, Selwyn—known for his deep and inspiring teaching, he has been writing "Every Day with Jesus" for more than forty years.

Ironside, H. A.—pastor of Moody Memorial Church in Chicago, Illinois, for many years.

Jameison, Robert—coauthor of the 1871 Jameison-Fausset-Brown commentary on the Bible.

James, William T.—author of more than a dozen books focusing on the end times; partner with Todd Strandberg in operating RaptureReady.com, the most frequently visited Christian prophecy Web site on the Internet.

Janssen, Al—senior director of resource development at Focus on the Family who has written, co-written, and edited numerous books and articles.

Jensen, Irving L.—retired professor and respected author best known for his Bible Self-Study Guide series.

Jeremiah, David—pastor and author whose radio and television broadcast, *Turning Point*, reaches thousands of people every day.

Killian, Rick—seldom-acknowledged author credited with writing *The Prayer of Solomon: Enduring Wisdom from the World's Wisest Man* for Bethany House.

Kolatch, Alfred J.—graduate of the Teacher's Institute of Yeshiva University and its College of Liberal Arts; ordained by the Jewish Theological Seminary of America; author of numerous books.

Kopas, Jane—Bible scholar, teacher, and writer who received her doctorate at the Graduate Theological Union in Berkeley.

Kroll, Woodrow—president and senior Bible teacher for the international media ministry Back to the Bible.

LaHaye, Tim—best-selling author of the Left Behind series, founder and president of Family Life Seminars.

Laurie, Greg—senior pastor of the Harvest Christian Fellowship in Riverside, California; author of several books; host of television and radio programs; speaker for public evangelistic events.

Lawrence, Cameron—staff writer for intouch.org, the Web site of Dr. Charles Stanley's international ministry featuring broadcasts in more than one hundred languages.

Leithart, Peter—professor of theology, pastor, and author of a number of books, including *A House for My Name: A Survey of the Old Testament*.

Levitt, Zola—late Jewish believer best known as the host for the national weekly television program *Zola Levitt Presents*. Also a widely published author, contributing author, and composer.

Lucado, Max—pastor of Oak Hills Church of Christ in San Antonio, Texas, and the author of numerous best-selling books.

MacArthur, John—pastor of Grace Community Church, founder of The Masters' Seminary, host of *Grace to You* radio program.

Martin, William C.—professor of religion and public policy at Rice University in Houston; author of numerous articles and books.

Matlock, Mark—president and founder of WisdomWorks Ministries; conference speaker; minister; author of *Don't Buy the Lie*.

McEachern, Alton H.—pastor, theology professor, and author of several books, including *Set Apart for Service*.

McGee, J. Vernon—radio Bible teacher of 1980s–1990s whose commentaries aired on his program, *Thru the Bible Radio*, and in print.

McKenzie, Steven L.—professor of Hebrew Bible at Rhodes College and author of many books on Bible studies, including *The Hebrew Bible Today*.

Mehl, Ron—pastor of a large congregation in Beaverton, Oregon, until his death in 2003. His books include the Gold Medallion winners *God Works the Night Shift* and *Just in Case I Can't Be There*.

Merrill, Eugene H.—distinguished professor of Old Testament studies; author of numerous books and articles.

Meyer, F. B.—pastor and evangelist in England; wrote more than forty books, including Christian biographies and devotional commentaries on the Bible.

Miller, Kathy Collard and D. Larry—frequent speakers who teach practical, biblical principles for restoring and reinforcing marital love, unity, and commitment.

Misslerm, Nan—partner with her husband, Chuck, in Koinonia House, a Bible study ministry; has written several books and study guides.

Moore, Beth—teacher and author of best-selling Bible studies, including *Things Pondered, A Heart like His*, and *Praying God's Word*.

Morris, Henry—Christian apologist and a founder of the Creation Research Society and the Institute of Creation Research. Wrote or edited some forty books, most of which focus on creation science and evolution.

Nystrom, Carolyn—Freelance writer who has written more than seventy-five books and Bible study guides; general editor for InterVarsity Press's Christian Classics series.

Phillips, Richard D.—retired combat officer for the United States Army who serves as a management consultant and is a frequent speaker on leadership and organization.

Plotz, David—deputy editor of the online magazine *Slate*; his offhand encounter with a dramatic Bible story inspired him to take a new look at the Old Testament.

Preus, Jacob A. O.—president of Concordia University in Irvine, California. He has more than fifteen published articles and books, including numerous sermon studies and reviews.

Price, Randall—research professor of archaeology and biblical studies at Oregon Theological Seminary who directs archaeological excavations in Israel and has written numerous books and articles on related matters.

Rainey, Dennis—president and cofounder of FamilyLife (a division of Campus Crusade for Christ) and a graduate of Dallas Theological Seminary. Daily host of the nationally syndicated radio program *FamilyLife Today*.

Richards, Larry and Sue—well-known husband-wife research and writing team; each also has written numerous books.

Rivers, Francine—author of numerous novels with Christian themes; she and husband, Rick, live in northern California.

Roper, David H.—author of and contributor to numerous publications; a leader in Peninsula Bible Church in Palo Alto, California.

Rossier, H. L.—Christian scholar and writer during the late nineteenth and early twentieth centuries who wrote commentaries on most of the books of the Bible, especially on the historical and prophetic books of the Old Testament. Was a prolific hymn writer as well.

Ryle, J. C.— nineteenth century English evangelist and prolific writer known for clear and lively writings on practical spiritual themes.

Sadowski, Todd—Christian financial adviser whose ministry involves enlightening and equipping Christians to become better stewards of the blessings God has provided.

Savage, Jill—author, speaker, and founder and executive director of Hearts at Home, an organization designed to encourage and educate women in the profession of motherhood.

Scott, Steven K.—author of five international best sellers and a popular speaker on the subject of personal and professional achievement.

Shirer, Priscilla—graduate of Dallas Theological Seminary with a master's degree in biblical studies; Bible teacher and motivational speaker in full-time ministry to women. Is the daughter of pastor, speaker, and well-known author Tony Evans.

Spangler, Ann—author of several best-selling books including, *She Who Laughs, Lasts!* and *Don't Stop Laughing Now!*

Spurgeon, Charles H.—called the "prince of preachers," his sermons held throngs spellbound at the Metropolitan Tabernacle in London in the nineteenth century and now in written form.

Stanley, Charles—senior pastor of the twelve-thousand-member First Baptist Church of Atlanta and a prolific author.

Stedman, Ray—the late, longtime pastor of Peninsula Bible Church in Palo Alto, California, and author of more than twenty-eight books, many still in print.

Strong, James—biblical scholar and educator whose best-known work is *Strong's Exhaustive Concordance of the Bible*, first published in 1890, of which new editions are still in print.

Swindoll, Charles—former pastor of the First Evangelical Free Church in Fullerton, California, and president of the Dallas Theological Seminary in Dallas, Texas. Author of many best-selling books.

Tripp, Tedd—pastor and author of *Shepherding a Child's Heart*.

Vos, Henry F.—professor of history and archaeology at the King's College in Briarcliff Manor, New York.

Walton, Don—founder of Time for Truth Ministries and a full-time evangelist and conference speaker.

Youngblood, Ronald—professor of Old Testament and Hebrew emeritus, Bethel Seminary San Diego, and author of numerous books.

Endnotes

2 Samuel 11, 12; 1 Chronicles 20
Conceived in Sorrow

1. Robbie Castleman, *King David: Trusting God for a Lifetime* (Colorado Springs, CO: Shaw/Waterbrook Press, 2002), 78.

2. Matthew George Easton, "Ammonite," *Easton's Bible Dictionary*, <http://www.studylight.org/dic/ebd/view.cgi?number=T212>.

3. Trent C., ed. "Ammonites," *Holman Bible Dictionary*, <http://www.studylight.org/dic/hbd/view.cgi?number=T212>.

4. Bob Deffinbaugh, "David and Bathsheba (2 Samuel 11:1–4)," A Study of 2 Samuel, <http://www.bible.org/page.php?page_id=565

5. Angie Peters, *The Life of David*, (Nashville: Nelson, 2008), 253.

6. Kathy Collard Miller and D. Larry Miller, *What's in the Bible for … Couples* (Lancaster, PA: Starburst), 215.

7. Robert D. D. Jamieson, A. R. Fausset, and David Brown, "Commentary on 2 Samuel 11," *Commentary Critical and Explanatory on the Whole Bible*, <http://www.studylight.org/com/jfb/view.cgi?book=2sa&chapter=011> 1871.

8. Charles R. Swindoll, *David: A Man of Passion and Destiny* (Nashville: W Publishing Group/Thomas Nelson, 1997), 184.

9. Billy Graham, *The Journey* (Nashville: W Publishing Group/Thomas Nelson, 2006), 157.

10. Liz Curtis Higgs, *Bad Girls of the Bible* (Colorado Springs, CO: Waterbrook, 1999), 31.

11. David Guzik, *David Guzik's Commentaries on the Bible*, <http://www.studylight.org/com/guz/view.cgi?book=2sa&chapter=011&verse=001#2Sa11_1>.

12. Ibid.

13. Robert Alter, *The David Story* (New York: W.W. Norton, 1999), 251.

14. Sue and Larry Richards, *Every Woman in the Bible* (Nashville: Thomas Nelson, 1999), 128.

15. Swindoll, *A Man of Passion and Destiny*, 185.

16. Sabrina Beasley, "Wishing He Were Your Husband," <Adapted from the January 2007 issue of The Family Room, FamilyLife's online magazine at www.FamilyLife.com/familyroom>.

17. Charles Stanley, *The Power of the Cross* (Nashville: Thomas Nelson, 1998), 195.

18. Francine Rivers, *Unspoken* (Wheaton, IL: Tyndale House, 2001), 186.

19. *Nelson's NKJV Study Bible*, "Word Focus" (Nashville: Thomas Nelson, 1997), 551.

20. William Smith, Dr. "Uriah" Smith's Bible Dictionary, <http://www.studylight.org/dic/sbd/view.cgi?number=T4398>, 1901.

21. Jamieson, Fausset, Brown, "Commentary on 2 Samuel 11."

22. Richard D. Phillips, *The Heart of an Executive* (New York: Galilee/Doubleday, 1999), 206.

23. Judy Bodmer, *What's in the Bible for … Mothers* (Lancaster, PA: Starburst, 2000), 288.

24. Matthew Henry, *Matthew Henry Complete Commentary on the Whole Bible*, 2 Samuel 12, http://www.searchgodsword.org/com/mhc-com/view.cgi?book=2sa&chapter=012. 1706.

25. Peters, *The Life of David*, 268-269.

26. *Nelson's NKJV Study Bible*, "Parables: More Than Stories," 1613.

27. Louis A. Barbieri Jr., "Matthew," *Bible Knowledge Commentary: New Testament* (Colorado Springs, CO: Victor/Cook, 2004), 33.

28. David Robinson, *God's Character Revealed in Judgment* (Texarkana, TX: Bogard, 2006), 92.

29. Steven L. McKenzie, *King David: A Biography* (New York: Oxford University Press, 2000), 160.

30. Kathy Collard Miller and D. Larry Miller, 220.

31. Francine Rivers, 201.

32. Judy Bodmer, 186.

33. Matthew Henry, *Matthew Henry's Commentary on 2 Samuel 12*, studylight.org.

34. Judy Bodmer, 282.

35. Henry Morris, *The Remarkable Wisdom of Solomon* (Green Forest, AR: Master Books, 2001), 16.

36. Richard D. Phillips, 250.

2 Samuel 13–19; 1 Kings 1; 2 Chronicles 1
The Man *After* the Man After God's Own Heart

1. Beth Moore, *A Heart Like His* (Nashville: Lifeway, 1996), 158.

2. Ibid., 155.

3. Judy Bodmer, 180.

4. Dennis Rainey, "How Do I Teach My Children About Sex So That They Will Stay Pure Until They Are Married?" <http://www.familylife.com/articles/article_detail.asp?id=1270.>

5. Sue and Larry Richards, 133.

6. Peters, Angie, *The Life of David* (Nashville: Nelson, 2008), 287.

7. *Nelson's NKJV Study Bible*, 532.

8. Richard D. Phillips, 230–31.

9. Ibid., 232.

10. Robert Alter, 284.

11. Ronald F. Youngblood, "2 Samuel," *Zondervan NIV Bible Commentary, Volume 1: Old Testament* (Grand Rapids, MI: Zondervan, 1994), 465.

12. H. A. Ironside, *Psalms* (Neptune, NJ: Loizeaux Brothers, 1984), 29.

13. Ibid., 27.

14. Richard D. Phillips, 178.

15. Alfred J. Kolatch, *The Jewish Book of Why* (New York: Penguin Compass, 2000), 283–84.

16. *Rose Book of Bible Charts, Maps and Timelines* (Torrence, CA: Rose Publishing, 2005), 24.

17. James I. Packer, Merrill C. Tenney, William White, Jr., ed., *The Bible Almanac* (Nashville, TN: Thomas Nelson, 1980), 302.

18. Steven L. McKenzie, 168.

19. Thomas L. Constable, "Notes on 2 Samuel," 2007 Edition, <http://www.soniclight.com/constable/notes>.

20. *Nelson's NKJV Study Bible*, 558.

21. Robert Alter, 364.

22. Billy Graham, *The Journey*, 170–71.

23. J. Vernon McGee, *Thru the Bible with J. Vernon McGee,* vol. 2 (Pasadena, CA: Thru the Bible Radio), 246.

24. *Ryrie Study Bible*, NIV (Chicago: Moody, 1986), 450.

25. Thomas L. Constable, "Notes on 1 Kings," <http://www.soniclight.com/constable/notes>.

26. Richard D. Phillips, 253.

27. *Matthew Henry's Commentary on 1 Kings 1*, studylight.org.

28. Thomas L. Constable, "Notes on 1 Kings," <http://www.son=iclight.com/constable/notes.

29. Billy Graham, *The Journey*, 135.

30. Peter Leithart, *Brazos Theological Commentary on the Bible: 1 & 2 Kings* (Grand Rapids, MI: Brazos, 2006), 30.

31. "Hold onto Christ" May 9, 2003, taken from "Words of Promise," 1996, Concordia Publishing House.

2 Samuel 23:1–7; 1 Kings 2:1–12
David's Death

1. Charles H. Spurgeon, "David's Dying Song," a sermon delivered April 15, 1855, <http://www.spurgeon.org/sermons/0019.htm.>

2. Bob Deffinbaugh, "Profiles in Courage (2 Samuel 23)," A Study of 2 Samuel, http://www.bible.org/page.php?page_id=578.

3. H. A. Ironside, *Psalms*, 79.

4. Ibid., 75.

5. Alton H. McEachern, *Layman's Bible Book Commentary: Psalms* (Nashville: Broadman, 1981), 10.

6. *Nelson's NKJV Study Bible*, "In Depth," 995.

7. Charles H. Spurgeon, "Commentary on Psalms 9:8," *C.H. Spurgeons' The Treasury of David,* <http://www.studylight.org/com/tod/view.cgi?book=ps&chapter=009&verse=008>. 1865–1885.>

8. Ronald F. Youngblood, F. F. Bruce, R. K. Harrison, *Nelson's Student Bible Dictionary* (Nashville: Thomas Nelson, 2005), 138.

9. Jacob A. O. Preus, *Just Words: Understanding the Fullness of the Gospel* (St. Louis: Concordia, 2000), 109.

10. *Nelson's NKJV Study Bible*, "Word Focus," 1059.

11. Robbie Castleman, 62.

12. Tim LaHaye, *Prophecy Study Bible* (Chattanooga, TN: AMG Publishers, 2000), 348.

13. Tedd Tripp, *Shepherding a Child's Heart* (Wapwallopen, PA: Shepherd Press, 1995), xvii.

14. Richard D. Phillips, 257.

1 Kings 2:13–46
Politics and Power

1. Mark Matlock with Christopher Lyon, *Living a Life That Matters* (El Cajon, CA: Youth Specialities, 2005), 37.

2. Larry Richards, *The Bible: God's Word for the Biblically Inept* (Lancaster, PA: Starburs, 1998), 210.

3. Roger Hahn, Voice Bible Studies, 1 & 2 Kings, Lesson 3, http://www.crivoice.org/biblestudy/bbkings3.html.

4. Thomas L. Constable, "1 Kings," *The Bible Knowledge Commentary* (Colorado Springs, CO: Victor/Cook, 2004), 492.

5. Matthew Henry, *Matthew Henry Commentary on 1 Kings 2*, studylight.org.

6. Sue and Larry Richards, *Every Woman in the Bible*, 80.

7. Jane Kopas, <http://theologytoday.ptsem.edu/apr1990/v47-1-article2.htm 4/20/07>.

8. Robert Alter, 380.

9. *Rose Book of Bible Charts, Maps and Timelines*, 74.

10. David H. Roper, *How to Handle Criticism Series: Life Together,* http://www.pbc.org/library/files/html/3239.html.

11. *Zondervan NIV Bible Commentary*, 495.

12. Sue and Larry Richards, *Every Woman in the Bible*, 112.

13. Dorothy Russell, *A Man with a Choice: A Study in the Life of Solomon* (Scotland: Christian Focus Publications, 2005), 13.

1 Kings 3; 2 Chronicles 1:2–13
Foreign Relations and a Famous Request

1. *Zondervan NIV Bible Commentary*, 495.

2. James Burton Coffman, "Commentary on 1 Kings 3," Coffman Commentaries on the Old and New Testament, http://www.studylight.org/com/bcc/view.cgi?book=1ki&chapter=003 (Abilene, Texas: Abilene Christian University Press, 1983–199).

3. Adam Clarke Commentary, "Commentary on 1 Kings 3," <http://www.studylight.org/com/acc/view.cgi?book=1ki&chapter=003>. 1832 9.)

4. *King James Study Bible for Women* (Nashville, TN: Thomas Nelson, 2003), 558.

5. Beth Moore, *Breaking Free* (Nashville: Lifeway, 1990), 16.

6. *Adam Clarke Commentary*, "Commentary on 1 Chronicles 1."

7. Jamieson, Fausset, Brown, *Commentary on 1 Kings 3*, studylight.org.

8. *Nelson's NKJV Study Bible*, 711.

9. David Guzik, http://www.enduringword.com/commentaries/1103.htm.

10. Henry Morris, 20–21.

11. Rick Killian, *The Prayer of Solomon: Enduring Wisdom from the World's Wisest Man* (Minneapolis, MN: Bethany House, 2007), 9.

12. Ray Bentley, 28.

13. David Guzik, http://www.enduringword.com/commentaries/1103.htm.

14. Mark Matlock, 37.

15. Cameron Lawrence, "Good Desire, Bad Desire," In-Touch website, http://www.intouch.org.

16. Peter Leithart, 44–45.

17. Ray Bentley, 30.

18. Mark Matlock, 38.

19. David Jeremiah, *Power Up! With Powerful Principles from Proverbs* (San Diego, CA: Turning Point for God, 2002), 11.

20. Charles Stanley, adapted from "Walking Wisely: Real Guidance for Life's Journey," 2002, pp. 8–12 http://www.intouch.org.

21. L. B. Cowman, *Streams in the Desert* (Grand Rapids, MI: Zondervan, 1997), 65.

22. F. B. Meyer, quoted in Cowman, *Streams in the Desert*, 103.

1 Kings 3:16–28; 4
Solomon—Chief Justice and CEO

1. *Nelson's NKJV Study Bible*, 1701.

2. Sue and Larry Richards, *Every Woman in the Bible*, 181.

3. Rick Killian, 105–6.

4. Guzik, comments on 1 Kings 3, http://www.enduringword.com/commentaries/.

5. Steven K. Scott, *The Richest Man Who Ever Lived: King Solomon's Secrets to Success, Wealth, and Happiness* (New York: Currency/Doubleday/Random House, 2006), 25.

6. Roger Hahn, www.cresourcei.org/biblestudy/bbkings4/html.

7. *King James Study Bible for Women*, 560.

8. William T. James furnished these comments upon request.

9. Jamieson, Fausset, Brown, "Commentary on 1 Kings 4:22–25."

10. Mark Matlock, 39.

11. Irving L. Jensen, *Jensen's Survey of the Old Testament* (Chicago: Moody, 1978), 212.

1 Kings 5; 2 Chronicles 2
Getting Ready to Build

1. Joyce L. Gibson, *The Book of Genesis: The Smart Guide to the Bible* (Nashville: Thomas Nelson, 2007), 55.

2. David Jeremiah, *Worship* (Atlanta: GA: Walk Thru the Bible Ministries, 1995), 10.

3. James Strong, *The Tabernacle of Israel: Its Structure and Symbolism* (Grand Rapids, MI: Kregel, 1987), 12.

4. *Rose Book of Bible Charts, Maps and Timelines*, 150.

5. Lambert Dolphin, "The Treasures of the House of the Lord," www.templemount.org/ TMTRS.html.

6. Angie Peters, *The Life of David*, (Nashville: Nelson, 2008), 227.

7. Charles H. Spurgeon, <http://www.biblebb. com/files/spurgeon/owpre.txt>.

8. Randall Price, *The Temple & Bible Prophecy* (Eugene, OR: Harvest House, 2005), 50–51.

9. Charles H. Spurgeon, <http://www.biblebb. com/files/spurgeon/owpre.txt>.

10. Lambert Dolphin, www.templemount.org/ TMTRS.html.

11. *Rose Book of Bible Charts, Maps and Timelines*, 75.

12. *Nelson's NKJV Study Bible*, 874.

13. Alfred Edersheim, *The Temple: Its Ministry and Services* (Peabody, MA: Hendrickson, 1994), 51.

14. Roger Hahn, www.cresourcei.org/biblestudy/ bbkings4/html.

15. R. K. Harrison, *Old Testament Times: A Social, Political and Cultural Context* (Grand Rapids, MI: Baker, 2005), 204.

16. Woodrow Kroll, "Solomon: Man of God, Part 1" in the series "Solomon: Good King/Bad King," 3/5/99 <http://www.backtothebible. org/broadcasts/radio/today.php/214>.

17. Alfred Edersheim, *Old Testament Bible History*, v. 5 (Grand Rapids, MI: Eerdman's, 1990), 71–72.

18. Ibid., 71.

19. Eugene H. Merrill, "2 Chronicles," The Bible Knowledge Commentary (Colorado Springs, CO: Victor/Cook, 2004), 620–21.

20. Leslie M. Grant, "Family Hour," <http://www. biblecentre.org/commentaries/lmg_11_1_ kings.htm>.

21. Matthew Henry. *Matthew Henry's Commentary*, studylight.org.

1 Kings 6; 7:13–50; 2 Chronicles 3; 4
The Specs for a Spectacular Building

1. Irving L. Jensen, 213.

2. Roger Hahn, www.cresourcei.org/biblestudy/ bbkings4/html.

3. Nan Missler, "Reflections of His Image: A Visual Picture of the Problem," Personal Update NewsJournal, August 2007, <http://khouse. org/articles/2007/728/>.

4. *Baker Encyclopedia of the Bible*, v. 2 (Grand Rapids, MI: Baker Book House, 1988), 2020.

5. Tim LaHaye, 474.

6. William T. James, gen ed., *Prophecy at Ground Zero: From Today's Mideast Madness to the Second Coming of Christ* (Lancaster, PA: Starburst, 2002), 45.

7. Daymond Duck, *Prophecies of the Bible: God's Word for the Biblically Inept* (Lancaster, PA: Starburst, 2000), 43.

8. *Nelson's NKJV Study Bible*, 568.

9. Thomas L. Constable, printout p. 21.

10. Matthew Henry, *Matthew Henry Commentary on 1 Kings 6*, studylight.org.

11. Randall Price, 69.

12. J. Vernon McGee, 260.

13. *Rose Book of Bible Charts, Maps and Timelines*, 157.

14. Dorothy Russell, 22.

15. Charles H. Spurgeon, *Christ in the Old Testament*, "The Spurgeon Archive," www.spurgeon.org/sermons/1600.htm.

16. David Guzik, comments on 1 Peter 2:4–5, Studylight.org.

17. Henry Morris, 23.

18. Adam Clarke, *Commentary on 1 Kings 6*, study-light.org.

19. J. C. Ryle, sermon preached in England, August, 1858, http://www.biblebb.com/files/ryle/ WARN1.TXT.

20. Tim LaHaye, 380.

21. Adam Clarke, *Commentary on 1 Kings 6*, study-light.org.

22. J. C. Ryle, http://www.biblebb.com/files/ryle/ christ_is_all.htm.

23. Joseph P. Free and Howard F. Vos, *Archaeology and Bible History* (Grand Rapids, MI: Zondervan, 1992), 143.

24. Peter Leithart, 64.

25. Alfred Edersheim, *Old Testament Bible History*, v. 5 (Grand Rapids, MI: Eerdman's, 1990), 86.

1 Kings 8; 2 Chronicles 5:1–7:11
The Dedication of the Temple

1. Ronald F. Youngblood, F. F. Bruce, R. K. Harrison, *Nelson's Student Bible Dictionary*.

2. Randall Price, 53.

3. Jamieson, Fausset, Brown, "Commentary on 1 Kings," studylight.org.

4. Zola Levitt, "The Seven Feasts of Israel," Prophecy Study Bible (Chattanooga, TN: AMG, 2000), 143.

5. Tim LaHaye, 991.

6. Beth Moore, *A Woman's Heart: God's Dwelling Place* (Nashville, TN: Lifeway, 1995), 81.

7. Larry Richards, *The Bible*, 295.

8. Priscilla Shirer, *He Speaks to Me: Preparing to Hear from God* (Nashville, TN: Lifeway, 2005), 48.

9. Oswald Chambers, *My Utmost for His Highest* (Uhrichsville, OH: Barbour, 1963), entry for 1/8.

10. David Guzik, *Notes on Hebrews*, 13:15.

11. Peter Leithart, 67.

12. Thomas L. Constable, printout p. 27.

13. Larry Richards, 294.

14. Alfred J. Kolatch, 121.

15. Matthew George Easton, "Shechinah," Easton's Bible Dictionary, <http://www.studylight.org/dic/ebd>.

16. Charles Stanley, January 2001, http://www.intouch.org/gen_content/index_627258_36658032.html.

17. Kenneth W. Collins, http://www.kencollins.com/pray-20.htm.

18. Don Walton, www.floridabaptistwitness.com/629.article.

19. John MacArthur, http://www.gty.org/resources.php?section=issues&aid=176359.

20. *Baker Encyclopedia of the Bible*, 2022.

21. Randall Price, 36.

22. Arnold J. Fruchtenbaum, "Fulfilled Prophecy and Israel," Prophecy Study Bible (Chattanooga, TN: AMG), 239.

23. John Wesley, commentary on 2 Chronicles 7:1–3 at www.studylight.org.

1 Kings 9:1–9; 2 Chronicles 7:12–22
Hazardous Conditions Ahead

1. Mark Matlock, 102.

2. Ray Bentley, 91.

3. Charles H. Spurgeon, "Essential Points in Prayer," a sermon on 2/10/1887, www.biblebb.com/files/spurgeon/2064/htm.

4. Dorothy Russell, 37.

5. Leithart, 71.

6. *Nelson's NKJV Study Bible*, "Word Focus," 930.

7. Bob Deffinbaugh, "The Reign of Solomon," www.bible.org.

8. Jenson, 213.

1 Kings 9:10–28; 10; 2 Chronicles 8:3–16; 9:1–28
Dealings with a King and a Queen

1. *Easton's Bible Dictionary*, <http://www.sacred-texts.com/bib/ebd/ebd068.htm>.

2. Steven K. Scott, 114.

3. Leithart, 76.

4. Morris, 25.

5. McGee, 267.

6. Sue and Larry Richards, *Every Woman in the Bible*, 135.

7. R. K. Harrison, 206.

8. David Plotz, "If He's So Wise, Why Did He Betray God?" slate.com/id/2153944/entry/2154058.

9. Matthew Henry, *Commentary on 1 Kings 10*, studylight.org.

10. Lee Strobel, *The Case for Christ*, 268–69.

11. H. L. Rossier, http://www.biblecentre.org/commentaries/hr_14_2_chronicles_1to20.htm.

12. Charles H. Spurgeon, http://www.biblebb.com/files/spurgeon/1600.TXT.

13. Rossier, http://www.biblecentre.org/commentaries/hr_14_2_chronicles_1to20.htm.

14. F. B. Hole, http://www.biblecentre.org/commentaries/fbh_53_ephl_3to6.htm.

15. Sue and Larry Richards, 135.

16. *Revolve: Psalms and Proverbs and Other WisdomBooks* (Nashville, TN: Thomas Nelson, 2004), 180.

1 Kings 11:1–8
The Godly King Does Ungodly Things

1. Boadt/West, *Stories from the Old Testament*, Vol. 2, 13.

2. Ibid.

3. Dave Breese, *Satan's Ten Most Believable Lies*, 26.

4. Greg Laurie, "Lessons from the School of Hard Knocks," WorldNetDaily.com.

5. Morris, 27.

6. Ron Mehl, *The Tender Commandments* (Sisters, OR: Multnomah), 41.

7. Carolyn Nystrom, *Old Testament Kings: A Lifeguide Bible Study* (Downers Grove, IL: InterVarsity Press, 1993), 20.

8. William C. Martin, *These Were God's People* (Nashville, TN: Southwestern Co., 1966), 155.

9. Sue and Larry Richards, 112.

10. Beth Moore, *When Ungodly People Do Ungodly Things* (Nashville, TN: Broadman & Holman, 2002), 66.

11. David Plotz, www.slate.com/id/2153944/entry/2154058/.

12. Beth Moore, *When Ungodly People Do Ungodly Things*, 4, 7.

13. Oswald Chambers, *My Utmost for His Highest*, 4/15.

14. Dennis Bratcher, "A Lost Future," http://crivoice.org/1kng3.html.

1 Kings 11:9–11; 2 Chronicles 9:29–31
The Wrath of God

1. Oswald Chambers, 10/10.

2. Charles H. Spurgeon, *Treasury of David*, v. 29.

3. Matthew Henry, *Commentary on Psalm 89*, studylight.org.

4. Alfred Edersheim, *Old Testament Bible History*, 114.

5. Max Lucado, *The Great House of God* (Dallas, TX: Word, 1997), 153.

6. Thomas L. Constable, "1 Kings," *The Bible Knowledge Commentary*, 501.

7. Ronald F. Youngblood, F. F. Bruce, R. K. Harrison, *Nelson's Student Bible Dictionary*, 251.

8. *International Standard Bible Encyclopedia*, http://net.bible.org/dictionary.php?dict=dictionaries&word=Ephraimite (ISBE).

9. Edersheim, *Old Testament Bible History*, 115.

10. Roger Hahn, http://crivoice.org/biblestudy/bbkings8.html.

11. *International Standard Bible Encyclopedia*, http://net.bible.org/dictionary.php?word=Light <ISBE>.

12. Ann Spangler, *Praying the Names of Jesus* (Grand Rapids, MI: Zondervan, 2006), 28.

13. Mark Hitchcock, *101 Answers to the Most Asked Questions about the End Times* (Sisters, OR: Multnomah, 2001), 217.

14. Larry Richards, *The Bible*, 84.

15. William C. Martin, *Layman's Bible Encyclopedia*, 357.

16. Henry Morris, 30.

Solomon's Song
It's All About Love

1. Robert Davidson, *Ecclesiastes and the Song of Solomon: Daily Bible Study Series* (Louisville, KY: Westminster John Knox Press, 1986), 100.

2. Bentley, 20.

3. Jensen, 305.

4. Spangler, *Praying the Names of Jesus*, 19.

5. Al Janssen, www.family.org/marriage/print.cfm?Module+3169.

6. Tim LaHaye, 684.

7. Thomas L. Constable, "Notes on Song of Solomon," 2007 Edition, published by Sonic Light, http://www.soniclight.com.

8. Ann Spangler, *Women of the Bible: 52 Stories for Prayer and Reflection* (Grand Rapids, MI: Zondervan, 2002), 158.

9. Lambert Dolphin, http://www.ldolphin.org/ssong.shtml.

10. Kathy Collard Miller and D. Larry Miller, *What's in the Bible for Couples*, 234.

11. Ibid., 235.

12. Jill Savage, *Is There Really Sex After Kids?* (Grand Rapids, MI: Zondervan, 2003), 26.

13. Alistair Begg, article, Familylife.com http://www.familylife.com/articles/article_detail.asp?id=1395&page=3&keywords=.

14. Kathy Collard Miller and D. Larry Miller, 109.

15. Matthew Henry, http://www.studylight.org/com/mhc-com/view.cgi?book=joh&chapter=15&verse=15#Joh15_15.

16. Jack S. Deere, "Song of Solomon," *Bible Knowledge Commentary: New Testament* (Colorado Springs, CO: Victor/Cook, 2004), 1023.

17. Larry and Thelnita Fincher, comments furnished upon request.

18. Jack S. Deere, 1024.

19. Alistair Begg, article, Familylife.com http://www.familylife.com/articles/article_detail.asp?id=1395&page=3&keywords=.

20. Kathy Collard Miller and D. Larry Miller, 246.

21. Dennis Rainey, http://www.familylife.com/articles/article_detail.asp?id=132&page=1&keywords=commitment.

22. Bentley, 23.

Proverbs
A Word from the Wise

1. Henry A. Halley, *Halley's Bible Handbook* (Grand Rapids, MI: Zondervan, 1965), 270.

2. James I. Packer, Merrill C. Tenney, William White, Jr., ed., *The Bible Almanac* (Nashville, TN: Thomas Nelson, 1980), 375–76.

3. Sid Buzzell, "Proverbs," *Bible Knowledge Commentary: New Testament* (Colorado Springs, CO: Victor/Cook, 2004), 901.

4. David Jeremiah, *Power Up! With Powerful Principles from Proverbs* (San Diego, CA: Turning Point for God, 2002), 14.

5. Gleason L. Archer, *A Survey of Old Testament Introduction* (Chicago: Moody, 1994), 515.

6. Billy Graham, *Day-by-Day*, Joan Winmill Brown, comp. and ed. (Minneapolis, MN: World Wide Publications, 1976), 8/14.

7. John MacArthur, "The Five Steps to Wisdom," transcript posted on Grace to You website, www.gty.org/resources/transcripts/GTY6.

8. Woodrow Kroll, Backtothebible.org.

9. Scott, 62–63.

10. Billy Graham, *Day-by-Day*, 2/19.

11. Wilfred J. Hahn, "Gilded Ages—Part 1: Solomon, 666 and Gold" Midnight Call, September 2007, p. 32.

12. Steven K. Scott, 194.

Ecclesiastes
The Search for Satisfaction

1. *Ryrie Study Bible*, 891.

2. *King James Study Bible for Women*, 996.

3. *Revolve: Psalms and Proverbs*, 193.

4. Lawrence Boadt, *Sayings of the Wise: The Legacy of King Solomon* (New York: St. Martin's Griffin, 1998), 16.

5. Ray Stedman, "Life in the Fast Lane" from a series, "Things that Don't Work: Ecclesiastes," RayStedman.org/eccles/3807.html.

6. Ibid.

7. Davidson, 22.

8. J. Stafford Wright, "Ecclesiastes," *Zondervan NIV Bible Commentary*, 1013.

9. *NIV Life Application Study Bible* (Wheaton, IL: Tyndale House and Grand Rapids, MI: Zondervan, 1991), 1139.

10. Angie Peters, *Designed to Build: A Woman and Her Home* (Texarkana, TX: Bogard, 2005), 46.

11. Selwyn Hughes, devotional for 3/21/05, Every Day Light: www.studylight.org/devos.

12. Davidson, 34.

13. *Quest Bible*, 918.

14. Wright, 1017.

15. Selwyn Hughes, "Go with Gladness," www.studylight.org/devos.

16. Ray Stedman, "Before It's Too Late," from *The Power of His Presence: A Year of Devotions from the Writings of Ray Stedman*; compiled by Mark Mitchell, posted on www.RayStedman.org.

17. *Life Application Study Bible* (Tyndale House, 1998, 1996), posted on studylight.org/devos/lws/index.cgi?FirstSelectMonth=09&FirstSelectDay=24.

18. *Bible Almanac*, 378.

Index

B

Baalath (region), 230
Baal worship, 162
Bahurim, 45
Baker Encyclopedia of the Bible
  on cost of Solomon's temple, 169
  on Solomon's understanding of Temple, 202
Barbieri, Louis A. Jr.
  on hypocrisy, 20
Barzillai, 73
Bathsheba
  Adonijah and Bathsheba, 84–89
  David and Bathsheba, 3, 4, 5, 8–15, 53–56, 81
  death of firstborn son, 23, 29
  motives of Bathsheba, 12
  parents of Bathsheba, 44
  power of, 5, 84–87
  Solomon and, 53–56, 84–85
Beasley, Sabrina, 13
Beersheba, 138
Begg, Alistair
  on premarital sex, 301
  on Song of Solomon, 296
Benaiah
  Adonijah and Benaiah, 52, 89
  David and Benaiah, 49, 131
  Solomon and Benaiah, 55–56, 89–91, 94
Bentley, Ray
  on Solomon's satisfaction with temple, 212
  on Solomon's thousand sacrifices, 112
  on Song of Solomon, 289, 302
  on wisdom of Solomon, 117
Bethel, 106, 194
Bethlehem, 4
Beth Shemesh, 194
Bible Almanac
  on ark of the covenant, 44
  on Ecclesiastes, 335

on Proverbs, 306
Boadt, Lawrence
  on Ecclesiastes, 322
Boadt and West
  on Solomon's rule, 250, 251
Boaz, vii
Bodmer, Judy
  on having sex when grieving, 23
  on Hebrew funerals, 17
  on role models for children, 31
body language, 200
Bratcher, Dennis
  on temptation to sin, 257, 260
Breese, Dave
  on Brook Kidron, 95
  on Proverbs, 306
  on Satan's gaining a foothold, 251
bronze
  in tabernacle, 109, 112, 150
  for temple, 151, 155, 180, 181, 199

C

cabul, 226
Calvary, 191
Canaanites, 42, 232–33
  Israel's slaves, 233
Canticles. *See* Song of Solomon
Castleman, Robbie
  on covenant between God and people, 71
  on loving and obeying God, 5
cedars of Lebanon, 140, 147, 160, 161, 163, 164, 179, 181, 182, 183, 188, 202, 225, 227, 239, 243, 297
Chambers, Oswald, iv
  on sacrifice through death, 193
  on spiritual relationships, 266
  on temptation to sin, 257, 260

chariots
  and claims to throne, 36, 52
  the Lord's chariots, 69
  Solomon's chariots, 140, 230, 231
Chemosh, 259
cherubim throne, 43, 149, 180, 194
children and discipline. *See* parenting
Christians
  behavior, 74–75, 229, 238, 259, 266–67, 334–35
  church, 176
  divine design, 55, 85–86, 328
  duties, 221–22
  faithfulness, v
  giving credit to God, 65
  marriage, 255–56, 293, 296–301, 333
  obedience, v, 4, 93, 177, 178
  planning, 172
  prayer, v, 15, 39, 158, 172, 179
  prayer posture, 199–201
  work, 202, 316–17, 328
  worship, v, 331–32
  See also Jesus; sin; wealth; wisdom
cities for storage, 230
Clarke, Adam
  on God's warning to Solomon, 175
  on sacrificing to God at "high places," 107
  on Solomon's Egyptian bride, 104
Coffman, James Burton
  on marrying within Israelite faith, 103
Collins, Kenneth W.
  on prayer posture, 199
concubines. *See* women of the Old Testament
Constable, Thomas L.
  on Absalom's flouting of God's will, 47
  on Adonijah as people's

Higgs, Liz Curtis
  on temptation of Eve, 11
high places. *See* altar
High Priest, 133
Hiram
  construction materials for
    temple, 159–60, 163–64,
    225–26
  generosity to Solomon,
    226–27, 234
  as Gentile in friendship with
    Israel, 163
  Solomon's gift displeases
    him, 226–27
  Solomon's ships and Hiram,
    234
Hitchcock, Mark
  on Jesus ruling from
    Jerusalem, 276
Hittites, 249, 253
Hivites, 232
Hole, F. B.
  on queen of Sheba visiting
    Solomon, 237
Holman Bible Dictionary
  on Israelite dislike of
    Ammonites, 6
holy fire, 206
Holy Spirit, 59, 311
  benefits of having with us, 57
Hophni and Phinehas, 90–91
horses, 140, 230
  cost, 231
  selling, 231
  Solomon's offense, 140, 231
House of Eli, 90–91
House of the Forest of
  Lebanon, 181–82
Hughes, Selwyn
  on good marital
    relationships, 333
  on strength through solid
    relationships, 330
humility, 117
Hushai, 44, 46

I

idol worship
  Ammonites, 6

incense, 162
integrity, 133
  Uriah and, 16
  See also righteousness
*International Standard Bible
  Encyclopedia*
  on Gentiles' coming to the
    light, 276
  on tribes of Israel, 272
iron, 25, 71, 155, 174
Ironside, H. A.
  on David as prophet, 67
  on David in God's hands, 39
  on Psalms as prayers of Jesus,
    66
  on suffering from sin, 40
Israel (ancient)
  census of David, 137
  children in Israel, 23,
    254–55
  chosen people of God,
    103–4
  early division, 92
  economy under Solomon,
    103, 234–35
  expansion by Solomon, 137
  funeral customs, 17–18
  God's promise to Israel,
    138, 205, 219–20
  golden age of Solomon,
    279–80
  governors under Solomon,
    136
  holy days, 188–89, 233–34
  marriage customs, 103, 252
  Northern Kingdom, 274–75
  Samuel's predictions for
    Israel, 62–63
  twelve districts of Solomon,
    134–36
  twelve tribes of Israel,
    271–72

J

James, William T.
  on God's promises to Israel,
    138
  on Temple Mount, 170
Jamieson, Fausset, Brown

on David and Bathsheba, 9
on feast chosen for temple
  dedication, 189
on meaning of "vine and fig
  tree," 139
on toleration of worship in
  "high places," 107
on Uriah's sense of military
  duty, 16
Janssen, Al
  on Song of Solomon, 289
jealousy, 65
Jebusites, 232
Jedidiah, meaning of, 23
  See also Solomon
Jehoiada, 89, 94
Jehoshaphat, 131, 134
Jensen, Irving L.
  on Solomon's ability as
    botanist, zoologist, 141
  on Solomon's spiritual
    leadership, 220
  on Song of Solomon, 289
  on temple as first large
    Israelite structure, 167
Jeremiah, David
  on design of tabernacle, 149
  on Proverbs, 306
  on wisdom of Solomon,
    118–19
Jeremiah (prophet), 279
Jericho, 42, 194
Jeroboam
  flight to Egypt, 277
  rebellion against Solomon,
    270–78
Jerusalem, 134, 187
  David's choice of, 40-41
  David's flight from, 37–38
  destruction, 278
  layout, 40, 152
  military importance, 25, 37,
    40, 275–76
  sacredness, 40–41
Jesus
  birth, 267
  contrasted with Solomon,
    241
  Jesus as light, 276–77
  love of Jesus, 289–90

model prayer of, 200
preincarnate, 215
resurrection of Jesus, 198
temptations of, 11
See also sin
Joab
Adonijah and Joab, 50, 59, 88, 93–94
census role, 91–92
character flaws, 93
David and Joab, 5, 6, 25, 35, 46–48, 73, 91, 93
death of Joab, 94
murder of Abner, 93
murder of Absalom, 47, 59, 93
murder of Amasa, 93
Solomon and Joab, 91–94
Joel, 68
Jonadab, 34
Jonathan, 45
Josephus, 49
Judah, 37, 48
as Southern Kingdom, 275
justice
demonstrating justice, 69, 126–27
God's strange way of, 129
as means of winning hearts, 35–36
perversion through corruption, 68
See also Hall of Justice

K

Killian, Rick
on Solomon's counselors, 112
on Solomon's proposed division of baby, 128
king, the, as God's representative, 220
King James Version Study Bible for Women
on Ecclesiastes, 322
on God's promise to Solomon, 137
on sharing altars with Canaanites, 10

kiss
forgiveness kiss, 35–36
romantic kiss, 2926
kneeling before king, 200
Kolatch, Alfred J.
on Jerusalem's importance to Hebrews, 40
on Ten Commandments, 196
Kopas, Jane
on biblical women and power, 87
kors, 139
Kroll, Woodrow
on Solomon's partnership with Hiram, 160
on wisdom and discipline, 312

L

LaHaye, Tim
on Davidic Covenant, 71
on God keeping His word, 178
on keeping the Feast of Tabernacles, 190
on Song of Solomon, 289
on Temple Mount, 170
Laurie, Greg
on marriage with non-believer, 252
Lawrence, Cameron
on resigning one's fate to God, 114
leadership, 70
delegating, 131–32, 160
managing people and, 74–75
seeking counsel, 132
selecting competent staff, 133
Leithart, Peter
on eyes as symbol of judgment, 216
on meaning of Adonijah's name, 58
on significance of Solomon's residence, 183
on Solomon asking God for wisdom, 117
on Solomon's Egyptian influence, 231

on temple and Mosaic Covenant, 195
Lemuel, 308
importance, v
strategies for, v
Levites, 149
Levitt, Zola
on significance of Feast of Tabernacles, 190
lineage, in Bible, 86–87
"living stones," 170, 175–76, 196
Jesus as cornerstone, 176
metaphor for God's house, 175
Lower Beth Horon, 230
loyalty, Uriah and, 16
Lucado, Max
on devil as God's tool, 268
Lucifer, 51

M

Maacah, 29
MacArthur, John
on importance of heart's position in prayer, 200
on studying the Bible, 311
Mahanaim, 46
Manasseh (tribe), 270
manna, 43, 201
Martin, William C.
on downfall of Jerusalem, 278
on Solomon's marriage alliances, 255
Matlock, Mark
on early pressure on Solomon, 82
on God's generosity to Solomon, 113
on satisfaction in finishing a project, 212
on Solomon's abilities as scientist, 141
on wisdom of Solomon, 118
McEachern, Alton H.
on Jesus and the Psalms, 67
McGee, J. Vernon
on arrogance of Adonijah, 52

on influence of Solomon, 236
on temple of Solomon, 173
McKenzie, Steven L.
  on Ahithophel's hatred for
    David, 44
  on David's son exploiting his
    harem, 22
Megiddo, 229
Mehl, Ron
  on marriage between
    believer and non-believer,
    252
mentoring, 82
Mephibosheth
  betrayal of Davaid, 44–45
mercy, 82, 96
  limits to mercy, 89, 96, 264
mercy seat. *See* cherubim
    throne
Merrill, Eugene H.
  on Solomon's reference to
    polytheistic gods, 162
Meyer, F. B.
  on surrendering willingly to
    the Lord, 119
Miller, Kathy Collard and D.
    Larry
  on David's temptation to
    adultery, 8
  on marital intimacy, 301
  on sin of rejecting God's
    love, 22
  on Song of Solomon, 289,
    294, 297
Millo, 229, 233
Missler, Nan
  on uniqueness of Solomon's
    temple, 169
Moabites, 249, 253
Molech, 259
Moore, Beth
  on Amnon's rape of Tamar,
    31, 34–35
  on Israelite's salvation
    through sacrificial worship,
    191
  on location of altars in Israel,
    106
  on temptation leading to sin,
    257, 259–60

Moriah. *See* Mount Moriah
Morris, Henry
  on God's chosen name for
    Solomon, 24
  on marriage between
    believer and non-believer,
    252
  on Solomon's guilt offerings
    at Gibeon, 111
  on Solomon's horses, 231
  on Solomon's turning back
    to the Lord, 280
  on temple as symbol of
    spiritual house, 176
Mosaic Covenant, 42, 195,
    215
Most Holy Place, the, 180
Mount Moriah, iii, 155, 169,
    187, 201
Mount of Olives, 44, 45
mourning customs, 17, 47
mule, 56
My Utmost for His Highest, 14

N

Naamah, 288
Nabal, 14
Nahash, 6
Nathan
  on Absalom's estrangement
    from David, 34
  Adonijah and Nathan, 52
  Bathsheba and Nathan,
    53–54
  David and Nathan, 37, 53
  David's sin against Uriah,
    15, 18–21
  David's strategies on Mount
    of Olives, 44
  David's triumphal return to
    Jerusalem, 48
  final days of Absalom's rule, 46
  message to Solomon about
    building temple, 151
  Solomon and Nathan, 55–56
Nebuchadnezzar, 168
Nelson's NKJV Study Bible
  on body-heat medical
    procedures, 49

on character vs. prowess, 16
on Exodus, 171
on God's blessing available
  to all, 126
on importance of fear of
  God, 70
on importance of heart to
  Hebrews, 217
on kiss of forgiveness, 35–36
on parables of Jesus, 19
on psalms as prophecies of
  Jesus, 67
on psalms as songs, 157
*Nelson's Student Bible
  Dictionary*
  on justice as measured in
    Bible, 68
  on omnipresence of God,
    188
  on twelve tribes of Israel, 271
*NIV Life Application Study
  Bible*
  on walking with God, 334
  on working hard with
    moderation, 202, 328
Nob, 90, 109
Nystrom, Carolyn
  on Solomon's marriages to
    pagans, 253

O

Obed-Edom, 194
obedience. *See* Christians,
  obedience
offerings. *See* sacrifices
oil, 164, 226
  importance of container,
    57–58
  importance of in Bible, 56
  Messiah and oil, 56
Ophir, 234
Ornan the Jebusite, 169

P

pagan gods, 217
parables
  man with lamb (Nathan),
    18–19

S

war in David's time, 153
  against Rabbah, 5–7, 25
  against the Philistines, 42
  expectations of David, 7
  ideal environment for, 7
war, spoils of
  David, 25
wealth, 315–16
  assigning portion to God,
    159
Wesley, John
  on God's acceptance of our
    prayers, 206
wisdom, 33, 119–20
  benefits, 311–12
  book of James and, 120
  discerning good and evil,
    117
  pursuit of, 119
  two kinds of wisdom, 120
  words and wisdom, 313
women of the Old Testament
  another man's woman, 22,
    46
  concubines, 38, 46
  children and, 254
  David's women, 14–15, 21–
    22, 49, 54
  idolatry and, 104–5, 253
  Jesus' lineage and, 87
  marriage alliances, 101–2
  mother of king. *See*
    Bathsheba
  primary relationship bond,
    102
  Proverbs 31 on ideal
    woman, 88–89
  Solomon's women, 105,
    214, 233, 252-57
  subjugation by men, 10–11,
    30, 48, 86, 87
  See also rape
Word, the, 120
Words of Promise
  on importance of altar's
    horns, 59
Wright, J. Stafford
  on Ecclesiastes, 328
  on signposts for living,
    332

Y

Yom Kippur, 190

Z

Zabud, 131
Zadok,
  David and Zadok, 37, 50
  Solomon and Zadok, 55–56,
    94
Zechariah, 190
Zeruah, 270
Zerubbabel, 168
Zeruiah, 91
Ziba, 44–45
*Zondervan NIV Bible
  Commentary*
  on David's loyal army, 38
  on Solomon's alliance with
    Pharaoh, 102
  on Solomon's execution of
    Shimei, 96

www.ingramcontent.com/pod-product-compliance
Ingram Content Group UK Ltd.
Pitfield, Milton Keynes, MK11 3LW, UK
UKHW052243240325
456661UK00008B/89